MIA ZAPATA & THE GITS

A STORY OF ART, ROCK, AND REVOLUTION

BY STEVE MORIARTY

ISBN 978-1-62731-150-2

There are photographs included that were gifted to the author over the years by friends and fans where the photographer is unknown. Feral House would like to thank these anonymous photographers by giving them, and all the fans that take pictures of their favorite bands, thanks and credit for documenting their scene. If you recognize YOUR photo, please contact us at: info@feralhouse.com.

Feral House
1240 W. Sims Way
Suite 124
Port Townsend, WA 98368
www.feralhouse.com info@feralhouse.com

Design by designSimple

Cover photo by and courtesy of Zannah Noe. Her work can be found at zannahnoe.com

Written in honor of Mia Katherine Zapata
and all those who loved her.

August 25, 1965–July 7, 1993

A portion of the author's proceeds from the sale of this book are donated to the Division of Trauma Recovery Services, Department of Psychiatry, University of California, San Francisco.

CONTENTS

1/23/89

Dear Steve, I very much did get your letter, And on a day I needed it very badly. I had told myself I needed to get some heartful soul from someone personal to me toaday. I was tring to seak my own straingth but I wanted to hear someone, not ju st talking at me but telling me they're on my side. And you had said ju st that at the end of your letter. A so unexpected one which just streingthens my belief in the supperstitions Thank you.

I believe you, your probably very cold. And even if your in your paremts warm house, you saw what was cold, and I believe it.

I've been cold too. Cold in thought. My mind stairs into the walls untill my body is numb. And when I walk, I try to forget where I'm going. Then I ussually end up in a bad neigborhood.,but I walk alone in this city of portland. Though all that I've done and seen is behind me, a clean slate stands clean, I just want to mess it up. Maybe in spight of all the things taken away from me. Chl Childish but I still have hope. That's why I needed to hear from you today. I want to believe in life, but nothings pretty and hardly honest. I don't want anyone to clean it up all pretty for me to look at it. I'll see my own beaty beauty. in whatever that will be to me.

I too, decidd ed I wou ld put a little trust, rather honesty in someone. But I've written and they have not. It's too bad and lied because they came to me from honesty but stepped out when it came down to it. It8s all part to why I sound cold. But I think somewhere inside me it dosen't want to believe it all dies.

Now I phrase the pains as another brick for my wall, and not one I'll stand behind. Feeling sorry for myself will turn me a drunkerd with my habits. I8ll try here for a little while but I don't want to stay.

I've painted you into one of my paintings. This time your not in a bar. Your cackling over someones shoulder like the wicked witch of the west.

So there. Ain't so sweet of a letter now is it?

I didn't want it to matter but knew

Letter from Mia to Steve, January 23, 1989. From author's archive.

PROLOGUE

Who am I, and who am I to write this book? I am not a journalist or an objective bystander. The stories I tell are true as I remember. The finer details—dates, places, people—are not as important as the spirit conveyed in the story. What I observed was the spirit of The Gits that came through the music. Our punk ethos guided and set the course for our young lives and, ultimately, the direction of our band—an ethos of humor, fairness, creativity, celebration, inclusion, resistance, resilience, and radical acceptance. In a way, it was a religion or a code of conduct—in some cases misconduct—especially when it came into conflict with society.

My bandmates and our musical mission remain a source of inspiration by which many of our fans and listeners live their lives as well. That became evident to me during an early screening of a 2005 documentary film about our singer, Mia Zapata. A man in his thirties in the audience stood during the Q and A after the screening and stated that he had long suffered debilitating depression. He related how once, after careful consideration, he had decided to end his own life. He then put on his stereo to mask the noise of his final act on earth and the Gits song "Second Skin" happened to be cued up on his mixtape. He paused to listen to Mia's lyrics and was inspired not to die.

A woman in France wrote that she gained the inner strength and resolve to leave an abusive man who beat her and threatened to kill her baby. The Gits song "Social Love" gave her the strength to escape with her baby despite the abuser's threats.

Another woman claimed that she discovered The Gits' music while listening to college radio in Los Angeles. She credits the song "Whirlwind" for helping her survive cancer.

Music inspires and motivates people everywhere. It's a universal language that unites people and creates community. It calms us down or gets us going, giving us an emotional outlet when needed. But these messages of courage, strength, and hope conveyed by complete strangers demanded closer examination.

The music of The Gits was born of the alchemy and chemistry between the members. My bandmates were rare and intense individuals. It has been daunting to represent their personalities and idiosyncrasies in writing. They are proud people and I have gone to great lengths to represent them with respect and reverence. I could not see a way to write about The Gits' music and the importance of the band in the wider cultural context without exploring their personalities and my interactions with them.

Of course, The Gits would not have been a noteworthy band without Mia Zapata. Her voice and the rare driving passion behind her delivery were unparalleled in rock music. Critics and fans noticed immediately, and she elevated the significance of the music in the cultural landscape of the time. For a band that had such a minor sales and performance record, to have such a moving impact on so many individual lives is remarkable. All this was prior to the rise of the Internet, let alone social media. This fact alone justifies devoting a book to the band.

That is not the reason I wrote this book, however. Nor am I motivated by monetary gain, because there is no money to be made writing books about cool bands than there is in being in one. There is no "Hogwarts" or action figures to market. There are no hobbits or vampires or zombies or whatever is trending in pop culture at the moment on which to capitalize. I don't have dreams of literary prizes or fame, but I do have a story to tell. I was there.

Unfortunately, and much to the distaste of those who knew and loved Mia, the true crime documentary and dramatization industry has seized on the circumstances of Mia's passing as a salacious story. This reality media obsession with violence against women, stalking, and even the murder of women has become entertainment for consumers. The topic has become debased to the point of fetishization of the victims. It is disgusting and an indictment of the television industry and media at large.

If one does an Internet search today for The Gits or Mia Zapata, information about her murder, the investigation to find the murderer, and the conviction of him ten years later predominate the results. The music, the lyrics, the people involved in creating the music are secondary or absent altogether. This cannot stand.

I wrote this book over the course of eight years to restate and reclaim the narrative of Mia's life and the career of The Gits. I was just the drummer; however, I was there. The Gits were my partners, and Mia was one of my dearest friends. I refuse to sit back and allow the story of The Gits to be told by those who wish to promote or capitalize on something unrelated and unimportant and ultimately hurtful instead of the art Mia and we created.

I loved being the drummer for The Gits, and I loved the members of The Gits. I believe in the power of music to effect positive change and improve the lives of people who embrace it. I am proud to have had the opportunity to contribute something meaningful to our community of independent artists and musicians.

Mia Zapata was one of the greatest rock singers to ever take the stage. Her contributions are significant. Not only did she write and record songs, but those songs continue to inspire the Art of others and has—by so many brave testimonials—saved lives. This is why I wrote the book. Viva Zapata!

On the floor in a dorm room c. 1985 at Antioch College. From the author's archive.

1

DRUNK

A letter bomb exploded at Barajas International Airport in Madrid the day after I boarded a 747 from their British Airways terminal. I flew first to New York, and then I transferred to a much smaller plane for Indianapolis. I had grown accustomed to such terrorist deviltries. Adroit punk kids at the high school I attended in northern Spain once placed a lunch sandwich, wrapped in foil, behind the toilets in the boys' bathrooms on exam days and someone else called in the bomb threat. The high school got evacuated by the bomb squad and everybody got sent home, hence more time to study. A remote-control bomb-extracting robot was dispatched. They blew up an egg sandwich right in the center of the concrete basketball court where we smoked at lunchtime. The school was declared safe until exams the next year. But I didn't bother returning to class.

I failed to mention these highlights in my letters home to Indianapolis. My poor mother had been devastated a year earlier when at seventeen I declared I was leaving high school in Indiana to study in Spain. I landed in a small town in the Basque region of northern Spain.

Speaking not a word of Basque and only four words of Spanish, I soon gave up on high school. I taught English and jazz drumming to a few locals. I joined a cover band and played gigs around Spain, Portugal, and France. I had to sing David Bowie songs because the guys couldn't understand the words and spoke no English. If I didn't remember the words, I'd sing mush mouthed English words and no one was the wiser.

Eventually, I learned to speak Spanish and some Basque by hanging out in cafés and bars listening and chatting, which was a national pastime. I liked to read Hemingway and Pablo Neruda, sip Spanish espresso, and wax philosophical in broken Spanish about the Spanish Civil War and the new rise of fascism in America with Ronald Reagan. I tried to fit in—I even bought a beret—but my impossibly blond hair gave me away as the village Yankee, and I did not blend in at all. Living in Europe at that age offered me a view of the U.S. from a completely different sociopolitical angle. Things were not as they had seemed in the homeland. I felt swindled and lied to by my teachers, coaches, and adults in general. I began to unravel all the big lies. I would have stayed in Spain and become an Anarchist or a bullfighter, but after a year my student visa expired, and it was back to the heart of middle America to find a job.

I was eighteen years old. A university soccer career somehow still waited for me in Indiana. I had been an all-state goalkeeper at my high school. In Barcelona I had seen homeless children playing in the street with wads of rags tied together for a ball who were better than the top strikers on my high school team. I had been scouted by university coaches. While away in Spain, I won a soccer scholarship to DePauw University, the self-described "Ivy League school of the Midwest." Being pummeled by speeding soccer balls at a traditional university felt like a return to the life I had escaped. To my parents' chagrin, I snubbed the scholarship at the Ivy League school of the Midwest and got a job. I worked on a landscaping crew hand-pulling invasive ivy from fences, and planting cut sod on my knees in the oppressive Indiana heat. In the Midwest in August, the sun and humidity are nearly intolerable. It made me reconsider my working-class identity and I quickly learned the value of a college education.

I happened upon a copy of the *U.S. News and World Report Guide to the Best American Universities* while waiting to have my wisdom teeth extracted. In a sidebar on page two was the heading, "Untraditional Bastion of Liberalism, Antioch College, Yellow Springs, Ohio."

Ohio, not Indiana. That qualifier was important to me.

Antioch College was indeed considered an oasis of liberalism and progressive education in the state of Ohio. Less Ivy League and more post-war progressive—post-Civil-War, that is. The campus was opened in 1850 and now is hidden in an ocean of genetically modified corn production, forty-three highway miles from Dayton, Ohio. An anomalous throwback to the 1960s. It had a grand neo-gothic Oz-like main building with ornate steeples. There was a "Red Square," so named in a nod to the Kremlin's

Red Square, where students gathered with a rope swing (not the type historically associated with the region of Southwest Ohio). Barracks-like co-ed dormitories for students were nestled between quaint colonial and Victorian homes, that served as an infirmary and classrooms. All surrounded by a business district that resembled a set from *The Twilight Zone*. That show's creator, Rod Serling, had been a student at Antioch, and some of the sets built for the show were based on the creepy vibe Serling observed while a student during the 1950s. The dissociated glazed look of Serling's characters in numerous Twilight Zone episodes was the same dead-eyed gaze of the townsfolk of Yellow Springs, Ohio. The accepting nature of the quirky, and often naïve, liberal reputation cultivated by the administration and alumni of Antioch attracted unusual students and professors from throughout the world.

Antioch's student body of the late 1980s was an eccentric cross-section of youth counterculture and outsiders—hippies, homosexuals, hicks, gender activists, single mothers, Christian fundamentalists, transgender kids, Deadheads, radicals, feminists, punk rockers, and computer geeks.

There were no sports teams at Antioch, no fraternities, no letter grades, and, by design, very few rules. Students were required to complete off-campus "co-ops" or internships for six months a year in an area of study, then the remainder of the year attend classes on campus. One could do just about anything for a co-op if it could be justified that the experience was educational. I would do a co-op semester doing social work at a Catholic social-service agency in the Florida Everglades and another at a public defender's office in Indianapolis. There was a co-op counting endangered sea turtles in the U.S. Virgin Islands. There was a co-op in San Francisco at a community youth center and punk-music venue called the Farm. One adventurous young woman had earned co-op credit doing sex work in Alaska.

My first roommate at Antioch was a rather sharp dressed guy from Cleveland named Ben London. He was an androgynous-looking kid who showed up on his first day of college with 200 records, a full-component stereo system, an enormous suitcase of well-ironed clothes, and a clock-radio tuned to top 40 and kept on all night. He also brought an old Vantage brand Les Paul copy electric guitar and amp.

I showed up with my backpack, a few T-shirts, one pair of ripped black Levis, a beach towel, and a shoebox of cassette tapes. Ben and I were suspicious of each other at first. We sized up one another in a Middle American territorial standoff for pop-culture supremacy. But neither of us flinched, and we became best friends.

"Hey, you play guitar?" I asked a couple of hours after our arrival.

"Yeah, you play drums?" asked Ben as he hung twenty-five pressed shirts on wooden hangers, edging my stuff to the recesses of the shared closet.

"Uh-huh."

"Where are they?" he asked, his tone mocking.

"At the 'rents' house in Indy."

Ben cocked his chin, as if to note my rank amateurism.

"I can get 'em in a week or so. I just needed to get outta Indy, and I wanted to be cool about our shared space and all." I sounded defensive even to myself.

Ben hung up his trousers and suit coats. Then out came the rock posters, clothing butler, stereo system, records, and books. Ben was reading *The Basketball Diaries* by Jim Carroll, so I thought he must be into sports. I was reading *Living My Life*, the autobiography of Emma Goldman. He thought I was an exchange student. We did not have a ton in common, but we both had a keen interest in music. We decided to find a bass player and start a band.

Ben's father, Edwin London, was a world-renowned avant-garde classical composer. My father worked at the hi-fi department at the local mall and struggled to make ends meet, but he bought me drum lessons. I played my first gig at age twelve. I didn't mention any of this to Ben. While I believed Ben was destined for greatness, like his father, I did not wish to follow in my father's footsteps.

I was very serious about music from the beginning. My teacher, Charles Mastrapolo, an old school jazz swing drummer, explained it this way: "A blacksmith makes horseshoes and works as apprentice for thousands of hours to become a professional. Same with lawyers, doctors, engineers, pharmacists, painters. They get paid accordingly for their work. You will spend thousands of hours practicing your drums. You will learn to read and write an entire language. You will choose the music, learn the notes, and perform it for people who pay to be entertained by your music. You must be paid for all your efforts. You must demand to get paid for your work playing music, or you lower the bar for all of us." It was the Workers Party approach to life as a musician. I was only twelve years old, but Charles Mastropolo privately told my father that I could be a great drummer; he meant one of the Greats. My father failed to inform me of this until years later.

In the next room, a kid was blasting a tape on repeat. I had never heard the band before, but, by the fifth play of the cassette, I knew all the words and could play the five-note descending pentatonic marimba part in my head. It was driving me mad. Peeking through the open door, I saw a guy wearing a flannel with sleeves cut, ripped black jeans, engineer boots, and wraparound Ray-Ban knockoffs. A strand of black hair hung over his freckled face. He was seated at a little study desk in one corner of the room. The tape turned over, and the album began for the sixth time. "When I'm out walkin', I strut my stuff . . . "

On the desk was a half-gallon bottle of vodka and a two-liter bottle of 7Up. The guy poured a shot into his collectible New Jersey Turnpike shot glass, then dropped it into a wide-rimmed highball glass filled with the soda. The shot glass sank to the bottom and, before turning his head to acknowledge my greeting, he placed one hand over the glass, lifted it up, and slammed it down on the desktop, sparking an eruption of 80-proof jet fuel. He hoisted the burbling concoction to his mouth and poured it down his gullet. It was a fine fuck-you to everything staid and conventional.

"Hey," I yelled again. "I'm Steve. I live next door. What's that tape you keep playing?"

"Violent fucking Femmes," he belched. Bam! Another depth charge down his throat. "I'm Matt. I'm not here for long, so I don't mean to get friendly with anybody at this fucking dump. I'm just waiting on my acceptance letter from RISD [Rhode Island School of Design]. I got my application in late, so of course I'll be getting the acceptance letter late. Duh!"

Matt's roommate was sitting on a filthy mattress, smoking a cigarette, and strumming floppy chords on a bass guitar. He tapped his foot to some avant-garde new wave tune he was hearing in his head, despite the Femmes playing on the cheap boombox hissing away in Matt's face.

"I'm Adrian," the roommate declared, extending a welcoming hand. "And this is my G&L bass guitar. 1978. Designed by Leo Fender himself. No ordinary instrument. One of the best. The intonation is impeccable. I played this in my hardcore band back in Pittsburgh. Me and my best friend, Guy. He's a genius and a skinhead." Adrian grinned and laughed aloud. "We'd each eat a whole sheet of acid and jam for like twelve hours. Our drummer is from El Salvador. He's a skinhead too. This one time, Guy was arrested for pissing in the street." He strummed a couple chords to get my attention. "Guy still had a sheet of acid on him, and so he ate the whole thing before the cops tossed him in a cop wagon. On the way to jail, the acid kicked in, and Guy kicked the shit out of three cops inside the van. They just let him go before they got to the station 'cause they were too afraid to admit to the other cops that Guy had kicked their asses."

"Sorry, I'm lost. Who's a genius?" I stammered.

Matt slammed another glass down before offering to pour one for me. "Jaco Pastorius!" he shouted. "'I'm the greatest bass player in the world!' That's what he used to say." Matt tossed his head back and laughed. "What kind of asshole says he's the greatest bass player who ever lived?"

Adrian lifted an eyebrow. "The greatest bass player who ever lived, perhaps?"

"You play bass too, Matt?" I asked.

He ignored my question. "Drink, Moriarty! If that is your real name." He lit a cigarette.

I realized that I was still wearing the Hello-My-Name-Is sticker on my jacket pocket.

Fashion disaster, but I decided to embrace the embarrassment, patting the sticker, making sure it was firmly secured.

Matt patted his chest to mock me, then mimed the technique for drinking a tequila slammer; I mimicked him. When I slammed the glass and drank as instructed, the 7UP erupted in my throat and came out of my nose, my eyes watered. But I could not taste the tequila.

"Lightweight" Matt chided.

"Fabulous!" I answered. "May I have another?"

"Thank you, sir, may I have another!" Matt yelled.

"What?"

"Say it!" Matt bullied.

"Uh, thank you, may I have another?" I asked, getting annoyed.

Half an hour later, I stumbled out of the dorm. I had to go to a rehearsal for Aristophanes' *The Birds*, a classical Greek play I had signed up for. I was playing Second Pink Flamingo. I had to stand on one leg for most of the rehearsal, but Matt's slammers made it hard to balance. After rehearsal, the cast threw a first-rehearsal celebration.

I thought I was prepared for college drinking, but during that first night I dyed my hair pink, lost my wallet, misplaced my room key, and started a band with my roommate Ben and our next-door neighbor Adrian. I got back to my room late and Ben had locked our door. Matt was passed out on the common-room floor, his clothes and his boots still on. The batteries had died in the boombox on the floor behind his head, and it lay silent. Exhausted and drunk, I wandered into Matt's room. I passed out face down on his empty bed. I awoke to discover that I had puked in the wastebasket and stained Matt's pillow and sheets with pink semi-permanent hair dye. Not exactly putting my best foot forward.

Directly across the hall from my room was a second-year student who had a private room, which I envied. His door was slightly ajar, and he was running through scales on an electric guitar that was not plugged into an amp. There were no decorations on the walls except for a single giant poster of a band called Poison Idea. The huddled band members wore ripped T-shirts and held bottles of Jim Beam and Olde English 800 malt liquor. Seated in the center of the frame was an extremely fat man dressed in stained white T-shirt and sweatpants. A tiny pair of John Lennon–type sunglasses sat on his face like two black buttons on a dirty bean bag chair. It was Pig Champion, the band's lead guitarist.

The resident of the room with the guitar noticed me staring at the poster and said, apologetically, "It's this hardcore band from Portland. Come on in."

"Cool," was all I could say. "Is that a Les Paul?"

He held the guitar up like a proud papa showing off his newborn. "Gibson Les Paul. I got it in New York City when I studied jazz and shit in Brooklyn."

"I'm Steve. I live across the hall." I jabbed a thumb over my shoulder. "I studied Jazz when I was a kid too."

He lifted his chin at me and looked me squarely in the eyes. "Cool. I'm Andy. Nice to meet you."

"Can I see it?" I asked, gesturing to the guitar.

"Sure. You play?"

"Naw, I just like guitars. Uh, I play drums."

Andy held out a gleaming black and silver teardrop Les Paul with one hand. On powerful forearms were tattoos of what looked like a dragon, a knife and a sea creature or a lobster. He was the first person I had met with any tattoo work. It was rare in the Midwest to see tattoos on anyone other than bikers and military vets. Tattooing was still illegal in New York due to the dangers of dirty needles and the city's reputation. And of course the looming AIDS crisis. I held the guitar carefully. The weight of the thing was surprising. I could barely hold it with one hand. It appeared incredibly unwieldy to play. "Fucking heavy," I said. "The dudes in that poster, Poison Idea—what do they sound like?"

"Really great hardcore band. Crushing," said Andy. "Here, listen for yourself."

"Hardcore." I repeated dumbly.

He pulled a cassette from a shoebox and popped it into the small boombox on his desk and poked the play button. The album, *Pick Your King*, featured black-and-white drawings of Jesus and Elvis. The lyrics, minor power chords, and insanely fast tempos caught my attention. How could they play that fast? I figured that most people would think this music was unlistenable, but I found it phenomenal.

I listened to the Poison Idea tape as Andy tightened the long laces of his steel-toed Doc Marten boots. His boot-tying technique made the laces look like perfectly parallel rungs of a ladder that ran from toe to his shin. He folded the cuffs of his Levis up twice and grabbed a green bomber jacket from the back of the wooden desk chair. I handed the Les Paul back to Andy, and he placed it carefully into its case.

"You wanna get some beer?" asked Andy.

It was only noon, and I was still hungover from the previous night, but I was down.

"Cool."

"The drinking age is nineteen in Ohio. You old enough?"

"Yeah, I'm eighteen."

He shrugged. "Okay, then let's go."

Matt, Adrian, and Ben were waiting outside.

Matt noticed my pink hair matched his pillows and he was livid. Pissed enough to hit me, so I tried, "Dude, sorry I got pink shit all over your pillow and puked in your bed last night." I felt incredibly stupid, but we all make mistakes.

Matt turned red, and I worried he thought I was taunting him. I wasn't, but he'd only known me for a few hours.

Andy followed, chuckling. I was relieved when he casually said, "Antioch is a messed-up place, but it beats working the docks in Brooklyn. That truly sucked!" Andy slapped Matt on the shoulder. "Matt, you wanna drink?"

"I think so, 'cause somebody puked all over my bed last night, goddamnit."

"You should remember to lock your door," added Andy, matter-of-factly.

Matt finally laughed out loud and said in a nasal New Jersey twang, "Yeah, guess you're right. And I'd better not give shots to kids from Indiana either."

"You passed out on the floor," I muttered.

The five of us walked from the campus to the tiny town center of Yellow Springs. We spat and cussed around ladies in leggings pushing baby strollers. It felt good to be with a group of guys, feral and free. When we came across an elderly woman with a walker, slowly crossing Dayton Street with traffic approaching, we stopped traffic to help her. A masculine force for good.

Marching down the main drag, we came upon a filling station that had been converted into a joint called Eddy's Drive-Through Liquor Store Too, next door to Ha Ha Pizza, famous for slices topped with seasonal psychedelic mushrooms. We passed a group of half-naked hippies changing their clothes in a VW mini-bus covered with Grateful Dead stickers, a soft-serve ice cream place called Dairy Freeze, and a tavern built inside an old train caboose. Every small town in the Midwest has something inside an old train car.

We traversed the entire village of Yellow Springs in about thirty minutes, until we arrived at a bar called the Dayton Street Gulch. Andy seemed to know where every place was in Yellow Springs and whether it had liquor, beer, or both. We walked through a set of Old West swinging doors to enter the Gulch.

"Beer and a shot, five bucks," Andy noted.

My new friends disappeared to the coin-op pool table in the dark recesses of the bar. I found myself standing against a wall, alone and underage, feeling like a target with bright-pink spiky hair in an Ohio redneck bar. When my eyes adjusted, I could see that the place was crowded with a sorry lot of afternoon drunks, disgraced hippie college professors, bikers, and dreary white guys in Carhartt jackets and John Deere caps. Nothing runs like a Deere, I thought. I needed to get the hell outta there—and fast.

"Hey, man. You look lost," called a woman's voice. "You wanna come sit with us?"

I turned and saw a pair of tall, wiry women sitting at a table in the shadows of the bar. They wore black sleeveless T-shirts, jeans, combat boots, and no bras. They looked like sisters.

"I'm Mia," said one of the women. "And this here's Jessie. She's cool. From New York City. People from the City are cool." She exaggerated the final word.

"I'm Steve," I said, my hands shoved deep into my pockets.

"We're just talkin' shit. Have a sit." Mia lifted her dimpled chin toward the empty chair at their table. "We're art students. What's your name? You an artist?"

"Naw, I think I'm gonna study journalism, but I'm not sure yet." My voice trembled. I had no idea how to be cool. "I play drums. Um, I guess that makes me a drummer."

Mia stared at me with curiously intense green eyes. "That makes you an artist, man!" No one had ever referred to me as an artist. I didn't quite buy it, but I liked the idea. "Ain't my friend Jessie here cute?" Mia jabbed the other woman with an elbow. "Come on over and have a seat." She pushed the chair from the table with her foot. "And of course you're an artist. A drummer's an artist."

Mia and Jessie sat very close and were very affectionate with one another. Sisters. I couldn't think of anything to say as I plopped down in the wooden chair and shuffled up to the little round table.

"You want a beer, Steve? Or a shot of tequila?" Jessie asked. Jessie was coy and pretty, which made my palms sweaty. I rubbed them on the legs of my jeans.

Before I could pick my poison, a brassy, obese barkeep named Cookie brought three Rolling Rock beers. Then came three shots of tequila with lime and salt. Cookie appeared to know the women.

"You like tequila?" asked Jessie.

I shrugged. "With the lime and salt, it tastes like nothing."

"Exactly," Jessie agreed.

"So, where you from, Steve?" asked Mia before she downed one of the shots of tequila. "I'm a Kentucky hick from Louisville. A Mexican Spic-hick from Louisville, actually."

"And you're from New York, Jessie?" I asked. She nodded. "Manhattan."

"I'm from India-no-place," I said.

Jessie grinned. "That's hilarious. I just met another dude from there."

"It's not far. Not far enough," I quipped.

Jessie licked the back of her hand and poured salt over the wet spot. "You don't like it there?"

"No, Indiana doesn't like me." I felt like I had said something cool, and my confidence began to sprout. "Hey, I saw a flyer in the student union. You ever hear about one of the Kennedy family speaking on campus? I'm gonna be a journalism major, and I wanna try to interview 'em."

Jessie's eyes widened. "You mean, like Jackie O? That would be so cool. Those outfits!"

A tough-looking guy sporting a short-cropped mohawk like De Niro in *Taxi Driver* pulled up a chair and turned it around so he could lean over the back of it. His sleeveless T-shirt revealed tattooed bands of barbed wire on muscled arms.

Mia gestured to the guy. "This is Michael Caselli, Steve. He's an art Nazi."

"Never play Yahtzee with an art Nazi," said Jessie, giggling.

"Hey," I said to Caselli. "I'm Steve. Nice to meet you."

"Fuck you both," he said to Mia and Jessie. To me, he said, "I'm Michael. Pleasure to meet you, Scott. You a student at the college?"

I nodded. "Uh-huh, and it's Steve."

"I'm looking for volunteers to help build the stage for the Kennedys show November 6th. I need help tonight. You wanna volunteer?"

Dead Kennedys' Antioch College performance on band's final tour, November 6, 1985. From author's archive.

“Totally,” I said, my voice overly enthusiastic. I pictured little John Jr. saluting his father in the coffin carriage passed. Maybe I could do a co-op at the *New York Times*. Holy shit, things were happening fast!

“So is Jacqueline Onassis coming?” I asked.

“No, Scotty. Just the four dudes.” He stood from the chair. “See you there at about six o’clock tonight.” To Jessie, he said, “You got those bolt cutters?”

Jessie reached under her chair and pulled out something wrapped up in an old wool blanket. “From the maintenance shed.”

“Borrowed ’em, remember?” Mia noted.

Jessie smiled and whacked the side of her head with her palm. “Right. I borrowed ’em from the maintenance shed.”

My mind raced as Caselli spun the chair back ’round in the proper direction and walked from the table out of the saloon doors into the early afternoon sun. I’d soon be rubbing elbows with the most influential family in the country. Maybe it would be Ted Kennedy and John Jr. It was weird that they were speaking at some podunk college in the cornfields of rural Ohio. It seemed like the Antioch College promotional materials were accurate when they said that Antioch was a very respected institution of higher learning.

2 WORK WORK WORK

At 6 p.m. sharp on November 5, 1985, a small band of art students, punk-haired kids, and rocker dudes gathered at the back doors of the abandoned theater on the edge of campus. We were bobbing in place and blowing on our cold, blue fingers. Caselli popped the padlock with the bolt cutters, and we went to work cleaning the dark theater space. The once-grand theater sat darkened at a forgotten edge of campus where Ohio State Route 31 entered town from the real world beyond.

We worked until sunrise, sweeping out pigeon shit and mummified rat carcasses. We built ramshackle scaffolds to hang stage lights, wired the place for electricity, and reinforced the stage so it wouldn't collapse.

I was dead wrong about the nature of the engagement, but it was one of the best gaffes I ever made. The "Kennedys" I had seen advertised on the poster were not the American political dynasty but the band Dead Kennedys, a San Francisco punk group. The show changed my outlook on rock music, and it may well have birthed half a dozen new bands.

It was 1985 and the Berlin Wall was standing strong, Ronald Reagan was serving his second term, and we were at the height of Cold War madness. CDs had only recently

Eastbay Ray, Jello Biafra, and Klaus Flouride at
Antioch College Theater on November 6, 1985.
Photographer unknown, from author's archive.

been introduced to the music market, and the Boston Red Sox hadn't won a World Series since 1918, the year World War I ended! Also in 1918, a Mexican revolutionary leader named Emiliano Salazar Zapata posed for a photo while decked out in his signature dress formals, wide sombrero of the local field worker, and bandoliers. He is standing still, holding the hilt of a saber and his prized Winchester semi-automatic repeating rifle. And that was the momentous year that the Bolshevik Revolution swept the Czarists out of Russia, paving the way for the Soviet Union, which would support Nigeria during the 1965 Biafra War, which gave a San Francisco punk rock singer his stage name. The year 1965 was also when my new friend whom I had met at the dive bar earlier that day, Mia Zapata, was born.

Late afternoon on November 6th, a mass of people queued for tickets outside the re-opened Antioch Theater building. Where the hell did all these people come from? Every punker, artist, anarchist, activist, and record collector within a 200-mile radius drove or hitched to Yellow Springs for the show.

Wright-Patterson Air Force Base was forty-five minutes from Dayton. The FBI had kept an eye on Antioch since the student faction of the Black Panthers closed the college down in 1970. What could be more subversive than San Francisco punk rockers in rural Ohio?

I was standing near the entrance to the theater when I heard someone warn, "Watch out! Men in brand new jeans and tennis shoes at nine o'clock." Government paranoia about anti-American insurgencies ran high.

I turned and saw several awkward, crew-cut men in mirrored sunglasses and new Chuck Taylors taking pictures of the people waiting to see the bands. They carried 35mm cameras around their necks and what looked like 9mms in their coats. They wandered about like tourists at the Eiffel Tower as they jotted notes on little pads. It was clear to the earnest G-men that this gathering could lead to a leftist coup and the destabilization of the bedrock of our American way of life.

A confident guy with hair to his butt loudly told the squares to abandon their cameras and new tennis shoes at the door if they wanted to enter the show. Punk kids gathered en masse around the not-so-secret agents, and the atmosphere intensified. The agents chose to abort the mission lest they expose their purpose and blow their cover. I was glad the show would go on unabated.

Inside the theater, Dead Kennedys prepared to blast through their sixteen-song set. Just before the show began, the singer, Jello Biafra, asked for a stool, claiming to have been jumped by skinheads (or he fell off the stage—it wasn't clear) the night before in Bowling Green, Kentucky. D. H. Peligro (the drummer), East Bay Ray (guitar), and Klaus Fluoride (bass) looked like normal enough guys in their late twenties, although they were terribly underdressed for the icy Ohio autumn. They took the stage while complaining about the cold, the lights, the stage monitors, and the food.

Without fanfare or introduction, the drummer counted off the first song, and the place came alive with frantic punk rock energy. The band was incredibly well-rehearsed. "Tight as a hippo's asshole," a young woman observed. The songs were furious and tight.

The bass drum through the PA felt like punches in my gut and the guitar was ear-splitting. The amplified noise of the amps and drums coalesced into a wall of thunder. It was the first time I'd seen stage diving, pogoing, slam dancing, and a seething punk-rock mosh pit. The "pit," I quickly learned, was the area in front of the stage where a sea of sweaty (mostly) boys danced in a spastic circular parade by lowering their heads, throwing up their elbows, and lifting their knees. I was amazed to see kids dive headlong off the stage and land safely on the raised hands of the "moshers" dancing in the pit. The stage-diver was balanced aloft for several seconds, then gently lowered to the floor, boots first. There was a careful protocol to follow in the pit. A few bloody noses and a concussion resulted, but for the most part it was an environment of camaraderie and creativity.

Dead Kennedys connected with the audience like preachers at a Southern Baptist tent revival. These weren't rock gods with long hair and inflated egos with cucumbers in their jeans. They were unassuming music nerds with ideas to share. They didn't show off with flashy solos or high-pitched screams. Dead Kennedys' style of punk music sounded oddly like the surf rock of the Ventures or the Beach Boys, only sped up. Jello Biafra spat radically political lyrics with a snide sense of humor. He wasn't related to the political Kennedy family, but he had run for mayor of San Francisco. I doubted the real Kennedys would appreciate the band name or the radical, satirical nature of Biafra's lyrics, but I did. I would never think of rock music in the same way.

I studied jazz drums since age ten, and I took piano lessons at six and sixteen to learn melody and dynamics. I could read music by sixth grade, and by tenth grade I'd won all the gold medals at state youth competitions in drum-set soloing, snare drum, and percussion combos. As a preteen I listened to artists like Max Roach, Elvin Jones, Dizzy Gillespie, Art Blakey, Oscar Peterson, Thelonious Monk, and Miles Davis. The first tape I got to listen to in my amazing new cassette Walkman knockoff was *A Love Supreme* by John Coltrane. I rode around on my prized Huffy three-speed chopper for hours, listening and trying to understand the music. I knew it was great, but I did not know why.

I had a prog-rock phase too. I liked the records, but I did not understand what the artwork had to do with the sincerity or authenticity of the music. The record jackets featured futuristic utopian worlds with white unicorns, flying whales, and nude sirens beckoning sailors aboard ships charting a course for the virgin seas (or some such shit). Genesis, Yes, Kansas, Styx, Jethro Tull, Klaatu, Asia, Europe, Marillion, Emerson, Lake and Palmer, and other "progressive rock" bands were top sellers when I was growing up. I tried to like it, but I didn't feel anything while listening.

I found the songs to be overly complicated for no reason, with odd time signatures and long-winded, pretentious lyrics written from the point of view of wealthy virtuoso rock-musician superstars obsessed with *The Hobbit*. The bands dressed in medieval robes, their long hair fixed in impossible curls and mullets. I felt nothing listening to these bands. I had a limited awareness of other types of rock music, therefore complicated prog rock seemed like an improvement over disco music and the Village People. Imported English punk, new wave, and hardcore were extremely hard to find or simply not available in my Indianapolis neighborhood.

One summer day in 1980, en route to soccer practice, I rode my bike by Karma Records, an Indianapolis record store and head shop. The *Kiss Alive II* window display that had occupied the front window of the store for months was finally gone. The life-size cardboard cutouts of the cat monster in platform disco shoes and the guy with the cow tongue sewn onto his real tongue were gone. Kiss was folded up in the 7-Eleven dumpster at last. I wanted to set it on fire, but I thought better of doing such a public service.

A simple gigantic black-and-white glossy poster had replaced the Kiss monsters in the display window. I could not take my eyes off it. A single ray of white light focused on a slender bass player as he swung the neck of his Fender Precision bass high above his head, as though he were swinging a sledgehammer. The bass violently smashed against the floor of a stage while his taciturn bandmates looked on and the crowd went wild. It was the iconic image of Paul Simonon of the Clash that graced the cover of *London Calling*.

All I could do was stare. It was a plain design. There was nothing to it, really. I had seen the Woodstock movie in which Pete Townshend of the Who smashed his guitar and Jimi Hendrix lit his guitar on fire with lighter fluid. Their instruments must have been giving 'em trouble, I supposed. But that was forever ago, the '60s even.

The Clash looked utterly dangerous. It was not unlike the *Jaws* movie poster of the fish about to eat the naked woman swimming in the ocean, or Carrie with her pig's-blood rinse. The Clash were uncontrollable. They were not like Kiss or Kansas or any band I had seen. I didn't know enough about punk music to know what the Clash stood for. How the politically tinged lyrics were antifascist and appealed to working-class youth in England. Short hair and combat boots. They wore no robes and sported no mullets. What could such a group sound like?

I was hit with a nose full of Nag Champa incense and a thousand musty vinyl records. It felt like a secret portal into the future—where I belonged.

"The Clash, *London Calling*, is a double gatefold album with a free booklet inside. It's an import from England on CBS Records," explained the smoking hippie tending the shop who was also my middle school Health teacher. I marched up to Mr. Moore, seated on his drum throne behind the counter. He was wearing this cool Daniel Boone frontier jacket with suede fringe and a T-shirt from the Rush *Fly by Night* tour.

I was in that shop nearly every day after that. "Hey man, I see the Clash poster in the window, but I don't see the records for sale." Out of courtesy, I always pretended not to know Mr. Moore outside of class.

"Cops said we can't keep 'em in the regular record bins. Too obscene for the fuckin' Baptists! They'll fuck their cousins and swindle their grandmothers, but they can't handle a little Bad Religion."

I never quite understood Mr. Moore, but he was one of the few cool adults I knew and knew more about music than anyone.

"Yeah." I didn't know if Mr. Moore was serious. "Dumb pigs," I said ruefully. Mr. Moore pointed to the back corner of the shop past the classical and show tunes sections. There was a long black curtain that led to the naughty video section. "The porno section!" he accentuated the P-word. "We gotta put the punk rock shit in the eighteen-years-and-older porno-tape section. You should check out the new Black Flag record, *Damaged*. And the Ramones, *End of the Century*. If you're into that crap," Moore added.

My father had given me a twenty-dollar bill to pay the parks department fee for the soccer league and instead I came home with three new records. I had to deal with my father and sell my skateboard to pay for soccer, but it was worth it. I still own those three records. To me, punks were Artists of the highest caliber—so dangerous their music had to be hidden behind black curtains.

I had not seen a punk band perform prior to Dead Kennedys. I was impressed, not so much by the didactic lyrics as by the raw energy and fearlessness of Dead Kennedys on stage. The music spoke of political absurdities, conspiracy theories, and broken government systems with a clever sense of irony. I wanted to make music that did all that but also reached people's hearts with truth and sincerity. My mind was craving something that spoke to me and to my generation, something that defined my experience as I created it. I wanted a soundtrack for my life.

"The Feds raided my home in San Francisco," Biafra bragged onstage. "The Feds are charging me with distributing harmful material to minors because I used a painting from H. R. Giger called *Penis Landscape* on a poster included with our new album, *Frankenchrist*. They recalled all the albums and charged me with distribution of obscene material just because of a guy's painting of a bunch of erect dicks and some innocent vaginas. It's ridiculous that they don't have other things to worry about, like the crack cocaine flooding our cities or the rise of the KKK here in southern Ohio. Are there any American Nazis in the crowd?" Biafra called out. "If there are, this song's for you. 'Nazi Punks Fuck Off!' One, two, three, four!"

I borrowed my friend Shelli's car the next morning and drove back to Indianapolis to retrieve my drum set. Academics could wait; changing the world through music could not. I started the Oldsmobile and a cassette tape played—Bad Brains' *Rock for Light* on one side and the dreary post-punk band Joy Division on the other. I let it play

Big Brown House open for Dead Kennedys' show at Antioch Theater in November 1985. Photographer unknown, from author's archive.

on repeat during the four-hour drive to Indianapolis and the four-hour drive back to Yellow Springs. I was floored by Bad Brains' drummer, Earl Hudson. He was faster than D. H. Peligro of Dead Kennedys. I had never heard a drummer play so fast or so precisely. I thought it impossible to play like that. It was clear that I had work to do if I wanted to play at the same level as Peligro or Hudson.

My roommate Ben and I had started a band with Adrian on bass. Roger Garufi—a sinewy, blond stoner kid with striking good looks and a deep voice—was the host of a roots reggae radio show on the college radio station WYSO. Roger barged into our second rehearsal, smoking a huge joint rolled like a cone. He listened for a few minutes and made himself the singer. Somehow, we settled on the name Big Brown House, and we were off and running, and we would open for the Dead Kennedys show.

Matt Dresdner, Adrian's roomie, also found inspiration at the Dead Kennedys show. He tracked down a second-hand Steinberger knockoff bass guitar at a pawn shop, and with Adrian's help he began to teach himself to play. Matt had never played an instrument, but within weeks he was in search of a singer for his own punk band. Matt enlisted Andy from across the hall because he thought Andy "looked punk rock." Matt heard Mia singing an Iggy Pop song, "The Passenger," while Jessie was strumming an acoustic guitar, and he later confessed that the sound of her voice made him cry. He immediately asked her to sing for his band. Although Matt did not know how to play bass, he had stumbled upon, arguably, two of the most talented and unique rock musicians anywhere. The three recruited drummer Bob Lee, another student, and the first iteration of the band that would become The Gits was born—or, since they identified as a punk band, I should say miscarried.

The following spring, students decided to organize another show at the Antioch theater building. Big Brown House would play. Matt decided to call his new band White Picket Fence, and they also signed on to play.

Mia fronted White Picket Fence and surprised everyone with her stage presence and powerful voice. Matt followed Andy's chords by watching his left hand on the fretboard and playing the root notes that corresponded to the frets on Andy's Les Paul. Bob was less experienced than I was, and he had trouble playing quick enough. Big Brown House were more experienced musicians overall, but White Picket Fence had something incredibly unique. Mia and Andy were forging melodies that were unorthodox and original from the very beginning.

The name looked great on the poster alongside Big Brown House, but before long it was changed to the Sniveling Little Rat-Faced Gits, borrowed from a skit in a 1970 episode of the BBC comedy show *Monty Python's Flying Circus*.

We all had a blast playing together on the stage of the Antioch Theater, but none of us could have guessed that the show would be the launch of a musical collective that would consume most of our time and attention for the next ten years.

Large painting of Emiliano Zapata and his brother Eufemio Zapata by Mia Zapata, 1985.
Photo by author of painting owned by Mia's dad, Richard Zapata, in 2018.

IT ALL DIES ANYWAY

3

I was sitting in the Antioch cafeteria as one of the local marijuana growers was walking among the tables of two and four kids. He had arms out, palms up, blessing the new students with offerings of free joints. He was introducing himself to make his services available. Every semester offered up a new cohort of customers. The place was thick with sweet, blue weed smoke. Mia walked by me without saying hello and slipped me a piece of paper with an address written on it. She'd cryptically invited me to her off-campus apartment for tea. She referred to her flat as her "dungeon."

It was raining and cold when I set out to find Mia's apartment. She lived in the basement of a multi-bedroom Ohio colonial on Dayton Street, not far from campus. At what I thought was her apartment, I found a door with a small, opaque window that offered up nothing. But I could hear music—the Pretenders' "My City Was Gone"—and the rattle of coffee cans and bottles inside. Not sure if it was the place,

I knocked lightly. Nothing. I knocked a little bit louder. When no one answered, I double-checked the address. I couldn't tell if one of the numbers was a "2" or a "7." And the one next to it could be a "0" or a "6." Convinced that I was at the wrong place, I turned to leave, and I noticed an old paintbrush tied to a string that ran under the door. Curious, I pulled the string. I heard a needle scratch over a record, and the music stopped. I heard cursing and more rattling bottles. The door creaked open. Mia was scowling, but when she saw me, her face relaxed into a wry smile.

"Hey, Steve. Come on in." She turned and walked away from the door. "I was just workin' on somethin.' Kinda busy."

Mia's basement flat was musty and smelled of hops and turpentine. It would have been totally dark, if not for a handful of candles dripping wax on the floor. When my eyes adjusted to the darkness, I saw on a table a mostly empty fifth of Jose Cuervo tequila next to a coffee can full of turpentine, a spread of paint brushes, and a color palette smeared with oil paint. A large canvas—sans frame—lay stretched out on the floor, looking like a rug covered in shit.

Turning her attention to the canvas, Mia said, "Shit, I'm so sorry. I forgot you were comin' by. I'm kinda busy right now."

"That's okay," I said, my arms tucked into my armpits. "I don't wanna interrupt. I can come back another time." I felt stupid.

Mia shook her head. "I ain't like that. You make yourself at home, pour yourself a shot of tequila." She handed me the bottle. There were no clean cups, so I took a swig directly from the nearly empty bottle. The swill at the bottom made me gag. I returned the bottle to the table, then looked down at the six-by-eight-foot canvas at my feet. The edges were held down by a speaker, a brick, a coffee can, and a big hunting knife. The browns, tans, and reddish blotches of paint (or blood) on the canvas had no real form. I couldn't make out anything in the mess of paint.

Mia held two paintbrushes in one hand and a paint roller in the other. She tilted her head and studied the canvas, seeing something buried deep in her mind's eye. It was something clearly beyond my vision. I guessed that a distant world was taking shape inside the colors. I admired her ability to dissociate from the present, to see things that only artists can see. I wished I could see it too.

Mia suddenly plunged the brush into a can of blue, then whipped the brush at the floor, splattering the canvas with color. She made that same whipping motion several more times, and slowly a vague image of a man with a hat took shape. She used the roller to form an arm and a rifle. I saw two men standing shoulder to shoulder, their hats made of browns and yellows. Mia moved to the opposite side of the painting, focusing her gaze on a dripping candle. Then she returned to the canvas. She added details to the painting here and there. I could finally see two men who appeared to be old-time soldiers with bandoliers, swords, and rifles. She painted eyes that were narrowed, intentional, and severe. The figures didn't seem so old-timey anymore.

Mia stepped onto the canvas in her combat boots. She aimed splashes and drips of paint at the canvas, unintentional and exploratory, like Jackson Pollock. I was fascinated, but I also felt like I was intruding.

"Mia, I can come back later if you want," I offered. "You're busy, and I was just in the neighborhood and thought I'd say hi."

"Hi," Mia said without looking up. "Hell no, Stephen. Don't go. Check out my painting. What do you think?" She pointed a brush at the canvas. "It's my great-great-grandfather, or somethin' like that. Emiliano Zapata. It's like my father told me."

"And the other guy is Pancho Villa, right?" I asked.

"No, it's his older brother, Eufemio!" Mia corrected me. "My father's been tellin' me about the family history, and apparently these guys were the heroes of the Mexican Revolution."

"No shit?"

"My dad's been tryin' to get to know me again. He's actually really nice, and he means well. He's tryin' to get me to go to Portland to stay with him, but I don't know, man. I don't wanna." Mia's face turned pensive for a moment. She shrugged and turned back to the painting. "Anyways, I'm tryin' to get to know my ancestors by painting their eyes and looking into 'em."

"Cool," was all I could think to say. I felt dizzy, maybe from the paint fumes and turpentine. Iggy Pop's *Lust for Life* was now playing on her turntable. Mia had that—a lust for life. At least her extroverted side did. Her introverted side was much more enigmatic. She dropped her brushes carelessly onto the surface of the big painting and turned up the music. She turned toward me and exhaled with a little growl that rose in pitch before rushing me with an open hand. Her palm connected with my sternum, and she pushed me hard. I fell backward against a cold, stone dungeon wall with a thud.

Mia pressed her face against mine and kissed until I pushed her away to breathe. We managed to avoid stepping on the wet painting, but we knocked over an easel, a speaker, a stack of books, and a wrought-iron fireplace poker. She was excited by the crashing noise, and I pretended not to be surprised. A dripping lit candle wavered on its wine-bottle perch and tumbled onto a paint-stained set of coveralls, setting them ablaze. Without releasing her grip on my shirt, Mia tossed her brush water on the flames. Then she resumed the attack on me. She was the hungry artist, and I was a willing subject. I refused to surrender as she bit my arm and neck. I might have been stronger and quicker, but Mia's irrepressible passion was unpredictable and indefatigable.

I let her pin me against the wall, but I slipped on a splotch of greasy green oil paint on the floor. My legs went out from under me, and I fell ass over tits to the hard stone floor below. I tried to rise to my feet, but Mia dropped her wiry 120-pound frame squarely on my gut.

It felt like some kind of dark dream. I could feel the heat burning between us. I could also feel the heat of a real fire . . . and the smell of smoke. Mia's coveralls were burning. Water! Mia emptied a full mug of tea she hadn't drunk at the flames.

She hopped to her feet and signaled me to follow. She grabbed the smoldering coveralls and pulled them on over her T-shirt and cutoff jeans. I snatched my jacket and followed her, still smoldering, out of the dungeon and into the cold night.

"Where . . . what are we doing?" I asked stupidly.

"Come on, Stephen. I know where there's a bottle of tequila. I buried it."

"What do you mean, you buried it?" I asked. "Why are we leaving right now? It's cold out."

"Come on, man. I'll show ya." She suddenly switched to a pidgin Spanish that almost sounded authentic, but I knew better. "*¡Ay caramba la gala ginta por las putas hombre, Esteban!*"

"That doesn't mean anything, Mia," I replied. "*¿Venga mujer, que hacemos en esta lluvia? Hace frio. ¡Me pones loco, Zapata!*" I said in Castilian Spanish.

We walked in the freezing November wind for several blocks before Mia stopped cold on the sidewalk in front of a large house near campus and pointed to a bush on somebody's property.

"It's right here on the lawn of . . . that house." She walked toward a hedge in the front yard, glanced fore and aft, then fell to her knees. She sniffed the trail like a basset hound. "I know I buried it here somewhere." It started to rain.

"You buried a bottle of tequila? Like actually buried it, like treasure?" I asked.

"Wait, not here. Over there." She pointed to another part of the yard, pulling a crumpled sheet of notebook paper from the pocket of her charred coveralls and looking around, as if searching for the lost clue in the darkness. "I made a map so I wouldn't lose it. No problemo, Esteban."

Mia scraped aside twigs and fallen leaves from a spot on the ground. She found a stick and began to dig.

"This is insane, Mia. What if the owner has a gun?"

"Have faith, Esteban," she said, digging faster now.

"What if the homeowner comes out and sees you?"

"Eureka!" she yelled. "It's here. Help me dig, Steve."

Unconvinced, I did as I was told. After a few moments of frantic digging, the stick seemed to scrape against an object in the dirt. There was something buried down there. "When did you bury this bottle? Why did you bury it?"

"Oh, I dunno. About five or six months ago, I reckon. Or could've been last week."

The rain was starting to really come down, and the dirt was turning into mud, which made digging a little easier. I wanted to get the bottle and go back to the dungeon, get warm, and pick up where we had left off. But nothing seemed to go as planned in Mia's world and this excited me.

My digging stick poked something flat, about the size of a large shoebox. I brushed away the mud and stones and uncovered the bottle's crypt. I removed the top and saw something wrapped in purple fabric. I pushed the dirt aside, uncovering something else in the shoebox.

What the hell was this?

Compelled by my curiosity and ready to move, I reached into the ground with two hands and gripped a wet, cold mush. A horrible smell assaulted my nostrils, then I saw squirming maggots between my fingers. I turned my head and nearly puked.

Mia stood and backed away. Then she simply turned and walked from the yard, mumbling something in pidgin Spanish.

"What the fuck is this, Mia?!" I shouted after her.

"Mr. Vengeance."

"My cat?!"

"I told a fib," Mia admitted.

"What the hell, Mia?!" I had asked her to watch my cat while away in Indiana to pick up my drums. When I returned, she told me that he had run away.

She stopped squarely on the sidewalk, turned, and yelled back. "He got hit by a car, and I didn't have the heart to tell you. I buried him so you wouldn't have to see him."

"I thought we were hunting free booze?" I exclaimed.

"Sorry. I grabbed the wrong map. I think the tequila is in the bottom drawer of my desk."

I had remnants of the dead cat all over my hands. I wiped my hands on the wet leaves at my feet and looked in Mia's direction for an explanation.

She gave a nervous shrug. "I thought you might want to say goodbye to your kitty."

"This is not my cat, Mia. My cat ran away."

"Hey, you wanna play drums with the Sniveling Gits?"

Before I could think of anything to say, she turned on her boot heel and walked in the direction of the dungeon. I said goodbye to Mr. Vengeance, a very good cat. I followed Mia back to her dungeon.

The smell of Mia's dungeon studio stuck in my throat—burned hair, turpentine, nauseating and intoxicating in equal measure.

"It's cold out. Just crash here tonight," she said, opening the half-drunk tequila bottle that was indeed in her desk drawer. She took a long pull straight from the bottle, then offered some to me.

I waved it away. “I am not accustomed to strong drink,” I said. It was something I had heard in a play. I grabbed hold of the bottle and took a pull.

“There ya go, Stephen, that’ll make the pain go away,” she consoled.

I followed Mia’s gaze to the man on the canvas. He carried the weight of the world in his eyes. I looked at her looking at him. She was lost in thought for a long moment before she felt my eyes on her. She was not a stereotypical beauty. Her hair was dyed blonde and poorly managed. She wore ill-fitting blue jeans and an old army coat. Her nails were bitten short, and she had trouble untying the wet knots of her combat boots, so I held while she pulled until the things came off her bare feet.

We spent the night laughing and shivering under a single gray woolen blanket. When she finally fell asleep, I lay there for a while thinking about everything that had happened over the past few days. Does she like me? Is she serious about me playing in her band? Am I in love? Can she really get to know her ancestors by painting them? My dreams circled the canvas as Mia’s great-grandfather Emiliano Zapata gazed and I traveled far beyond the safe college plains of rural Ohio to a time of horrible smells, unimaginable suffering, and tremendous heroics. I was now the drummer of The Gits.

First band picture taken post gig, Yellow Springs, Ohio, c. 1986. Photo by Jan Julicker.

The Barfing Blues Band was Matt, Mia, and Steve with Chris (Birdman) McCullough.
C. 1986 or 87, from the author's archive.

BARFING THE BLUES

I woke up at 8:07 a.m., already late for class—again. I made a cup of instant coffee, grabbed my textbook, then hopped on my ruby-red Schwinn three-speed. I sped to class in the cold drizzle, balancing the cup of coffee in one hand and steering my bike with the other, the book shoved in my pants. My anthropology professor gave me shit for showing up late for his class—again. I took a seat behind a guy wearing feather earrings and a dress and a woman in a matching tie-dye T-shirt and skirt. When the professor asked me if I'd done the reading about pre-Columbian Mexican art, I was still half asleep. I described how *curanderas* advised generals during revolutions, and how they shapeshifted into jaguars and children of the dead. Then I shrank back into my chair and tried not to fall asleep.

When class was over, the professor asked me to wait. After the classroom had cleared out, he asked if I was on drugs. Before I could deny using, he asked if I would procure said drugs for him. I wasn't high, but I told him I'd see what I could do. He erased the word "late" from next to my name. I nodded and walked out of the classroom. The sun was shining brightly. I enjoyed riding my bike through the sparkling puddles en route to my next class, French.

"Hey, man!" called a low voice from behind me.

I turned and saw Mia approaching on her bike.

“Let’s check out the old music building before they tear it down,” she yelled. “I hear it’s haunted.”

“Bonjour, mademoiselle!” I called back to her. “Shouldn’t we wait ’til it’s dark?”

“You crazy? It’s haunted,” said Mia as she turned and rode off toward the old music building. Of course, I followed.

Antioch was once considered a great liberal-arts college. Antioch’s first president, Horace Mann, was an attorney and a congressman from Massachusetts, a well-known abolitionist and social reformer. He was considered the founder of public education in the United States. He believed that a well-educated populace was essential for a strong democracy. In his first graduation speech, Mann implored the Antioch graduates to “be ashamed to die until you have won some victory for humanity.” That sounded like a good punk-rock chorus to me.

It was of the first colleges to admit women and African Americans. It welcomed gay, lesbian, and transgender students as early as the ’40s. Coretta Scott King, Rod Serling, Stephen Jay Gould, and a few notable intellectuals studied there. Martin Luther King, Jr., gave the commencement speech in 1965. But by the 1980s Antioch had become progressive to the point of institutional suicide.

The lax admission policy and a curriculum based on progressive idealism without a focus on fiscal responsibility or an endowment resulted in a great college on the verge of bankruptcy. By 1985, Antioch was in danger of losing its university accreditation, and many interesting (and non-essential) programs had been terminated and professors laid off. Several buildings were shuttered, including a music and theater building. Wishing to win one more victory for humanity, we took it upon ourselves to “officially” resurrect the theater stage with a punk-rock show and revive the music program by starting rock bands.

Cecil Taylor, one of John Coltrane’s pianists, taught at Antioch in the late ’60s. When the college could not pay him his salary he rented a truck, backed it up to the loading dock late at night, and stole Antioch’s ten-foot Steinway concert grand piano. It was Taylor’s personal severance package. The resources of the institution had been squandered during the radical ’60s and ’70s, but that was a gift to us. We could use what remained of the school’s reputation and entertainment budget to serve our needs. It was, as we saw it, a “do it yourself” education, and we did whatever the hell we could imagine. We took that responsibility very seriously. We organized our academic lives, created our own academic majors, and sought internships to complete a degree. No one else would do it for us. Economists believe that a liberal-arts degree offers negligible return on investment. That may be true, but the cultural insights and emotional intelligence I developed during the four years I studied at Antioch would be invaluable for navigating the fraught years to come.

Mia and I dropped our bikes and walked through the overgrown weeds to the back door of the old music building, which was scheduled for demolition. We pried the door open with a claw hammer and stepped in. Although the floor inside seemed a little uneven, it felt solid. There were a few wretched upright pianos in practice rooms. Steps led to the record library in the dark, dusty basement. Remarkably, much of the collection was intact, but it was scheduled to be destroyed with the building in the coming days. There were hundreds of classical records in sleeves adorned with Rembrandt and Botticelli paintings. Strauss, Schubert, Wagner, Tchaikovsky, Beethoven—the masters would all be crushed by the wrecking ball.

Deeper in the stacks we found fragile acetate blues and jazz 78rpm records, produced by labels such as Decca, Smithsonian Folkways, Black Swan, Okeh, and Chess Records. A ten-by-ten-inch box held a collection of 78s labeled simply "Race Records," which included four platters of blues musicians from the 1930s and 1940s. Lead Belly, Ma Rainey, Robert Johnson, Bessie Smith, Ethel Waters, Sister Rosetta Tharpe, Sippie Wallace, and the guitarist Memphis Minnie, whose songs Janice Joplin and Led Zeppelin made famous.

Mia grabbed hold of the records and clutched them to her breast. She was like a small child in a big mall, reuniting with her parents after being lost in a sea of knees and nobodies. Mia found her sacrosanct family elders. She shoved the records into her backpack.

"Mia, I don't think that's how you check out records from a library," I mocked.

A security guard, likely alerted by a campus do-gooder, called out to us in the darkness. "Hey! You can't smoke pot in there, kids. It's a fire hazard. You can smoke in the cafeteria if it's too cold outside," she suggested.

She chased us away, but not before Mia smuggled more than an armful of blues records to safety.

While we were in college, our academic and intern schedules didn't always sync up, and there were months when Mia and I were not in the same town at the same time. At one point Andy was in London, studying for a semester, leaving me, Mia, and Matt without our band. We didn't feel like we could be The Gits without Andy.

I didn't run into Mia for a week or so after our big blues-heist break-in and I thought she must be hiding out. I was late again for anthropology when Mia called after me as I was riding my bike to class. "We should just start a blues band while Andy's away."

I stopped pedaling and turned to look at her. "Let's get Matt on bass," I suggested. Matt had picked up the bass only weeks earlier, and already he was developing into a proficient player.

"I got a friend who can play guitar like that, so let's get started," she continued. "I just need to play. It's all I need right now, man. We gotta get this shit together, Steve."

Later, I saw Mia sitting on a curb with her head in her journal. It was clear that she'd been crying, and she looked as if she hadn't slept.

"What happened?" I asked.

"Can I borrow five bucks, Steve?"

"I don't think I have that much. What do you need it for?"

"I need gin, man. It's five for a pint."

I dug into my pocket and pulled out a few bills and coins. I counted them, then said, "I've got $4.35."

"Never mind." She waved it away. "You gotta eat."

I held out the money. "I already ate today," I lied.

"It's okay. I'll ask Jessie," she said.

Mia was shaking, and I was concerned. Why gin and not just a beer? I didn't know how to help, which made me angry at myself. Maybe starting a blues side project would help her stay busy and feel better.

Much later I'd learn that, although Mia was creating art and painting wildly, she was also drinking a lot and failing to turn in her work. She was flunking out of a college that gave no grades. Her father, Richard Zapata, was pressuring Mia to move to Portland and attend outpatient rehab under his care. Mia had been living on her own for three years, and going to live with her father was a step in the wrong direction. Mia had not grown up with her father. Moving to Portland felt like failure to Mia, however they both sought connection with one another. While Mia was aware that she was drinking too much, it would have to get seriously out of control before she would acquiesce to her father's request.

Mia had struggled with learning disabilities throughout her childhood. She was quick-witted, emotionally intelligent, and creative beyond words, but dyslexia made it hard for her to keep up in subjects other than art. Mia sometimes misspelled her own name, and she once wrote the band name as the "Gitts." Paradoxically, Mia wrote incessantly, filling journals with her thoughts, reflections, and drawings, revealing the most beautifully expressive prose. Grammar and spelling were a hindrance to her creativity and workflow. She found inspiration in the lyrics of great blues singers who, like Mia, enjoyed little academic success. Mia's lyrics were, from the very beginning, fully formed ideas with carefully considered meter and counterpoint.

Matt was up for the challenge, and he agreed to play bass in our blues project. But when the time came for our first rehearsal he wasn't feeling well. He left the practice complaining of nausea before we even started. The next morning, the blues band guitarist, a biology student named Chris "Birdman" McCullough, also called in sick. Then Mia caught the bug. So, when we needed a name for our side project, the choice was perversely clear: the Barfing Flu Blues Band. We eventually shortened to the Barfing Blues Band, or just BBB. What's in a band name anyway?

We started rehearsing the blues songs, paying special attention to our dynamics. Mia and Chris chose songs from the liberated stack of 78s from the doomed music library. We practiced at low volume since there was no PA to amplify the vocals and, for the first time, I could hear the full range of Mia's voice over the instruments. Her singing voice already sounded seasoned and completely original. It made me shudder, as though I'd been given access to a privileged realm. I knew that I'd been invited by a genius to a life-long place in music if we could just keep it together.

Blues music transported Mia. She absorbed the melodies and the lyrics into her being. She understood the music innately, and she appeared to channel the soul of a long-forgotten voice, breathing new life into the old songs and integrating her own lived experiences.

Mia somehow understood the sui generis nature of the blues and she brought new energy to the forgotten tunes. She drew upon her own anguish and lonesomeness to create something beautiful and healing. The exercise of delving into the history of the blues influenced her lyrical content in The Gits too. She was authentic while also remaining reverential to the old-time masters. The personal lyrics she sang were honest and made her vulnerable. She invited her band and audience to join her. Whatever the personal hell, we would get through it together.

I knew that jazz traced its origins back to the blues. I loved both. When the Barfing Blues Band rehearsed, it was the most natural music in the world to play. I loved the lazy tempos. To accentuate the feel, I played just a wee bit behind the beat. Matt kept the bass parts simple and had no problem learning the blues songs. Our playing styles, while different in many ways, jibed very well.

Mia's parents were television and radio professionals, so as a girl Mia was exposed to the headphones and microphones of recording and broadcast studios. She knew how to use a microphone for effect, developing a kind of growl she no doubt gleaned from the 78s. She used her throaty, chesty voice to great effect.

Shortly after we started practicing, the Barfing Blues Band landed a real gig at the Canal Street Tavern in Dayton, Ohio. It was a small, legendary blues and bluegrass club that welcomed the college crowd because students drank expensive imported beer and tipped better than the regulars. We were only able to rehearse twice, but we managed to prepare a forty-five-minute set in just a week. The songs we chose to play were primarily lifted from Mia's coveted 78s, but we also transposed tunes by Iggy Pop and James Taylor and an original into an odd semblance of blues music.

One of my beefs with rock musicians is that most have one trick: turn up the volume on their amplifier. They will not or cannot play with dynamics. Drummers often have the same blind spot. When our blues project played too loudly, we couldn't hear Mia, and she was the only one of the barfing bandmates who knew the song structures. Plus, when we played too loudly during rehearsal on campus, we got shut down by the police. Because we'd practiced at a low volume, we performed the same way, making our music more accessible to the audience.

At the Canal Street Tavern, I noticed the audience leaning in toward the stage to catch every word Mia sang. Tavern regulars and the younger college set were rapt with attention. Mia could sense the symbiosis with her audience, and she looked into their eyes as if in conversation with each and every audience member. She apologized for not doing justice to the original artists, and she sparred adeptly with hecklers to win over the unconvinced. Mia was a natural on stage, and it was beautiful to behold.

After a break between sets, Mia sat behind a tired old upright piano on the stage and started playing an old tune. Until then, I hadn't known that she could play piano. The lyrics told of dying and going to hell, where she danced with the devil and sang with demons. "Their eyes dripped blood, and the demons clacked their teeth, for they were glad she came . . . down to that brimstone flood!" Holy shit!

When the song was over, there was no applause. Silence. Crickets. Mia did not say anything, but I could tell she was mortified. Dejected, she called for Matt and me to join her on stage. Still no applause. I felt bad for her because I thought she sounded great. It was not an easy song, but at least she had tried. But then a tall, skinny older (over forty) guy sporting OshKosh overalls and a straw hat spun on his to bar stool to face the stage. He slid off his perch, stood, and clapped his hands slowly and boldly with approval. On cue, the entire bar erupted in applause, and they didn't stop until Matt and I were on stage, and I counted off another song. Mia blushed visibly and turned away, then we sat back down to play an encore. Mia had the crowd in the palm of her hand.

It turned out that the man who clapped was the legendary bluegrass and folk-country musician John Hartford, who was performing the next night. He knew then what I wouldn't know until years later—that he'd been a witness to a genius finding her voice.

A few years back, I discovered live recordings of our little Barfing Blues Band. Mia could have been a pop or jazz singer of the caliber of Amy Winehouse, Rickie Lee Jones, or Lana Del Rey, but she didn't have the temperament of a cool jazz torch singer or an old-time blues revivalist. She certainly drew inspiration from those uniquely American art forms, but her soul was restless and raw. She loved the frantic tempos, the tribal rhythms, the urgency that makes punk music. Patti Smith, Bonnie Raitt, Billie Holiday, Nina Simone, Johnny Rotten, Iggy Pop, Bessie Smith, Big Mama Thornton—she absorbed them all with equal relish. Mia too was one of the greats. My personal quest was to show the world that greatness and accompany her all the way to the top, whatever that could mean.

I couldn't sleep after the show. I was alone at my flat in Yellow Springs and it was hot and muggy as hell. My head was still buzzing from the music, the cheering of the audience, and the remarkable endorsement of John Hartford. I called Mia to see if she was still awake. She was, of course. She asked in a faux-courtly tone if I'd like to have a nightcap. She'd be right over with a six pack of Black Label beer. I sat on the stoop of my apartment and waited.

It was still 91° at 3 a.m. when I heard a distant tinkling bell ringing out gaily from the darkness. Mia approached on her bicycle, weaving between parked cars, swerving from sidewalk to street and back again. The glass beer bottles were in a basket lashed to the handlebars. I thought she was clowning. She was approaching too fast, ringing the bell with one hand and piloting her red girl's Schwinn with the other. She looked up and laughed nervously but she was not slowing down. I stood up and jumped from her path, barely avoiding a collision. Mia and the bike came to a stop in a big thorny juniper bush next to the stoop.

"Aww, fuck!" she yelled from the bush. "Shit, man. The brakes don't work."

"Nice landing, Amelia Airhead," I teased.

"Nice show tonight, Stephen," she said from inside the sticker bush. "Can you give me a hand please?"

I helped her to her feet, then picked up her bike and leaned it against the stoop. When she bent down to retrieve the beer, she discovered that all but two of the bottles had broken. She offered one to me and kept one for herself.

Crickets droned everywhere on that muggy Ohio night. The mosquitos drowned out the constant ringing in my ears borne of the hundreds of hours of bashing drums and loud guitars.

It was too warm to hang inside, so we walked a few blocks from my flat to a city park with a shimmering cobalt public swimming pool. We were sticky with the sweat we had earned from a night of loading gear and playing our hearts out in a sweltering, smoky bar. At the park, the pool looked so refreshing I wanted to drink from it, but, alas, it was closed for the night.

"How annoying, they close the public swimming pool after sunset. Ridiculous. An outrage, actually. An affront against the People! I am going to write the mayor!"

"Shut the fuck up, Stephen! We are getting in that water."

We ducked behind some bushes and scoped out the area. We saw a Yellow Springs police officer making the rounds in his squad car. He pulled into the lot adjacent to the pool bathhouse and shined his spotlight on the empty pool. Convinced it was all clear, he flipped a U-turn and continued on his rounds. I checked my watch: one minute, two, three, four minutes and thirty-eight seconds, then he pulled into the lot again and shined his light on the water. As we polished off our warm beers, we watched him a third time. The moment he turned his back to the pool, we made our move.

Like a couple of slinky coyotes, Mia and I scaled the pool fence, wiggled out of our clothes, and dove into the wonderfully reviving, over-chlorinated waters of the public pool. As we treaded water in the deep end, I could think of nothing but kissing Mia's glistening lips.

I glanced at my Timex. We had thirty-eight seconds before the cop returned. We hustled out, grabbed our clothes, and got back into the bush for cover. When the officer shined his light on the pool, he obviously saw the trail of wet footprints that led from the water to the fence. He scanned the perimeter, but we were well hidden. I wondered how many times he had dealt with desperate pool-hoppers during the muggy Ohio summer slump. He stuck around for a few more minutes, listening for the sounds of giggles and trespass. Eventually he gave up and flipped a U-turn to continue his patrol. We ran for the pool a second time. It felt so fucking good.

Steve, Ben London, and friends after some costumed sporting event at Antioch College in 1989. Photographer unknown, from author's archive.

The Gits play Rock -n- Roast Festival at Antioch College in Yellow Springs, Ohio, 1989. Photo by James Moriarty, from the author's archive.

AIN'T GOT NO RIGHT

5

When they demolished the Antioch music building, we were left with no place to develop songs and rehearse. Other kids, taking their cues from us, suddenly showed an interest in starting bands. A dozen musical projects might be brewing on any given night. There were blues bands, cover bands, performance-art rock bands, punk bands, pop bands, reggae bands, soul bands, spoken-word and poetry slams, Grateful Dead jam bands, and of course, my bands. We tried practicing in our campus dorms, in off-campus houses, and in classrooms, but nothing lasted long. The cops always showed up with some neighbor who had complained about the college kids partying. Frustrated, I decided to go to the administration with an official appeal for rehearsal facilities. I was directed to the Antioch College Dean of Men, Stephen Schwerner.

What an ominous title! And what a band name.

I wrote a proposal in pencil on a legal pad and made an appointment with Dean Schwerner. Greta, the dean's daughter, was a brilliant theater major who lived down the hall from me. I asked her for advice about speaking with her father. Her response was surprising. She said that her father might be sympathetic to our cause because he loved jazz and had a long-running jazz radio show on the campus public radio station, WYSO. Greta's uncle, the dean's brother, Michael Schwerner, had been one of the civil-rights leaders who went down to Mississippi to organize and register voters in May of '64. Michael Schwerner and his partners, James Chaney and Andrew Goodman, were hunted down and summarily murdered by the KKK, then their bodies were tossed into a swamp. Not surprisingly, their killers were acquitted at trial. How scared those guys must have been. And how brave. We would have been roughly the same age. What a heavy burden for their families!

"Look, Steve, just talk music," Greta advised. "My dad'll help you out."

When I arrived at the dean's office, I found the door slightly ajar. I would have knocked but I suddenly got cold feet. The man's brother had martyred himself for a righteous cause, and here I was about to start bitching about playing loud music. My childish issue wasn't worthy of this man's time. I turned to leave. He must have heard me through the crack in the door, and he called out to me.

"Oi?" he said. "You there! Who is it?"

"Oh, shit," I said aloud.

"What is it, man? You in trouble? Come in," said the dean. I sheepishly pushed the door open.

He shook his head to see me standing in his doorway. "The goddamn school year hasn't started, and you and your cohort are already causing havoc everywhere, destroying the campus and drinking all night." He waved me in. "Angels by day, but when the sun goes down all hell breaks loose. Reminds me of myself, before I became the James Dean of men." He smiled and snickered. "Come on, get in here. Have a seat. What's on your mind, boy?"

I wiped my hands on my jeans, then I launched into a semi-scripted plea. "There's a crisis on the campus," I blurted. "The Federalist troops have taken our land, and we have no place to play music."

Obviously confused, Dean Schwerner furrowed his mighty brows. He interlocked and cracked the knuckles on his great hairy fingers and queried, "What the hell are you talking about?"

"There's no functional instrumental music program at the college. We have a great lecturer named John Ronsheim, who teaches classical and jazz cultural history, but we have no musical instrument classes or instruction and no place to play."

He nodded. "Okay, I'm listening."

"Me and my . . . I mean, many of the students want to play instruments and practice, but we can't. We want to form . . . uh, combos and quartets, jazz bands and things like that." I thought it best not to use the words "rock" or "punk."

He grunted.

"I've studied jazz since I was eleven years old, and I need a place to practice drums . . . and other stuff too, you know?"

The dean glared at me from behind a thick gray beard and black, heavy-framed glasses. I figured he was trying to measure my destructive capabilities, the way a beat cop checks out the new kid on the block with an MS-13 tattoo. I was convinced that I'd overstepped my bounds. What a stupid idea this had been.

Dean Schwerner fixed his stare on some long-lost dream hiding in the corner of his office, hidden among the towers of books piled to the ceiling and a stack of records on the edge of his desk. Slowly, the dean stood. He was tall and balding, potbellied, and shrewd. His beady eyes were transfixed on something I couldn't see, and that terrified me. He sat back down, then placed a hand reverentially on a Miles Davis LP called *Birth of the Cool*. He sank into his high-backed leather chair and secret music enveloped his soul. His fingertips ever so slightly tapped the ding-ding-a-ding of the swinging ride cymbal on the armchair, while Miles's trumpet became his empathy and his mission to serve . . . like his big brother, Michael. He turned his gaze on the gangly kid in ripped jeans standing before him.

I thought Dean Schwerner looked absolutely pissed. I sat in silence, my anxiety spiking. I was planning a strategic retreat when the dean's eyes widened, and he slammed a fist on the great oaken desktop. "I have a jazz show on WYSO. Ten years running, every Wednesday night. If you wanna really learn to swing, man, you gotta get the hell outta Dodge. Go to New York City. That's where it all happens. In the City you live, breathe, eat, and drink jazz. Uptown! The Roxy! Birdland! You wanna play jazz, you need to go to New York. Jazz is the only true American art form. You must be her ambassador, young cat. You might be hungry, you might be cold, and you might even die, but you'll be living the music, and the music will live through you. Life is jazz!"

I could only swallow and nod dumbly.

"There are Antioch alumni in New York. Knock on their doors and find a place to crash. Practice and play in the subway. Get a gig at a club. Be a coat-check girl, or bus tables. Go up to Harlem and take in the culture. When you start to dig it, you'll start to live it. When you sing, you'll start to swing. 'Cause it don't mean a thing—"

"If it ain't got that swing!" I interrupted.

He nodded in approval. "I'm a jazz fanatic! Trane, Monk, Mingus, Miles, Evans, Roach, Peterson, Parker, Blakey—all the greats!"

I mentally noted that he hadn't mentioned Cecil Taylor.

"The titans of the only true American art form. You'll soar, man. Spread your wings like Icarus, and you'll be on fire. Just be cool."

I blinked silently. I was dumbfounded by what he was telling me. "But . . . I just signed up for journalism, anthropology, sociology, and French classes this semester, and I was planning to finish college and all that."

But maybe I was wrong to want to finish college before making a go of a career in music. The dean's brother had sacrificed his life in pursuit of his dream of a fairer America. Why should he be willing to make the ultimate sacrifice when I wasn't even willing to sacrifice a college degree to pursue my dream? Civil rights, Dr. Martin Luther King, Jr., Joseph Lowndes, Rod Serling, Miles Davis, Charles Mastropolo—they had all done whatever was necessary to realize their potential. Why shouldn't I?

We fell into an awkward silence. I'd forgotten why I'd come.

Looking at his watch, Dean Schwerner said, "I beg your pardon, but what was your name, son, and why . . . what's the trouble, boy? Are you in trouble?"

"Not yet. No problem, sir," I mumbled.

"Always glad to help the movers and the doers. Good man. Carry on and enjoy the rest of your college tour. And don't miss my show, Friday at 6 p.m. That's tonight."

“Not a chance I’ll miss it,” I said, backing out of his office into the grand marble floored lobby of the main building.

I went looking for Ben, Adrian, and Matt.

Prior to my meeting with the dean, the guys had scouted for a place to practice. Among the rundown campus buildings, they had discovered an entire dormitory that had been closed since sometime in the ’70s, when it housed the student wing of the Black Panther party. West Hall was a three-story brick building. The first two floors were divided into a dozen small dorm-rooms, and the attic had a twelve-foot ceiling apex and no windows. Perfect! We envisioned each of the sixteen dorm rooms serving as a music rehearsal studio, and the grand attic would be our recording studio.

When the dean was on air and his radio show started, we went to work on the doors. We had to jimmy the lock on the heavy steel doors of West Hall. It was already dark. We had tools and a matter-of-fact attitude, so no one could tell we weren’t a maintenance crew. Once in, we barricaded the doors and went to work sweeping out the halls and picking up the mess inside. We soundproofed the rooms by leaning old mattresses against the windows or stuffed blankets under doors and chimneys. We worked until early in the morning. Next day, we fetched our gear and rocked out in the attic until the next morning. There were no noise complaints, no cops, and no deans to get in our way . . . yet.

Within a week, Antioch students with musical dreams had occupied a dozen of the former dormitory rooms. Guitars, drums, pianos, and horns could be heard blaring away. It felt good to have solved the problem for so many students.

Mia performs in red dress with The Gits at Antioch College, c. 1986. From the author’s archive.

Joseph Lowndes, Andy Kessler, Jay Ruby, and Steve Moriarty at Antioch College, Yellow Springs, Ohio, c. 1988. Photographer unknown, from author's archive.

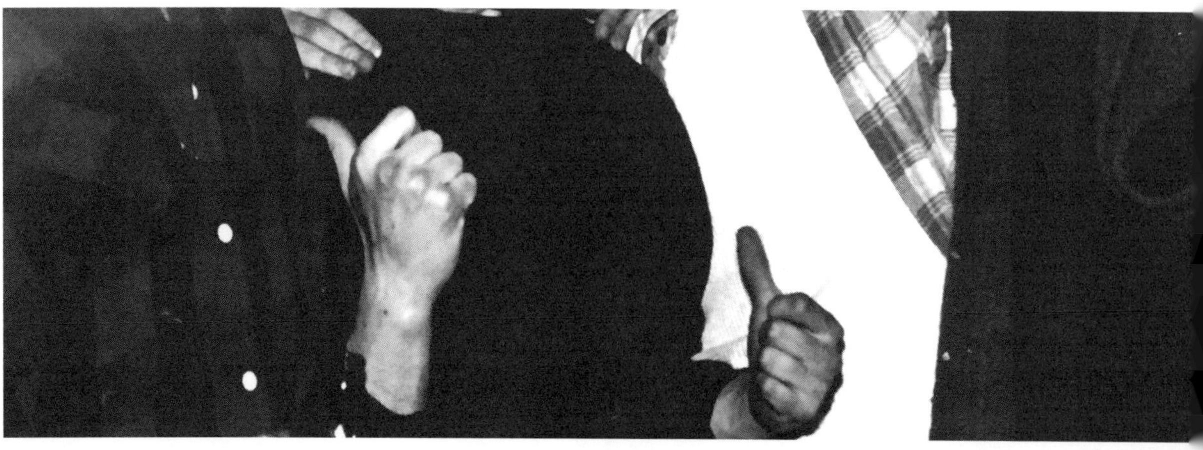

6

BEER AND BLOOD

During my second year of college, Mia, Matt, and Andy left Yellow Springs to complete their internships. The three found work at a special project called the Farm, a nonprofit community center located in the Mission District, a low-income, largely Latino neighborhood on the edge of San Francisco. The Farm was founded in the early 1970s by the influential artist and educator Bonnie Ora Sherk and the taxi driver and trumpeter Jack Wickert. It contributed to the culture and vibrancy of the Mission District. An Antioch alum, Andy Pollack, took the helm and kept the collective active until 1987. The vision was to create a small farm with a garden and some animals to teach the neighborhood children and young adults about collectivism, community, and healthy food and where it comes from.

The Farm maintained its programs by putting on music shows in a large community room on the property. The bands were local to San Francisco, such as Dead Kennedys and Frightwig. Also, many of the now-legendary underground American and English punk and hardcore bands played the Farm: Discharge, Social Distortion, the Descendants, the Mentors, 7 Seconds, MDC (Millions of Dead Cops), RKL (Rich Kids on LSD), Dirty Rotten Imbeciles, Raw Power, the Accused, Redd Kross, Soundgarden, and Bad Brains, to name but a few.

Matt, Mia, and Andy ran the stage, did the lighting, took tickets, and promoted the shows all around the Bay Area. Many of the bands that Andy and Matt had seen at CBGB in New York played at the Farm. It was no doubt an incredible and inspiring experience for the three. The Gits (with Bruce Ducheneaux on drums) played the Farm too. Years later, when we played San Francisco, The Gits were fondly remembered and well loved.

Between 1985 and 1989 there were periods of three to nine months that The Gits were neither studying nor working in the same city. When together, we made fast use of the time and wrote music and played live when we could. When apart, the four of us pursued our individual projects.

I played drums with Big Brown House prior to being asked to join The Gits and divided my time between the bands. It was exhausting at times, but, at twenty years old, my physical and mental health were not of notable concern. My skills improved as a drummer and contributing songwriter.

I worked to combine my swing jazz chops with the tempo and power of rock drumming. I played the tom-toms of my drum set like a set of melodic instruments. I experimented with found objects like radial saw blades and iron pipes laid out like a vibraphone. Somehow, I was keeping up with my studies, but I was burning the candle too late, and it was taking a toll.

To gain credits for the independent study off campus, Big Brown House hatched a plan to move to nearby Ann Arbor, Michigan, and there we would rent a house for a few months where we could all crash and play and record our music. We could focus on being a band and writing music. The final project for college credit was to record and present a cassette of our original music. We had six months.

Adding to the allure of Ann Arbor was the fact that Iggy Pop, the Stooges, and MC5 were from there. That made it seem like the music scene was "real," even though the aforementioned bands were no longer any part of that same scene. Detroit, the home of Motown Records, Stevie Wonder, the Temptations, John Lee Hooker, Alice Cooper, and Parliament/Funkadelic, was a short drive from Ann Arbor.

It was as if we believed that these various iconic music stars might be seen at any moment strolling downtown Ann Arbor, with Stevie Wonder holding on to the arm of Ted Nugent and David Bowie holding hands with Iggy Pop at the U. of M. undergraduate library.

We bought a dime-bag of weed and some beer for the journey. Sufficiently supplied, Roger, Adrian, Ben, and I piled ourselves and our gear into Roger's '74 Dodge "love machine" van, complete with shag carpet on the walls, surround-sound stereo,

CB radio, swiveling captain's chairs, and a huge rumbling 400-cubic-inch motor—all made in Detroit, Michigan, USA.

It was April. None of us had money, so when we rolled into town we found ourselves effectively homeless. We slept in parks or in the van when it snowed. We loitered around town and avoided arrest for a few days until Roger discovered a flyer on a health-food store bulletin board advertising a summer sublet. It was a student group house, a big, beige thing at the intersection of State and Packard. It had five bedrooms, three bathrooms, and an empty basement where we could write and record our music. We sprang into action. One of the guys convinced his parents to wire money and we signed the sublease for $500 a month.

We moved in, set up our gear, and started to write and practice new music. We also had to find work and gigs and somehow record an album during the next five months. It was slow going because the country was in recession, but we found various jobs and made it work.

One day, I was hanging out near the University of Michigan campus when I stumbled into a Take Back the Night march, protesting sexual and domestic violence. Thousands of women were marching down the street, shouting and carrying signs. I decided to march along, but they told me that men weren't allowed to participate in the TBTN march. But I could stand on the sidewalk and clap if I chose. Standing there, I spoke with an older woman wearing a pink miniskirt and Mickey Mouse ears who told me about the rampant sexism at the university.

Women were organizing to stop an epidemic of campus date rape and sexual assault that was being covered up by university authorities.

It made me feel awful. I walked along the sidewalk for a few blocks, inspired by the marchers, but I also felt overwhelming sadness. And I was angry for not having known about this. I wondered why guys feel like it's okay to force women to have sex. But then I read the marchers' placards and signs. The media encouraged men to think of women as objects, without feelings or value, read one sign. I simply had to open a magazine or watch any television show or movie for confirmation of that truth. A culture of rape, bullying, intolerance, violence, and murder made America a dangerous place for women and girls. I had not thought of this obvious affront until then.

The marchers were serious and angry. Some women cried; others marched silently with distant stares, remembering. Their pain enraged me, in part because it made me feel so powerless. I went home wondering what I could do to make their lives better. Truth is, I could not change their lives by doing any one thing. I could only work on myself. If I did nothing, then I would simply be part of the patriarchy and thus a part of the problem, not the solution. I walked along the sidewalk with the flow of the march, but eventually faded remorsefully off on a side street and slumped back to our corner to tell my friends.

Next morning, I awoke feeling sort of ill. I had no idea what was wrong with me, but the feeling had been gnawing at the edge of my mind for weeks, and now it was hollowing me out. I felt exhausted and utterly alone. Fucking depressed. I was tired all the time, but I couldn't sleep. I felt weak, but I couldn't eat—not that I had an appetite. And I couldn't communicate to my housemates—or anyone, for that matter—how difficult it was to face the day. I felt tremendous regret, as though I'd done something terribly wrong, but I didn't know what it was. My mind wandered to dark places, and I drank beer in search of relief. But when I sobered up the old fog enveloped me once again. I became increasingly self-aware and obsessed with the meaningless routines, but I became fixated on the futility of trying anything. My waking moments were filled with the constant pressure of guilt, regret, shame, hopelessness, and crushing sadness.

Catastrophe seemed to loom on the horizon, and I found myself considering suicide.

At band practice with Big Brown House, I felt clumsy and inept behind the drums: I couldn't feel the tempo, and I kept dropping sticks. I thought that everyone could tell just how insecure I was feeling, and I was convinced that I couldn't perform as they expected. But the guys didn't seem to notice. I had to expend so much energy to act as if I didn't feel dead inside, but no one could see through the front.

That changed when my morose disaffection and clumsiness caught up with me. My hand slipped while I was playing drums, and my index finger smashed into the sharp, jagged edge of a broken cymbal. Blood pulsed from the tear, splattering my drums with carmine blood spots. I wrapped a bandana around the cut, but I couldn't get the bleeding to stop. I tried to speak up, but I could not find words over the loud tuning guitars. I simply stood up and went upstairs to treat the wound. I made a sling from an old Joan Jett T-shirt and slung my hand above my heart. But the bleeding still would not stop. I could hear the guys still tuning and riffing in the basement rehearsal space. I left the house and walked barefoot a couple miles to the university student medical clinic, where I waited a few hours to be seen. An intern put a few stitches in my finger and sent me home with a script for Percocet and a pamphlet about HIV/ AIDS transmission.

I left the clinic and shambled over to the steps at the entrance to the University of Michigan undergraduate library. Students, professors, and eccentric college-town residents in tie-dyed shirts and sweatpants surrounded me, but an invisible wall made it impossible for me to interact or even to make the most basic decisions, like which way to walk. I felt as if I were dying inside. I needed some kind of help. I was sure that my bandmates would not understand. I was alone.

A middle-aged woman wearing a muumuu and holding a clipboard walked out of the library and paused beside me for an uncomfortable moment. I tried to maintain a blank stare, but she stepped closer. Oversized Native American silver and turquoise necklaces jangled inside the cleavage of her mammoth sunburnt bosom. She flopped down next to me. She smelled of sweet patchouli and cigarettes, which turned my already nervous stomach. Annoyed by the interruption, I turned to complain.

"Nickel for your thoughts," she said.

I glanced up. My eyes met hers. She wore large, round Janis Joplin–style glasses with a silver librarian chain around her neck. "Uh . . . my thoughts? Not really worth a nickel," I said, my voice glum.

I wanted her to get up and walk away, but she wouldn't leave me alone, and I didn't even have the energy to insist that she leave. The pain behind my flat expression left me mute. An ache began to burn in my stomach. I wanted to bury my face in her enormous, sweaty middle-aged-hippie-lady breasts, purge my sorrow and grief, and drink from the tit, like in the last page of *The Grapes of Wrath* . Then I would rise again, resplendent and saved. Like Bono, I would be born again (but in the USA, not Ireland), guiltless and absolved, free of my blackened conscience forever.

The hippie lady shifted and struck a match, holding it to her Marlboro Light 100. Her mustache glistened with sweat from the unseasonably hot May weather.

"Whatever's bothering you, it can't be that bad," she croaked. "You look like your dog just died. I'm a school counselor. Are you a student?"

"No, not here. I'm just a drummer," I replied.

"That's wonderful!" she exclaimed. "A healing drum circle is a sacred and transformative spiritual practice."

"Yeah? I'll have to give it a try sometime. Mostly I play music."

"There's a great gathering on the summer solstice. It's literally the new dawning of the Age of Aquarius." She broke into song.

I wanted to break into a run, but I was hypnotized by the turquoise undulating between her breasts.

"The stars will align in a perfect line in the night sky," she continued. "It's the Harmonic Convergence—Venus and Mars, Saturn and Uranus. It means that a new paradigm dawns, and the energy will shift all society toward enlightenment and world peace. We're so lucky to be alive at this moment in history. Be very grateful!"

I wondered if the harmonic convergence would help the Nicaraguan and Guatemalan peasants the U.S. was bombing. Reagan had announced that Nicaraguan communists were massing on the border of Mexico to invade Texas. What a fucking idiot, that Reagan. Nicaraguan communists coming to Texas? Really? We all figured that he or Bush would start a war soon, and there was talk of a draft. My friends and I were just the right age for service.

"It could mean the coming of Jesus. We just don't know," she rasped. "We'll be here on the steps of the library tonight. You should join us. Bring your drum. I have a sense that you and I have a special connection. You can't deny that there's powerful energy between us."

"Uh . . . I don't really do that kind of drumming," I said, wondering about that energy connection.

She suddenly thrust her hand into my pants.

"Jesus, lady!" I barked, slapping her hand and standing up. Fucking patchouli and the harmonic convergences. Of what? "Goddamnit, lady!" I started jogging away from her. Shaken, I had not seen it coming. Did I allow that to happen? Had she been stalking me? Did my female friends deal with this shit every day? I think they did. I was feeling worse than ever. Maybe I should just quit the band and disappear to Spain or Italy. I could learn the art of winemaking. Just become a new, less conscientious male somewhere else.

I arrived back at the band house exhausted, thinking of nothing but a cold shower to counter Michigan's muggy heat. In my room I found a rude note from the Big Brown House guys pinned to my door: "You can't just walk out of rehearsal and not come back. It is a violation that could lead to expulsion from the band or other consequences."

Friends?! What wankers! How dare they pull that on me. The backstabbers! I was ready to quit. But what would I do? I grabbed my towel and a cold beer to drink in the shower. In the bathroom, I stripped and turned the cold water on. Something didn't smell right. I looked into the tub and saw a stone-dead, five-pound largemouth bass, looking up at me from a whitened eye that oozed slime. That was all I could take. I seized the cold bass by the bottom jaw, lifted it to my eye, and said, "What the hell are you doing here, man? Taking a bath? Of course, you are. Silly question."

Without returning my pants to my ass, I carried the unfortunate beast down the stairs, dripping blood and goo on the stairs to the living room floor. I asked if anyone knew how the bass got into the shower. The figures watching TV on the couch and easy chair shrugged without looking up.

"Fine," I growled.

Out the front door I went with the ol' largemouth, a smelly slime trail marking our path. I dropped the fish on the boiling hot sidewalk, then stopped for a moment to reflect. The concrete was cookie-sheet hot, and the nearby flies, gnats and hornets were becoming excited. I pulled out my ever-handy black Swiss Army knife (with tweezers and corkscrew, of course), kneeled over the bass, and splayed it gills to tail, spilling an enormous mass of bloody blue and black guts at my bare feet. Holding the slimy body down with my left hand, I used the tiny Swiss saw blade to hack off the head. It made a hollow, squishy rattle as the creature's cheeks slapped against the ground, its glassy eyes pleading with mine for mercy.

"Fine!" I yelled.

My hands were wet with pong and blood. Scales got in my hair. What a way to go. Gasping for air while imprisoned in a filthy white tub. Looking down on the mangled

Advertisement for Take Back the Night March. Courtesy of the Lansing State Journal.

fish corpse, my mind waxed philosophically. What had brought me to this primal food ritual? How had this fish come to be in the shower? Who was I? Why this poor fish, giving me life by its death? Was this what the insurance documents meant by "accidental death or dismemberment"? If karma was real, would I be unceremoniously dismembered on a boiling hot sidewalk someday? Was this going to make it harder to live here?

"Hey, Steve. You havin' a fish fry for my birthday?" called a familiar voice from behind.

I spun around and discovered Mia, standing there in a cheery yellow sundress.

"Mia, what are you doing here?" I asked, astonished.

She gave me an affectionate hug, not seeming to care about the blood and guts.

"I was just in New York, and I lost my ID on the Lower East Side, so I needed my birth certificate to get a new ID in Ohio, and I had to go to Chicago 'cause I was born there." She shrugged. "Figured I'd take the Greyhound to see ya. Y'all ready to party or what?"

"Wow. Cool. Um . . . happy birthday. It's so good to see you, Mia." I was tripping over my words, tongue-tied by this mystical sylph standing before me. "Sorry, I'm covered in blood and guts."

"Aren't ya always covered in blood and guts?" she teased.

I looked down at my gory hands. "Only on your birthday."

"It's not really my birthday." She smiled and fidgeted with her fingers. "But might as well be."

"Did you say, 'Marcus . . . Welby . . . M.D.'?" It was a serious question. I hadn't caught that last part.

"No, dummy. It's Doogie Howser, M.D.," she corrected.

"But what does that have to do with your birthday?" I asked stupidly.

"You're a strange one, Esteban." She started walking toward the house, then she called over her shoulder. "You got any beer in the fridge?"

"Maybe."

Before I could go inside to check, Mia bounded up the porch steps and threw open the front door. "Hey, y'all. Ready to party or what? Hi, Roger! Ben! So good to see you. You all making music here? Where's the album at? I can't wait to hear what you've been writing. Ima make you skinny boys some dinner."

I forgot myself just long enough to laugh aloud. The day could not be more ridiculous.

Mia showing up was completely unexpected and gave me hope.

Big Brown House was Ben, Steve, Roger, and Adrien. Winter, 1987.
Photo by Lynn Peterson, from the author's archive.

KINGS AND QUEENS 7

Mia wanted to have a family dinner that evening. The main course would be my one-time bath-mate, the bass. Mia graced the table with two round jugs of Riunite wine, the kind that comes wrapped in straw for some reason.

"Riunite on ice—that's nice," she repeated several times as she floated around the dining-room table, filling wine glasses as if riding a cloud. Not that we had ice.

The warm sparkling red wine flowed over the rims of the glasses and stained the tablecloth. Mia covered the spills with the chipped and cracked plates she discovered at the back of the cupboards and with a can of Spam and some creamed corn, both of which were on the menu.

Once the daffodils had been properly arranged in beer bottles and set on the big oaken dining table, Mia tied an old rusty brake drum to a clothesline and whacked it with a drumstick to call everyone to the table. Ben, Adrian, Roger, and their visitors wandered into the dining room and took their seats.

Roger had befriended a mute homeless guy with long hair and a big bushy beard. We did not know his name, so we called him Jim Morrison. He did not smell too bad, so we let him sleep on the porch because his presence kept other members of the local homeless community from using our grand front-porch sitting area as a toilet. He wandered into the house during the day and made himself at home on the couch in front of the TV. When he joined us at the dinner table, he reached for the wine.

Mia had cooked the bass with a pinch of herbes de Provence and a splash of Olde English 800 (it is never too late to marinate). The poor creature almost looked edible when I laid his golden-brown corpse on the table. I asked several times how the fish had ended up in the bathtub, but no one would cop to the crime.

Mia raised her glass and tapped it with a little spoon. "One second, guys. I have a little somethin' I'd like to say tonight," she announced.

"Speech! Speech!" I urged.

Standing up, Mia said proudly, "I'd just like to thank y'all for your kindness and hospitality. And Stevo, Roger, Ben, Adrian . . . I want to—"

Jim Morrison could not wait to eat, so he thrust a hairy-knuckled hand at the baked bass, knocking over Mia's arrangement of flowers and weeds, soaking the table, and filling the bass platter with the sweet, warm wine. Mia's eyes narrowed, and she turned her attention to Jim Morrison.

"Down in Louisville, where I'm from, we got a way of treatin' one another called Southern hospitality." She didn't have much of a Southern accent, but she could affect one for effect. "I know you got a few nice records with that Doors band of yours, which is pretty good . . . 'cept for that organ. Ya gotta lose that organ, man!"

She spoke rhythmically and at times nonsensically, as I imagined a '50s jazz musician would, alternating real words with made-up slang. She could hold a completely coherent informed conversation with virtually anyone. She did not smoke, but her deep, sometimes mannish voice sounded as if she smoked three packs a day.

Mia could conduct a formal cocktail party or host a table of brunching ladies with equally casual yet measured attention. Upon meeting Mia, I do not think that anyone could imagine the superhero she could become onstage. Alcohol could fuel the extroverted performer in Mia, but it was also her kryptonite. She downed a half pint of the red wine and fixed her gaze on Jim Morrison. "I'm talking to you, mister! *¡Ay, Chihuahua, la gala ginta!*" she said in her pidgin Spanish. "You gonna shut up now or . . . ?" She waved a hand at him. Then she remembered her manners: "Ah, never mind. I am happy you could come to be here with us today. But next time bring your band along, Mr. Morrison."

"I don't think he can even hear you," said Ben.

"Hmm," grunted Mia, shifting gears. "Well, while I have y'all's attention, I'm gonna do you a little magic trick." She made a grand gesture to the table. "If y'all ladies and gentlemen would kindly remove your wine glasses and cigarettes from the surface of the table, I will now remove this ol' nasty tablecloth, leaving every piece of china perfect on this table right here."

Roger's eyes widened, and he pushed back his chair from the table. "Mia, don't," he muttered.

Adrian sat dumbly smiling and Ben was trying to drain the Riunite from the fish platter when Mia grabbed the tablecloth with both hands. In a single motion, she snatched it back over her head. Plates, flatware, and cups filled with wine went flying in all directions. We let out a collective gasp as Mia stood proudly, holding the tablecloth up high like the victorious matador, splendid and fearless, cheating death without a flinch.

She surveyed her handiwork, then spoke a single, magical word, "*¡Mole!*"

"*¡Mole, mole!*" We applauded. And to Mia Zapata we raised our glasses, and our spirits were high. "*¡Mole!*" we cried, "*¡Mole!*"

It was 86° Fahrenheit by 7 a.m. the following day. Impossible to sleep. I made a cup of instant coffee, then wandered out to the front porch to read the Detroit *Free Press*. A heat wave, AIDS, a recession, a brand-new crack cocaine epidemic—there were so many issues making life difficult in Rust Belt cities like Detroit. The *Free Press* was running a count of youth killed with guns that summer: closing fast on 500, mostly African Americans around twenty years old. I was twenty years old.

"Mornin,' Stephen," said Mia in a cheery voice. "Morning," I grumbled.

"Whatchu doin' today, Stephen?" she asked.

"Nothing. Working." I had a job digging holes and landscaping an apartment complex with Adrian and Roger. Ben got a night job making doughnuts. I hated the work. The foreman was a jerk, and it was stinking hot on the job site.

Mia pulled a plastic baggie from her backpack and held it up for me to see. "You ain't workin' today," she said. Inside the baggie were spindly dried mushrooms with iridescent, gray-purple caps. "You're takin' the day off. It's time for you to take a little trip."

I knew what they were. Psychedelics were popular on campus, but LSD was the drug of choice for most people I knew. I steered clear. I didn't even like marijuana because it made me feel dissociated and paranoid. I needed to feel in control. I didn't like the idea of tripping my brains out and learning the meaning of life. That's why people lose their minds. They learn the meaning of life and are changed so fundamentally that they go mad. Or they are enlightened such that society deems them insane. They will lock me up or put me in a straitjacket, like Frances Farmer. I wasn't ready for the vulnerability a drug trip brings. I had a million reasons not to dose. But I decided to do it anyway. I hoped Mia would be there for me if I wandered too close to some scary cave of psychological horrors. So, I popped the acidic-tasting mushrooms into my mouth—two caps and three stems—and washed them down with lukewarm coffee. Mia took twice that amount. We left the safety of the porch for a little walk.

I wasn't wearing shoes, and the concrete sidewalks and streets were baking hot. Sweating, Mia and I walked toward campus, stopping at a liquor store to buy two cold cans of Foster's Lager. We continued to an older part of town, cutting through an old cemetery, its ancient iron gate crawling with sweet jasmine and morning-glory vines. The grass was sweet relief for my scorched feet. Then the grass became something much more—rolling waves of vivid green, an ocean of ghosts resting peacefully beneath. Broken sprinklers came alive, their spray tickling our faces and making Mia's dirty-blonde hair glisten golden in the sun. I was dizzy from the heat and afraid of losing control.

Mia's eyes, a deeper shade of green accented with hazel flakes, met mine, and time stopped. I was restless but frozen, staring at a woman so strong and feminine, fragile, and fearless. Was I staring at her for hours or minutes?

I barely knew her, and I had no clue what she was doing here with me. Why would she want to spend time alone with me? What was her motivation? Was it a cruel joke? I guessed that she would soon run away, laughing, leaving me terrified and alone in a horrible cemetery while tripping. I'd go insane and never find a way out. I'd fall into an open grave and be buried alive in the frigid caverns of my blackest nightmares.

"How long will it last?" I asked, trying to sound cool, but my voice trembled. I needed to know. Would I be overwhelmed with the consequences of my life's choices?

I must have looked disturbed because Mia slapped me. "Steve, you're trippin'! Just go with it. Don't be scared. I'm not goin' anywhere. It's okay. You're just high. Chill. Let's walk."

We wandered between the tombstones and crypts, moving from shade tree to shade tree. The sprinklers created mystical rainbows, and plastic flowers came alive and marched shoulder to shoulder like a faded zombie army. Clumsy bees bumbled above our heads, scaring the mosquitoes that wanted to suck our blood and add welts to our salty, sunburned skin. Fuck, this was cool.

Sitting in a shady spot, we talked about our lives growing up in Indianapolis and Louisville. Our hometowns were just two hours apart, but we lived on either side of the historical and cultural divide between North and South and the hostilities were still evident between people on either side of the Ohio River. We both struggled to live outside the racism, bigotry, hyper-Christianity, and oppressive conservatism so prevalent in our hometowns.

The only way to escape the places where we grew up was to play the game until we could find a clear pathway out. We had both chosen to use whatever advantages we had to attend college in the hope of breaking free, allowing us to pursue our dreams. Going away to college was salvation.

Getting up, Mia broke into a run, headed up a steep hill to an important-looking marble headstone. She turned to look at me. I followed, wading through the grassy waves and the sprinkler rainbows. When I reached out to her, Mia grabbed my hand and pulled me to the ground, near a ninety-one-year-old gravestone belonging to Betty J. Carson, a loving mother, wife, and friend. Mia asked Mrs. Carson for permission to lean on her grave marker. A fat baby angel sat nude atop Mrs. Carson's stone, his white cherubic eyes looking skyward, a wee hand outstretching as he offered a little birdie to Jesus. Fly away to heaven with Betty J. Carson's soul, little birdie.

Reaching out her own hand, Mia gently pinched the little angel's penis, giggling like a pervert. I smiled stupidly as our gazes crossed. She placed both her hands on my chest and pushed me against the hot granite stone, then she pressed her mouth on mine and kissed me so deeply that I forgot to breathe. I might have died right then because my beleaguered young soul left my body. I found myself floating above it all, looking down. I saw Mia, a youthful Betty J. Carson, and the little baby angel.

Mia's mouth tasted of soil, sweat, and honey. We crushed clusters of orange and white impatiens growing around Betty Carson's grave and she approved. No day had ever looked as colorful and vibrant as that day. No chorus of birds ever sounded so harmonious and well-rehearsed. The air smelled only of good things: flowers, water, cut grass, marijuana smoke, Mia's kiss. I experienced a wave of electricity that brought to mind a childhood experiment with a pair of blunt scissors and the kitchen AC outlet. The spray of the sprinkler tickled my neck and my every cell connected with Mia's own and for just a millisecond we became One.

In a little, forgotten Ann Arbor cemetery on a Monday afternoon in 1987, the medicine in the psilocybin rewired my brain. Something broke loose in my consciousness. Psychedelic illumination put the dead past to rest and sewed together the frayed neurons of my brain. A weight lifted from my shoulders and for a single salient moment I witnessed a profound connection to a woman and the wider world. My busy, confused brain floated peacefully with Betty Carson and her cherub. Mia and I were as close as two young people could be. We were spiritual beings alight, hovering weightless between the worlds of the living and the dead, the past and future. We were a single mass of light energy with the Goddess's holy perfection in heaven. I ceased to exist in a physical form and all that remained was the essence of ethereal, pure love. Until Mia pinched me for spacing out.

"Steve! Vamos! Let's go."

"Ouch!"

"Come on, man. I gotta pee!"

Mia took my hand and pretended to pull me up from the ground with great difficulty. We ran through chirping sprinklers, leaped over tombstones, and pinched the noses and toes and toes of the angels perched here and there atop the tombstones. We ran down the steep hill at the back of the cemetery and scurried through a hole in the fence like two skinny rats, emerging on State Street in the center of the University of Michigan campus. We cut through an alleyway, where we pissed behind a dumpster.

The scalding afternoon was reaching its breaking point, the skies turned an eerie yellow-green, and storm clouds gathered on the horizon. Lightning struck the earth with a terrible hair-raising cymbal crash. My bare feet floated above the bubbling molten surface of the pavement like magic air-hockey pucks. The hair rose on my arms and neck, and I could smell ozone in the air. A clap of thunder shook the earth, followed by a few fat raindrops. We challenged the great rage of Zeus in heaven with outstretched arms, our thirsty mouths agape. The rain fell on our faces as a cool humid gust blew ahead of the sudden pressure drop. Mia and I ran for cover down the street, in the direction of our sublet house at State and Packard.

Lightning cracked and thunder boomed above like enormous bass drums. The sky opened and, in an instant, we were soaked. We made for the wide veranda of a lovely two-story brick building that might have been a library or an old hotel. Its front door was open, so Mia walked right in. I followed, passing through a cluttered foyer and into a great room, where I saw a grand piano with a life-sized plaster bust of Beethoven staring disapprovingly over the keys.

I called out, but no one answered. Mia called. Still no answer. On the wall was a pair of giant Greek letters, delta and chi. Unknowing, we had waltzed right into a University of Michigan fraternity house. Thankfully, no one was home. Mia's eyes glinted and a puckish smile spread across her face.

"Oh shit, Mia. We have to decorate this place." I was peaking on the shrooms. Grinning wickedly and nodding her head, she said, "I know."

The walls were a lovely eggshell white. We opened closet doors and cabinets until we found cans of old paint and brushes. We each grabbed a can and began decorating the walls of the great room, with its grand piano, tiki bar, fireplace, and racist statue of a black-faced jockey holding a riding crop. Above the fireplace, with great care and attention to detail, I wrote in orange paint, "SEXIST, RACIST HOMOPHOBES." Mia had three paint cans open and was working on a barnyard scene with what looked like a rooster, a pig, a donkey, and a crooked little farmer.

"Mia, we gotta be quick. This is a frat house, and they could come home any minute They'll kill us if they catch us."

"Aw, quit yer belly-achin.' I'm workin' here," she replied over her shoulder.

I heard feet on the stairs and drunken laughter.

"Seriously, Mia. We gotta split . . . like now," I pleaded.

Three big-ass frat boys walked in and caught us red-handed.

"Can we help you?" asked one. He sounded as dumb as he looked.

These were corn-fed, Midwestern linebacker types. Two of them carried a beer cooler, one guy on each handle. They were sunburned and drunk, and they had stumbled into their house to find two tripping Gits, dressed in black T-shirts and cutoffs, painting the walls of their home-away-from-home. I decided to distract the enemy to give Mia a chance to get away. I gestured for her to hide the paint cans she held, but she gave me a confused look. She was oblivious to the threat just out of her sightline.

"Hello, gentlemen," I said in my best imitation of a professional voice. "We're the painters you called. We're just testing some colors to see what will look best on these walls. It's vital that the paint match the décor, the furniture, and . . . things," I stammered.

One of the kids carrying the beer cooler spoke up. "I think the red and purple are pretty."

"Doofus!" His buddy punched him hard in the upper arm.

The smarter one took charge. "Hey, we didn't call any painters."

"It was supposed to be a surprise for somebody's birthday. His parents ordered it. Jason or Freddy or Frank . . . um, what do you think of the combination of purple and orange?" I asked, turning toward the wall, and stroking my chin.

"You don't look like painters," said a fourth jock, obviously destined to be a professor.

Mia stumbled in. "Zat is because vee are not za painters," she said in a terrible attempt at some kind of Chinese-German accent. "Vee are international frat-haus designers, not za stupid painters. Vee come from Holland, and vee do not speak good English, so vee just finish here and go back to da hotel. Ya, okay? Vee choose das colors, zen da student painter guys come and zey paint. Starving student painters—you know zem, no?" Mia dropped one of the paint cans to the floor with a thud.

The first frat boy looked suspicious. "Who's that?" he asked me, gesturing to Mia.

"Why, that's Fräulein Nina Häagen. Surely you've heard of her. She's only the most famous haus artist in all of Amsterdam. Fräulein is an overly sensitive artist. And you must not talk with her now. One must never disturb her creative process." I cupped my hand over my voice to indicate a secret message. "She could have an attack, a nervous breakdown. She starts to yell. The cops will come."

The more assertive kid scratched the crewcut under his Michigan Wolverines cap. "This doesn't seem right at all. Why is paint all over the chairs and table, and what the hell did you write on the wall?" He motioned to the other three frat boys. "Guys, go upstairs and call the housemother, and we'll find out what the hell is going on."

"Okay, okay, you boyz go up das stairs and find out vat is goings on. Vee don't do no more color testings until you good boyz call your fadders. Don't vorry. Vee is vaiting here vile you go up zere to bringing our payment. Is only $500 . . . dat's with your discounts. Vee wait right here." She pointed to the ground and crossed her arms indignantly.

Mia eyed me and raised an eyebrow, which I took as a plea for an exit strategy. I didn't have one. My ears were burning, and my arms were quivering from fear and from the air conditioning. I locked eyes for a moment with the bossiest kid.

He looked away nervously and said, "Okay, sir. We'll get the checkbook and pay you the five hundred bucks for the color testing. But please don't do any more color testing until we find out who decided to paint the house."

I shrugged and looked at Mia, who couldn't believe our luck. Were we really going to walk out of there with $500?

"Can you make zat cash?" she shouted.

That one was a bridge too far, and neither of us could contain our laughter. The mushrooms were revving in high gear, and I began to feel slightly evil and ghostlike—not of this world, which made me invisible and fearless.

"Back door," I said in a whisper.

"Go!" yelled Mia as she knocked a full can of forest green latex paint off the grand piano and onto the large, ornate Persian rug. She nearly slipped as she walked past the ten-foot Steinway. She managed to regain her footing. She snatched Beethoven from atop the piano, holding the old genius in a headlock and followed.

We ran down a wide hallway, through the first floor, and into the kitchen. The back door was wide open, so we bolted out, then we raced around the side of the house and dashed down an alley and out to State Street. Beethoven scowled as we hightailed it back to our safehouse, where the odds would be better if the frat boys caught up and tried to murder us.

"Kidnapping is a pretty serious offense," I quipped. "Not if the victim is a dead bust!" Mia retorted. "We can return him later."

"Tell 'em it was just a joke and apologize. That way they won't beat us up."

I nodded. "Sounds fair enough." But I doubted that they wouldn't want to beat us up.

Storm clouds darkened the sky anew, like a cloud of locusts descending to consume everything in sight. Or maybe a tornado that would suck up cows and send little dogs squealing like cats in dog suits. A twister had sent my family to a shelter when I was six and when we emerged the neighbor's Pinto was lodged in a sycamore tree. I understood the new peril we faced. There was an eerie silence, and the sky darkened such that the streetlights flickered on above. Before we could make it to the safety of the porch, where our odyssey had begun, hail the size of golf balls pelted our heads and the parked cars around us, setting off the alarms.

We took cover at a bus stop and lashed ourselves to a signpost, watching in amazement as rain fell in vast waves and Odin shook the bus shelter with murderous rage. The gutters became rivers, and the avenues became seas. Poseidon emerged from the waves and glared at us for taking drugs and disturbing the dead. Then, just as quickly as it had started, the downpour ceased, and the brilliant sun showed through a perfect pinhole of blue sky. I didn't know it at the time, but at that very moment we were in the eye of some kind of Lake Michigan superstorm— part hurricane and part funnel system—a once-in-a-century weather event. Beethoven's expression soured. I wondered if maybe he had summoned the storm as punishment for stealing him from his new American home.

The sun carried with it an envelope of warm dry air to grace the calm. Mia's eyes sparkled in the light. Tendrils of dirty blonde crisscrossed her forehead. Her cheeks glistened as rain dripped from her strong jaw and dimpled chin. Standing beside me, she shivered, still clutching the bust to her breast. I felt the mushroom high waning.

I took Beethoven from her. The lightning struck the tip-top of the First Baptist Church of Ann Arbor steeple directly across from us on Packard Street. Sparks cascaded from the transformer on the traffic light poles at the big intersection at Packard and State. Then a deafening thunderclap—a thousand war drums shook the ground, rattling the safety glass of the bus shelter. Hail fell like a machine gun strafing us from above. The skies opened yet again, and sheets of rain fell. Was this the harmonic apocalypse? Had the hippies been too optimistic regarding the true dawning of the Age of Aquarius?

Inspired, Mia unbuttoned her shirt, wadded it up into a ball, and tossed it defiantly into the mad river raging in the gutter. "Run!" she cried, taking off toward Main Street, wearing nothing but cutoff Levis and leaving me dumb with the unflinching Ludwig Van.

I told the maestro to hold on tight as I dispatched my T-shirt in like fashion and followed after Mia. The torrential rain flooded the intersection as we ran for our lives to the safety of our rented house.

State Street descended a steep hill, joining Main and Packard at the intersection. The five-way intersection had become a knee-deep lake beneath the battered traffic lights, blown horizontal, flapping in the gusting winds.

"Not here!" Mia exclaimed, seizing Beethoven. She waded up the slope of Packard Street, now a raging river free of vehicle traffic, save for the foolhardiest four-wheelers. She centered the bust of the mighty composer in the road, facing uphill in the center of the road, directing his steely eyes upstream, barely above the rapids. It was there that he made his stand.

Ludwig van Beethoven, the proud and defiant decomposer, daring drivers to pass—an evil troll demanding tribute for entry to the depths of Hades.

Mia and I waded across the big intersection to the whistles and applause of the members of Big Brown House, their girlfriends, and Jim Morrison. Wearily we ascended the steps to the safety of the porch. Mia and I plopped down on a ratty little loveseat someone had dragged onto the porch. I took Mia's hand, but she pulled it away and pointed to the street. The bust appeared absurdly human, a severed head directing a macabre orchestra. Vehicles piloted by drivers-turned-mariners

cautiously approached Beethoven, wondering how he had come to deliver his final furious coda in the middle of a flooded Michigan street. We all were awed by his stoicism as the plaster of his cheeks and eyes melted in the warm rainwater, distorting his severe features.

Eventually a stone-white '73 Chevy Malibu motored down the flooded causeway and stopped just short of smashing Beethoven's ashen head. The driver, a woman wearing sequined horn-rimmed glasses and cherry-red lipstick, looked familiar. Her car door swung open slowly; I could plainly see the silver turquoise necklace dangling in the valley of her ample bosom as she leaned out the door. The gaze of the handsy hippie from the library met mine. I shuddered as she leaned out of the car, grabbed Beethoven by the throat and heaved him out of the water and onto the passenger seat beside her. Slamming the door, she continued forward through the rapids, running the red light and leaving a wide wake behind. We never saw the great composer again.

Mia and her WWII-era bomber jacket at Antioch College in 1988.
Photographer unknown, from author's archive.

that is
Mia Zapata

JUST LIKE MY FATHER TOLD ME

8

There was a little place to sit on the fire-escape ladder outside my window. Mia and I sat there in the cool night air, talking for hours. I listened without speaking as Mia recounted the family history that her father had recently told her. I felt honored that she shared with me what she was learning about herself and her history. She told me a little about her immediate family— her parents, brother, and sister—but she also went into detail about some of the stories her father had told her about her great-grandfather Emiliano Zapata.

Mia adored her mother, and after she left home for college she felt some responsibility for her mother's well-being. Mia explained that her mom had climbed the ladder to become one of the highest paid TV executives in the country. Donna had a New York City office, complete with her own staff. She lived in a beautiful penthouse

Sketch in personal letter to the author from Mia, sent in June 1989. From author's archive.

with a view of Central Park, but she spent far more time working long hours in her office than in that apartment. Mia did a co-op with an aspiring Antioch filmmaker, Fred Liss, in New York in 1986, so she could visit her mother regularly.

Mia introduced me to the work of artists who inhabited the underground arts world of New York's Lower East Side: Andy Warhol, Jean-Michel Basquiat, Robert Mapplethorpe, the Ramones, Johnny Thunders, William S. Burroughs, and more. Mia studied how Jim Carroll, Patti Smith, and Lou Reed, artists who fused poetry with rock and roll, formed bands as literary experiments to challenge pop music with the depth of their written expression. Mia's older brother, Eric, owned a salon in Hollywood, called ZAPATA. Mia was obviously very fond of Eric, but, like all big brothers, she would call him "a big fat jerk." Her younger sister, Kristen, was bright, accomplished, and beautiful—near perfect in Mia's eyes. Mia looked sad as she talked about her siblings, even when she shared details about their happiest childhood moments. She clearly missed her family, but, like me, she was restless and aspired to create something special.

I had little to say. I felt lucky that she shared so much. I was a more accomplished listener than a talker. Getting to know Mia during those summer days in the upper Midwest was a privilege I will cherish. We saw one another in a way I did not think possible. I wished Mia had been my sister. Perhaps she was. She had a unique and intimate relationship with Matt and Andy, too. There was no envy for her attention. Mia was authentic and serious about the sacred nature of true friendship. It was one of her most precious values. She loved being in The Gits and she loved having us as brothers. I could see it in her eyes. I think she felt safe with the three of us.

Perhaps without knowing, Mia had given me a reprieve from my jumbled emotions. The last thing I remember communicating to her before slipping into a long, satisfying sleep was thanking her for setting me free. And the last thing I heard Mia say at the end of that magical day was, "We're in this together, Steve." She whispered into my ear: "And nothin' can keep us four from crushin' the world." In a hand-written letter a few months later, she wrote, "Our friendship will stand strong as one half of a perfect circle with Andy and Matt."

When I awoke the next morning, Mia was gone. I found a letter waiting for me under my keys. I sat back and allowed a renewed feeling of optimism to wash over me. She had graffitied or tagged my wall with lipstick on her way out the door. It read, "Never forget the Squawking Vixon [*sic*] Chicken Bitch." How could I forget? How could I forget any of it? Now I had to clean the Sharpie and lipstick off the wall in my room.

The despair and insecurities I felt had lifted at last. The remaining melancholia became a gentle morning fog burned away by the sun. I wanted to remember the previous day's storm. I would capture the mighty lightning in my calloused palms and harness the deafening thunder to power my cymbals and bass drum. I'd seize the collective force of every living organism and every god in the heavens and bring it crashing down like the Precision Bass of Clash bassist Paul Simonon onto the stage on the cover of *London Calling*. I wanted to bottle the feelings, so I could pull it off the shelf and take a whiff whenever I needed a reminder of my purpose.

The thought of a physical relationship or exclusive couple-hood with Mia felt ridiculous. I had no desire and no right to expect anything more. I liked having a sister. Andy and Matt completed the perfect circle of camaraderie and solidarity. Our purpose was not romantic. The goal was never to live happily ever after. Giving meant more than getting and the musical mission trumped my personal aspirations for family or fatherhood. The musical mission of The Gits was the most important epic of my young life. I believed our songs could influence people who could then shape world events. Mia was there to define and deliver the invitation to anybody who would listen and understand the communique.

Big Brown House cassette cover, c. 1987. Photo by Joe Hirsch, designed by Matt Dresdner, from author's archive.

9 DRINKING SONG

Big Brown House finished writing twelve songs for an album. We recorded them on a Tascam four-track cassette recorder in the basement of the house in Ann Arbor at the end of the summer of 1986. We produced a cassette and called it *Scrappy James*. Transformed by friendship and creative accomplishment, I returned to the Antioch campus and the mission of The Gits. Although I had spent every day for six months writing and playing with Big Brown House, my allegiance shifted to playing in The Gits, whatever may come.

For the time being I played in the two bands, practicing five or six nights per week. My drumming chops improved exponentially. I focused on reading the jazz drum solos my old teacher shared and the up-tempo punk and hardcore beats I heard in the Bad Brains and Dead Kennedys songs, as well as the new bands I learned about during my travels like Bad Religion, Misfits, Minor Threat, Social Distortion, and the Pogues.I listened to the songs with headphones and played along to the recorded songs. I also discovered a love for playing the laid-back odd timings inherent to reggae artists like Jimmy Cliff, Burning Spear, Peter Tosh, Culture, and Bob Marley. My objective was to incorporate swing, bebop, and reggae drumming into the Gits' music.

Mia's dad had been urging her to join him in Portland and attend outpatient rehab. We felt an urgency to document the music we had created prior to her going away. It was time for The Gits to record. We had written a lot of songs and there was a professional recording studio in little Yellow Springs. What if she decided to leave the group after rehab? She wanted to finish some classwork and a few art projects, but she wished to put energy into the band. She insisted on rehearsing whenever possible and put an enormous focus on writing lyrics. Her lyrics were expanding beyond songs about personal heartbreak and anger about the end of her relationships. Her lyrics became more universal. She changed pronouns from "me" to "we" in several cases, adding a level of maturity and insight. During this time, she penned "Social Love," "Ain't Got No Right," "Cut My Skin—It Makes Us Human." All three became popular songs in our set list for years to come.

We pooled our money and booked as much time as we could afford at the Yellow Springs recording studio, about six hours. We knew little about recording, but we knew that it could get expensive very quickly. Bands typically recorded eight, sixteen, or twenty-four tracks onto analog tape. This method allows for overdubs and the ability to fix mistakes and cut and paste parts to perfect (or ruin) a song. We decided to record directly to the master tape. No overdubs, no studio tricks, just hit record and play our set, one song after the other, live, thereby recording all the songs in our repertoire in one go.

The recording constraints did not bother Matt, who noted that his favorite band, Minutemen, had recorded more than thirty songs on their magnum opus *Double Nickels on the Dime* the same way. In just three hours we recorded seventeen songs, more than enough for an album. It was The Gits' first demo recording, but I always considered it to be a complete album that represented the band's development during its first three years of existence.

Mia's voice soared as she improvised or changed many of the lyrics during the recording. I played odd times and accented Mia's inflections by laying off playing flashy drum fills and allowing the slower songs to breathe. I did not want to overpower the guitar or vocals. Andy's melodic counterpoint to Mia's vocal phrasing was unusual and original but also sympathetic and supportive of Mia's delivery. I came to understand that my role in the band was as accompanist, to accompany the others, like the spark to the pistons that creates power to an engine.

All the parts must run smoothly for the motor to operate efficiently. And when our motor was well oiled and warmed up it was unstoppable. We each had unique roles in the band, and we respected the skills the other members brought to the table. Andy brought song idea after song idea and the three of us added parts. We arranged the music around the lyrics and Mia always delivered. She listened to the songs in practice or sat with Andy someplace private. Quietly they combined ideas into thoughtful, unusually crafted rock songs. Despite the collective ideal, Andy and Mia were the primary songwriters.

The music was different in ways that could be confusing to those who tried to categorize us. Some songs were straight-ahead midtempo rockers. There was a swing feel and lilting blues flavor to other songs. We often repeated parts three, five, or eleven times instead of the typical four refrains. I could not have been prouder of the music. It sounded indefinable and powerful, and I felt honored to be a part of the project. I hoped that the demo of recordings would not be the end of it all. Our tenure as college students would be ending soon.

We'd been calling ourselves the Sniveling Little Rat-Faced Gits. We wrote to the Monty Python comedy troupe for permission to use the name and, to our surprise, the Pythons agreed. But the unabridged version of the band name did not fit on the spine of the cassette, so we shortened it to The Gits. It sounded more like a real rock band, and so The Gits became our chosen nickname from then on, but Sniveling Little Rat-Faced Gits was the formal version.

After we settled on a name, Matt silkscreened a hundred cassette covers with a picture of me in blue and yellow ink, lying on my back, laughing (or gasping for air in an asthmatic fit; I can't remember which). We sold out in a few days. In 1996, Broken Rekids would re-release the songs on CD and vinyl with the title *Kings & Queens* (named after one of the songs on the album). The label advertised it as our first demo recording, and it sold several thousand copies.

We gigged as much as we could when we were all in the same place at the same time. We were limited to shows around Ohio—Columbus, Dayton, Cincinnati—and live radio shows, high school dances, bowling alleys, and house parties, and we arranged to open for the bands I brought to perform at the college: Camper Van Beethoven, the Flaming Lips, Das Damen, Die Kreuzen, Firehose, Scrawl, and any band we could intercept as they toured the well-paying college towns in the Midwest.

Mia was honest about her struggle with alcohol. After dropping out of school the middle of junior year, she could no longer use her studies as an excuse not to attend rehab. The hangovers and her dad's insistence won the argument.

I felt stupid for not recognizing that Mia was struggling. I was too wrapped up in my own ridiculous existential angst and self-pity to see that she was suffering.

That was why she needed money for the gin, I realized. It had never occurred to me that she was drinking more than any of our peers and she might need help. We all drank too much. It was the culture of celebration and it helped to dilute the pressure of social awkwardness and the shadowy torment of whatever childhood trauma. I did not understand the complicated forms that addiction takes. Mia was so young and already physically and emotionally exhausted from the struggle. We joked about getting fucked up and being ragged, sloppy alcoholics. It was funny.

We wrote songs about it. It was revelry, celebration, and a form of defiance. How naïve I was about the toll alcohol dependence can take.

One morning in Decemeber, I rode my bike through Yellow Springs and discovered Mia bundled up in her leather bomber jacket, crying at the Greyhound stop. She was sitting next to Andy. They were hugging. I sensed the heaviness of the moment but they both smiled, so I approached.

"How long you gonna be gone, Mia?" I was beginning to comprehend how inextricably linked our dreams for the future had become. I didn't know if she was coming back. The Gits could be finished before we even started. I could think of nothing to say. I took off on my bicycle and retrieved an old Kay acoustic guitar that I had never learned to play. I gave the guitar to Mia as she boarded a Greyhound bus. I hoped that it would help her keep the dream alive.

That night, I pored over the seventeen songs we had recorded. During the next year I always kept a cassette copy of the songs with me. I listened to Mia's lyrics and analyzed every mistake I made on the drum parts. I played it for others. I gave copies away and allowed people to make copies. From Minneapolis, Seattle, San Francisco, and L.A. to squats from London and Liverpool, Amsterdam to Sarajevo, Bilbao to Barcelona, I traveled and shared The Gits. Most people, especially the punks who listened, loved the songs as much as I did. I was encouraged. I compared the songwriting to that of the bands I loved, such as the Clash, Stiff Little Fingers, Joy Division, even Bad Brains. The Gits sounded appropriate nestled between the Damned and X-Ray Spex on my mixtapes.

We had become dependent on one another for emotional support. The band had become the foundation of our life. We watched out for and supported each other in all things. I was concerned that Mia would come to believe that the band was incompatible with sobriety. It may have been, but the three of us agreed not to pressure Mia. Her well-being was paramount.

I conceived of a way to do most of the remainder of my degree while traveling. I would travel the U.S. and Europe during the year to come and return to campus in spring of 1989 to graduate. I liked to muse that I was a "Road Scholar," unlike the distinguished Rhodes Scholars. My version of a Road Scholar was that of a starving student of life. I would simply land somewhere, learn something, write about it, and, like the sex worker in Alaska, collect college credit.

I enrolled in a poorly organized urban-studies program in Europe for six months. It was led by a self-important conservative political-science professor from another

small liberal arts college in Wisconsin called Beloit College. The professor's caustic personality and fragile ego created problems from the onset of the trip. He insisted on holding all the passports and he lost mine. He was condescending and drank too much and made inappropriate advances on the female students.

The urban-studies program began in Sarajevo, Yugoslavia. (Serb nationalism was simmering and would reach a boiling point when political violence would consume the Balkans not too far in the future.) I did not feel safe traveling with a group of hapless American college students and their clueless teacher, so I left the program after a week to travel solo. I was a Road Scholar at last!

Somewhere in Europe at age 21, c. 1988. Photo by and courtesy of author.

Squatted mansion in the south of France, c. 1988. Photo by and courtesy of author.

BEER AND MORE BLOOD 10

Standing in the lobby of a Sarajevo hotel enjoying a final farewell (because it was final) with the college professor, a woman in a leather motorcycle jacket approached and mercifully interrupted. "I must have listened to the 'Private Lubs' tape 1,000 times." She pulled out a copy of the Gits demo tape from her backpack as proof. "I've been dissecting Mia's lyrics. I keep finding deeper and deeper meaning and inspiration with every listening. It's fucking brilliant."

It took me a minute, but I recognized Valerie Agnew. She was always up front at The Gits' shows at Antioch. She was a couple years younger than me, but she was wonderfully assertive and self-confident. She had a smile that slayed dragons and an easy, free laugh that caused strangers to stop on the street and smile. She was a Feminist Studies major who happened to be touring Europe with a Women's Studies program.

We left the hotel to have a beer together and we bonded instantly over music and politics. She was sick of traveling exclusively with humorless women, she confessed. "Too much drama, man!" She wasn't on board with typical feminist rhetoric. Valerie's feminist views were more radical. Her struggle was more urgent, and she believed that social change demanded even more direct action and was urgent enough to require the backing of men allied to the cause. She had been sexually assaulted while working at a Planned Parenthood in Philadelphia and, when she told me the story, my heart felt the rage too. Our minds aligned. We were like Mars and Venus, trading roles and sharing an orbit, while we tested our mettle. We abandoned our cohorts and disappeared together into the shaky political landscape of the Balkans and Eastern Europe.

We talked until late at a café and when it got too late we wandered into a city park and talked until morning. She listened with her whole body and gave her full attention. She could talk to anyone and made friends easily. She was well read and held uncompromising political beliefs rooted in feminism and social justice. I did too.

Although the two of us were barely twenty-one years old, we were similar in that we felt that we were fully formed politically and we needed to test our resolve in the cruel world. We aggressively sought meaningful challenges to apply our principles of social justice and radical solutions to. Sometimes that meant risky business. Neither one of us was risk-averse, in fact we were hungry for it.

From Sarajevo, we traveled to Zagreb, Mostar, and Ljubljana, Yugoslavia. We traversed Germany and Austria and finally arrived in London, where we slept outside a few nights, holding one another close to stay warm on Hampstead Heath during a November freeze. Hoping to check out the punk scene and see some English bands, we found a cheap flat with some friends near Camden Town, the center of London's punk rock scene. We walked the aisles of secondhand junk tables in search of old punk 45s at the Camden Market. We saw a few mediocre punk bands and, against the advice of a ticket taker at the tube station, we went to the London suburb of Brixton to see Fela Kuti, the famous Nigerian musician and activist, perform at the Brixton Academy. We saw police beating a couple Black kids in an alley. We felt we had betrayed our principles by not stopping to help. On our way back to the flat we bought bread, cheese, and bottles of cheap wine. Already money was running short.

Valerie charmed her way into a job at a pub, where I could hang out and drink free pints when her boss wasn't around. At the pub we heard about a safe new drug that was invented for psychiatric healing and had become trendy at after-hours clubs. I hated the music that they played at those dance clubs, but we went anyway so we could buy hits of ecstasy. I grudgingly paid my five quid to get into the club, then I wandered around the dark disco until someone without eyebrows emerged from the shadows and the thump-squish of the House music, pressed an index finger against my left earlobe, and yelled, "E?"

"Gimme four, please. Cheers!"

"Eighty quid, mate!"

In the late '80s, £20 equaled $40, which meant that they were charging $40 per hit of ecstasy. It was a pricey high, but it was a powerful feeling, quite different from mushrooms. An hour after a dose, I was overcome by a sense of overwhelming euphoria and communion with my fellow human beings, no matter any past resentments. The drug made gratitude and forgiveness so easy. The empathy that the drug conjured in my mind stuck around for weeks. It was like a life lesson from God or a moving meditation session. But it was a lot more expensive than natural forms of communion. God may have been close, but our landlord was closer, banging on our door and demanding rent.

"Maybe they'll forget to collect rent this month," I said, only half-jokingly, to Valerie as we pooled our money to finance another ecstasy trip. We escaped out the rear door into the garden to avoid the landlord at the front door and caught a double decker bus to an anti-fascist demonstration in Trafalgar Square.

The National Front and the English right wing, emboldened by the Reagan–Thatcher love affair, were active in London. We got wind that skinheads from the National Front were coming on buses to counterprotest an anti-Thatcher march. Fights broke out and the cops just stood back and watched. The march was not well organized and, despite a bit of pushing and yelling on both sides, the march didn't start moving for hours and we got bored after getting into a few shouting and shoving altercations. We walked into a pub where we heard the London Irish band the Pogues. The bar and all the tables were taken, but a group of punks who had seen us scrapping in the fray with some skinhead kids invited us to their table and bought us pints. They offered us cigarettes that they were rolling from the butts of other patrons' ashtrays. I declined a smoke.

We sat down and Valerie hit it off with the punks immediately, a couple of whom obviously took a shine to her. They invited us to a football match policed by an army of bobbies on foot and on horseback. We sneaked in through an opening that someone had cut in a wire fence, and we took seats in the nosebleeds. Two teams with a long-standing rivalry were facing off: Liverpool and Arsenal. Fans of the two teams had to be separated by barricades topped with barbed wire. That didn't stop them from throwing rocks and bottles over the barriers. I saw someone lob a lawn dart at the opposing fans' section. When the match was finally called a draw, I was happy to get the hell out of there in one piece. It was exhilarating to hear thousands of fans chanting together. The choruses swelled to a fever pitch and then crashed with a collective "aaaaaw!" when a goal was missed or a shot saved by the goalie. The soccer chants sounded like the choruses I heard on the punk records of the Clash, the Jam, the Dammed, Sham 69, and Sex Pistols, all London-based bands. These bands were writing songs about the actual lives they lived, not fairytale myths or tropes about how rich or cool they thought they were.

Returning to our flat the next day, Valerie and I found our things on the sidewalk. The landlord had also posted an eviction notice on the door and changed the locks. Frustrated but not surprised, we gathered our gear and went in search of the squatters we'd met the day before, hoping that they could put us up for a while. The squatters, who were in their twenties, identified as Anarchist punks. They loudly espoused the virtues of the working class, as well as the inherent right to live on the government dole and not work. They took a perverse pleasure in schooling the wayward American college students on their favorite fanzine editions of the works of Peter Kropotkin, Karl Marx, and Penny Rimbaud.

The Anarchist squatters shared some intel with us: there was an abandoned council flat on Elmwood Avenue in Wood Green, a North London suburb. Our pals could supply us with tools we could use to break into the flat so that we could establish a new squat, adding to the half-dozen squatted flats making up their community of punks. So, in the dead of night, we set out with a crowbar, a pair of flashlights, and screwdrivers to claim a new home for ourselves.

According to the squatters, if you could set up a bed and a chair and install your own lock, the local police would have to obtain an eviction notice to evict, all of which could take weeks. But if we were lucky, we could make a case for leasing the flat from the city and we could stay there indefinitely. I loved this plan because I fantasized that it would be cool to have a summer flat in London. Valerie and I could come after graduation and start a radical life together.

Breaking into the building was easy, but the wood around the door was rotting and we found it difficult to remove the old door handle to replace the lock. The other squatters had told us that the neighbors would not notice us because they would be too busy watching the "telly" at that hour. That turned out to be flawed intel. The neighbors were on the lookout for idiots like us, and they called the police.

When the blue lights began flashing and four cops stormed the house, we tried to run for it but felt like running in water. At the back fence, I gave Valerie a leg up. She flopped over the top and hit the ground running on the other side. But when I tried to pull myself up after her, my strength failed me. I had not eaten in twenty-four hours, and I was too weak to run. I just put my hands up and turned toward the fence. A blow from a leather club in the small of my back dropped me to my knees.

"That'll be far 'nough, punk," growled the officer, proving that, though he didn't carry a gun, he could still hurt me. I felt cool being called a punk, although it was not a moniker of respect.

A pair of cops took me to the lock-up at Wood Green station, while two others, I assumed, went looking for Valerie. They put me in a cell alone. I was exhausted, hungry, broke, and in a jail 5,000 miles from home and, on advice of the squatters, had left my passport behind. Still, I remember thinking, this is gonna make a great story if I ever get out. I also thought about how disappointed my mother would be to bail me out of a London jail. If she were to discover I was there.

Sitting on a slab of concrete that served as a bed, I studied the bits of graffiti scratched into the concrete blocks of the cell wall: "You American fuckers think you tuff shit. You ain't shit. I will kill you."

I wondered if I could pass as Canadian. I lay down on the concrete bed and closed my eyes. I could only think bad thoughts. I couldn't sleep, although it had been two days since I'd even rested.

I was mercifully on the verge of some kind of slumber when I was jolted up by the sound of a jail door opening. I looked toward the opening door and saw Valerie, handcuffed, being led to a cell on the other side of the hall.

"Val, I'm here, baby," I called out, waving. "Over here. Don't be afraid. It's gonna be all right!"

"Hey, Steve," she said, laughing. She sounded relieved.

"No talking between inmates, right!" bellowed the officer escorting her to a cell.

They let me stew for a few hours before a sergeant finally arrived at the jail to question me. As far as I could tell, he would decide our fate. He asked me what I was doing breaking and entering while he was trying to watch the Cubs game on the telly.

I struck what felt like an appropriately contrite look, then I launched into my apology. "We're starving students—like literally starving. I haven't eaten in more than a day. And we have no place to stay. We had to find a place in an abandoned house. We're sorry, and we won't do it again."

The sergeant frowned at my answer. He put a bloated phone book on my lap and asked me to find the name and address of the squat where I was staying in London. When I said that I couldn't give him an address because we had no place to stay, he whacked the phone book with a leather truncheon. It didn't hurt much. It was more of a warning, but it served its purpose. But then he hit the book a second time, slamming my testicles. It felt like I had been punched in the gut. Still, I had a feeling he was holding back, like he didn't have the heart for a proper beating that night.

I discovered then there's something oddly romantic about being tortured and interrogated while calling out for your lover across a cell block.

"Don't worry, Elektra," I called. "We haven't done anything wrong. They'll let us go. Be strong!" Elektra the Assassin was a hero in a comic Valerie was reading when I met her.

I thought of Winnie and Nelson Mandela and their enduring love. I could be Steve Biko from that Peter Gabriel song. And someday the punks would write a song for Valerie and me—martyrs for the Cause.

Whack!

"Ya did indeed do sumpin' wrong," said the copper. "You come into my district where you got no business. Now tell me who give yas the tools to bust into that flat and where they is. And what about the other one? Why'd ya drag her into this mess? What she doin' here, and why'd she leg it when we'd seen yas in the council flat? It's drugs, ain't it, boyo?!"

I didn't know the squatters who had helped us in our foiled attempt because they were smart enough not to give us their real names, and I didn't know the address of their squat. My mind searched frantically for an escape, but I was a rat in a cage. I was starting to think that we could do hard time for this. Be brave, be brave, I told myself.

At 4 a.m., the cop brought me a cup of tea and a piece of blueberry pie on a nice plate.

Feeling heroic after surviving the torture, I made a wisecrack that I imagined would be the chorus of the song someone would sing about us someday: "I ordered a cappuccino, not tea."

When the cop didn't respond, I told him I was from Chicago and that there were a lot of cops there. Then he asked if I supported the Chicago Cubs or the White Sox.

A strange question. I replied, "The Cubs, naturally."

Engaged, he said he'd had a pen pal since primary school who lived in Chicago, and the two of them would soon be married. He was moving to the States to be with her. He showed me a snapshot of a corn-fed Midwestern girl. She wore a toothy grin and a big yellow sundress, a regular Illinois farm girl.

"She's very pretty," I lied. "Congratulations, Officer. You're a very lucky man." I hoped I wasn't laying it on too thick, but the cop brought me a blanket an hour later and winked as he handed it to me. He managed to warm my heart and send a chill down my spine at the same time.

I tried not to watch the clock because a political prisoner doesn't count the minutes. Plus, I suspect that they set it intentionally too slow to break my spirit. Remembering that I'd picked up Morse code when I was a kid, I tapped a simple message to Valerie, who was locked up around a corner. "Shave and a haircut." . . . I waited . . . "Shave and a haircut." . . . I waited some more. I hoped she wasn't being tortured . . . or worse. At last, I received her cautious yet clear reply: Tap, tap. Two bits. I cried tears of joy. I was so in love.

Just before noon, our captor came to my cell and handed me my passport. The squatters had given us up completely. They turned over our backpacks, which contained our passports, our student visas, and the odd textbook. We were summarily expunged from the rolls of the East London underground Antifa Squatters Group and supporters of the Arsenal Football Club, but we were also expunged from the jail. Satisfied that we were simply dumb students, our jailers unbolted the cell door and kindly invited us to fuck off, saying, "Never be seen in the district of Wood Green again, or I'll send yas to the Tower of London to be hanged, get it?"

"You'll love Chicago," I said to the Wood Green constabulary as I turned to exit. "Loads of cops there." I gave him a genuine smile to thank him for a lesser beating and picked up the pace.

The cop bobbed his head at me. "Good afternoon, mate. Nice chattin' with ya. Made me night go much quicker. Don't wanna see ya again but stop by anytime, now. See yas."

My vision was blurred by the elusive early afternoon London sun that greeted me outside.

Looking around, I found Valerie waiting nearby on a park bench smoking a roll-up. We embraced as if reunited after decades of separation. Then we made a mad dash toward the tube station, soaring past lines of sullen commuters, thrilled to be out of jail. The moment felt electric, charged with passion and relief. We were so happy to have found one another. Once out of the Wood Green district, we found a pub, the Green Man, and I bought two pints of Guinness Stout with the six quid I had left to my name. Beer never tasted so good.

The Gits on stage, c. 1992. Photo by and courtesy of Lu Hanna.

TICAL

Valerie called home, and her parents wired her some money. A trick I could not perform.

We had a few weeks before we had to return to Antioch to try to validate our experiences for college credit. We sold our cameras and some Levis and used the money to travel to northern Spain, where I had friends. In San Sebastián we crashed in a little cave overlooking "La Concha," a little bay lined with fishing boats and a wide promenade. We were young and in love. I was convinced that this was the beginning of forever.

I had been traveling for over a year and was still enrolled at Antioch College. It was time to finish the degree. I returned to Ohio to see if it would be possible. A letter from Mia was waiting for me in the student mail room. She wrote that she had been sober for several weeks, but she was having a tough time living with her father. Mia did not include her plans, but I hoped that she would come back to Ohio. I could not be sure.

Mia showed up late to Matt's graduation party with a wilted bouquet of wildflowers and weeds tied with a broken piece of barbwire. Reunited with all my bandmates. I organized an impromptu "last show" on campus with The Gits and Big Brown House and a new band, D.C. Beggars. The

Lost in thought, c. 1992. Photo by Jackie Ransier courtesy of C/Z Records.

Beggars' founder, Julian Gibson, had followed his girlfriend from Washington, D.C., to Yellow Springs where she would attend college. The relationship didn't last, but Julian wasted no time starting a band with his home city as the namesake. He became part of our Antioch band scene and a friend to all of us. It felt great to be back in my safe Mid-American home, with Valerie and so many of my friends.

To qualify for a bachelor's degree in clinical social work, I had to complete a final project. I chose to lead a music-therapy group with inmates at the Lebanon Correctional Institution, a maximum-security state penitentiary in rural Ohio.

Matt, a visual-arts major, also had to complete a project. He swore on his life that he would make one thousand teacups baked in a kiln with some ancient Japanese glaze. The project was an example of Matt's ambitiousness and sense of humor. Matt and I were different in many ways, except when it came to making music in The Gits. When I sat behind drums, my focus was every bit as myopic as Matt's. While I played, my mind pushed racing thoughts onto another track, and my focus tunneled on the task at hand. I learned to step out of my body and into the flow of rhythm. An indescribable confidence took control of my hands and feet. At twenty-one years old, I had been playing the drums daily for over a decade. I looked down to see my hands playing syncopated polyrhythms that emerged from years of formal training, forming patterns and mathematical equations solved by muscle memory. In rare moments, I was a musical alchemist, conjuring the elements, spirits, and the four winds into a transformative experience for others to find strength and joy. I simply had to let go of the controls and accept the force.

I once spoke to Mia about the experience, and her face lit up. "Yeah, man. I know what you mean. It's like you lose time and forget everything, and you become what you're doing and then you give it away without askin' why."

"Yes! Exactly!" I exclaimed.

"It's like when we're crushin' it on stage—nothing matters but the song, the energy, and the crowd. You just feed on the energy, and it gives you strength and hope," she added.

We walked together as we discussed our shared experience of catharsis, until we encountered Andy, who was drinking a bottle of German beer on the student health clinic stoop. Andy and Mia had started college a year before Matt and me, but neither had graduated. Andy was the smartest person any of us knew. He read books the titles of which eluded my comprehension. He had taken every class he wanted, and he was done with school.

Perhaps drawing on legendary punk music icons like Rat Scabies, Richard Hell, Joe Strummer, and Sid Vicious, Andy adopted a stage name to separate his personal life from the band identity. Andrew Kessler thus became Joe Spleen.

Mia dropped out when she went to Portland. Mia and Andy were just waiting for Matt and me to finish college. Time was fast approaching when we would have to strike out as a band or quit.

Andy and Matt were deep in thought and appeared worried. Mia sat down and the three told me that they had assumed that I would either quit The Gits and get on with a career or commit to my other band, Big Brown House. I had not communicated any commitment either way, and they assumed the worst.

The bubble of privilege would be no more. No more free lunches, easy friends, and university resources for our bands to exploit. We booked a final Ohio show to serve as a graduation ceremony for Andy and Mia and scheduled a meeting to discuss the future.

Big Brown House was, by now, a strong band with an interesting melodic sense and Ben's unusual and accessible lead guitar style. Ben was just as committed as any of us to making a go of Big Brown House in a real city. Ben was also concerned about which band I would choose.

I was too busy or just unwilling to decide what to do after graduation. I avoided choosing between the two bands, because I didn't want to disappoint any of my friends or miss an opportunity by quitting one of the two projects. I spent the better part of four years playing drums in both bands. Big Brown House had written dozens of songs and had developed an original sound that could be commercially successful in the right environment. The Gits had come along a little later yet had an undeniable originality and intensity. I had to make a choice. The decision was made late one night before the graduation ceremony. Adrian, bassist for Big Brown House, quit the band due to "artistic differences" and declared in a signed resignation letter that he would not be joining Big Brown House after graduation.

I seized the opportunity and went in search of Matt. He was at his pottery, still throwing little teacups on the road to one thousand. Would he make it?

"Matt, join Big Brown House on bass and we will become the tightest rhythm section that ever played in a band." I urged. "You'll be better than Jaco Pastorius in no time." I added.

"Impossible, don't be stupid," Matt replied without looking up from the white-hot oven at his feet.

"Are you gonna play in The Gits after graduation?" he logically questioned.

It was a fair question. I had to be definitive. "I will if you will play with Big Brown House," I said.

Members of The Gits, Big Brown House, and the D.C. Beggars and a few trusted supporters—including my paramour Valerie—gathered in a makeshift war room in the student union. I pinned a U.S. road map on the wall. It didn't take long to find consensus. We all agreed to get as far away from Ohio as possible. But where would we go? San Francisco was too expensive, according to Mia, Matt, and Andy. Chicago was too close to Indianapolis, according to me. Los Angeles was too close to ridiculous. New York was just too much. What about Seattle? It was not expensive, nor too hot, too cold, nor too close. Mountains, ocean, and that band Soundgarden. That was all any of us knew about the place. The rock-music scene in Seattle wasn't yet on anyone's radar.

Somehow we were picking up on something in the ether, a magnetic pull that would draw so many young people and bands during the coming decade. The city would soon become synonymous with alternative rock music. Alternative to pop music and ol' time rock and roll, like Elvis and Buddy Holly and, well, Bob Seger. Seattle in 1989, in my view, must have been like San Francisco just prior to the Summer of Love, 1967—a spawning ground for rebellious creative youth striking out on their own.

None of us could be certain that the others would show up. Nevertheless, we agreed to meet in Seattle sometime in the autumn of '89. The plan was implausible—arrive broke in an unfamiliar city, find work and housing, land gigs, and thus simultaneously launch the careers of The Gits, Big Brown House, and D.C. Beggars. We'd done it before on a smaller scale in Ann Arbor, Michigan, and we would do it again in Seattle.

Soundgarden had released their *Ultramega OK* album, which I got in the mail from a booking agent. I liked the record a great deal. Chris Cornell's incredibly piercing voice was haunting and sounded complex. The odd time signatures and rhythm section were powerful and tight. Mudhoney was another band I recognized from Seattle. They sounded a lot like the Stooges to me and there was not much wrong with them, I thought. Big Brown House could play a show with Soundgarden, and they would certainly take us under their wing when they saw us live, I believed. Mudhoney would certainly love The Gits, and then we could help the D.C. Beggars. One big family of like-minded musicians. How naïve I was.

Valerie and I crossed the country in a little blue Dodge Colt that my father sold to me to "start my adult life." I had my set of drums and records, a bag of clothes, and four boxes of books. Valerie had even less. We drove through Canada to Seattle because we heard that gas was cheaper up there. It was, but only when calculated in liters.

Andy, Julian Gibson, and Carla Sindle (the guitarist and singer for D.C. Beggars), Mia, Roger, and Ben would drive out to Seattle in the old Dodge van that we had taken to Ann Arbor. I hoped that I would see them in Seattle, but I had doubts. It's not easy to get a dozen people to agree on anything, let alone move to an unknown city and start over. "Communists," I said, as if shocked. "We are Communists!"

Valerie and I arrived in Seattle in August '89. "Bullshit," I exclaimed after hearing that it rained a lot in Seattle. The weather was beautiful, and it didn't rain a drop until Thanksgiving of that year. Then the rain did not let up (unless it was snowing) until the Fourth of July 1990.

It got a little rough. I searched the classifieds for work and for rental houses in the low-rent (crime-ridden at the time) Capitol Hill neighborhood. We came across a decrepit four-bedroom house at Nineteenth Avenue and Denny Way in which to live and rehearse. Strangely, there was a medicinal buckeye tree shading the front porch. (Buckeye is the state tree of Ohio and the name of their state's sports teams.) Stranger still was the landlord, a self-proclaimed White Warlock, for all intents and purposes. When signing the lease (or what passed as a lease), he explained how he maintained a house free of infestations. There had been cockroaches, yes. They had all been vanquished using simple warlock alchemy: several roaches had to be captured and put into a pot with a touch of sherry, salt, and pepper. Place on medium heat and simmer for ten to fifteen minutes or until bugs are dead and soft, then eat the stew. (It doesn't taste all that bad with the wine, or so he said.) The colony of insects will smell that a roach-eater lives in the home and bugs will pack their bags for safer digs.

"And are there mice?" I asked, expecting to catch him off guard.

"No mice. Had rats once but they were no problem. I caught one rat in a trap. A big fella. I used a lighter and just burnt his tail."

"Oh god, you ate it," Valerie gasped.

"Oh no, never. I let the poor fellow go and he went back to their nest. Well, if a giant did that to you, would you stick around? No way! The burnt rat told the others, and they followed the roaches."

I could see no sign of pests, so we rented the place and named it, accordingly, the Rathouse. Andy, Mia, Julian, and Carla moved in with Valerie and me. It became our home and base of band operations. We rehearsed in the cellar, had parties in the common space, and hosted touring bands from around the world. Ben and his partner Rosanne moved across the street, and before long a new Seattle community of ex-pat artists, musicians, and punks took shape with the Rathouse as the hub. The rent was $580 split six ways. Somehow, we were all still broke.

We found ourselves outsiders and unwelcomed by the established Seattle bands. Bands such as Mudhoney, Mother Love Bone, U-Men, Blood Circus, the Accüsed, and Soundgarden had known each other since high school and some since elementary school. It was a Seattle boys' club, but we soon found our place with other outsiders. Valerie and I had become unapologetic political activists since spending the night together in jail. We made friends with squatters and anarchists in Seattle as we had in London. Valerie was outgoing and gregarious, and she made friends easily. She soon found a job at Pike Place Market, where her circle expanded rapidly. I was shy and more reserved, but I volunteered at an anarchist book collective called Left Bank Books and got to know people there.

Valerie and I wanted to model the Rathouse on the Dischord House in Washington, D.C., and the CRASS Collective in England, two overtly political groups of friends who also created music. I sought to create a music-focused collective of friends who modeled progressive ideals by building inclusive community; not self-serving and competitive, it was a music collective that was also political. Sadly, our efforts were mostly lost on our comrades. I realized that trying to reinvent a band to have a side of political activism was neither progressive nor fair, so I gave up. Then Bush #1 launched Persian Gulf War #1, and all of us protested the bombing of Iraq with a few thousand others in the streets of Seattle. It was inspiring to agitate for change. There were skirmishes with police on horseback in riot gear. We yelled and carried signs and banged on drums for hours, but the war happened anyway.

We wanted to get to know other musicians, and we needed to release some music on vinyl. None of the local record labels we approached seemed interested in helping us to achieve this goal, so we started our own record label, Rathouse Records. Rathouse's first release was a compilation called *Bobbing for Pavement: The Rathouse Compilation*. We approached bands we liked, including some who were also new to Seattle and others who had been playing in Northwest garages for years.

D.C. Beggars, The Gits, and Big Brown House contributed two tracks each for the LP. Gas Huffer, Hammerbox, My Name, and a punk band called the Derelicts also contributed songs. Andy recruited a brilliant photographer friend from Antioch, Dale Montgomery, to create the cover. He came up with a visually compelling photo collage of filthy, rejected doll heads. We convinced a young graphic artist named Lisa Orth (the founder of Big Flaming Ego Records) to design the album package, and we raised the money to press a thousand vinyl records—although 200 arrived warped. The Rathouse compilation on Rathouse Records sold out in a month and is highly collectible today.

The Seattle music scene was not well known beyond the Pacific Northwest at that time. The curmudgeonly Washington Liquor Board had established a litany of rules and regulations limiting live music and the promotion thereof. They passed a "teen dance ordinance" which made it illegal to post flyers advertising events, limited the hours minors could be out, lowered the capacity of venues, and fined clubs and people for noise levels above a whisper. It made bars and community centers unwilling to risk having live music, it discouraged landlords from leasing their places for performances, and it levied huge fines on violators in random, biased ways that kept us all guessing and running when we noticed a police car. Jaywalking could get you a ticket in the hundreds of dollars. A club could be fined $200 per flyer for posting handbills advertising shows on public telephone poles. Not only unfair, the legislation was also openly hostile toward the music community.

This was the era of acronyms against creative individuals doing it themselves. Al Gore's misguided wife, Tipper, had established the Parents Music Resource Center (PMRC) to fight against naughty language and sexual innuendo in music. It required that a consumer of music containing English expletives be over eighteen years old. By design, the enforcement of this industry-wide policy blatantly targeted heavy-metal bands, Madonna, and hip-hop artists. The rule required labels to add those silly little stickers that say "Parental Advisory—Explicit Content." However, the rule backfired. Records that had the "obscenity warning" enjoyed increased sales, which then caused bands to create explicit content in order to earn the warning label!

Bumper-sticker membership organizations like MADD (Mothers Against Drunk Drivers) were soon parodied with stickers that read, "DAMM (Drunks Against Mad Mothers)." Signs posted along the I-5 corridor asked drivers to call 764-HERO to report drunk drivers. Sure enough, the number was too often used to report drivers of color. Seeing a clever way to subvert the mandate to snitch, while gaining free promotion, an indie rock band called themselves 764-HERO, yet another example of the rebellious humor and subversive cleverness of some of the groups in the Northwest.

In the '80s and early '90s, the idea of civic responsibility was perverted by conservative zealots and liberal do-gooders to include locking up minor drug offenders, rolling back welfare to poor mothers and the disabled, deregulating banks and the stock market, and of course the movement to ban women's right to abortion. The reign of the grinning, demented U.S. president, Ronald Reagan, was over, but his legacy lived on, and his former number two, George H. W. Bush was now in charge.

The more I connected the dots, the more I was compelled to consider the term used for the music we played, punk rock. It was more than rock music; it was a statement. We would ignore opportunities that compromised our ability to write and perform the music exactly as we saw fit. Mia cussed at will in our songs. This made our songs unplayable on commercial radio. We ignored rules we found ridiculous. We were determined not to compromise our musical ethic just to be played on the radio or sound like other bands or make a better class of friends. Our mission was bigger than becoming mainstream.

Mia Zapata and Andrew Kessler (a.k.a., Joe Spleen) at live show c. 1989-90. Photographer unknown.

Band meeting and photo shoot with vintage Kodak Box camera at the Rathouse, located at 19th and Denny in Seattle, Washington, c. 1992. Photos by and courtesy of Joe Hirsch.

12

WHILE YOU'RE TWISTING, I'M STILL BREATHING

Seattle in the late '80s was an isolated working-class port city, a four-hour drive from the nearest "big" city, Portland, Oregon. The country was in recession, and unless you were an engineer working at Boeing or a laborer on a fishing boat there were very few jobs.

Drugstore Cowboy, *My Own Private Idaho*, and *Twin Peaks* accurately reflected the urban, drug-addled desperation and dewy, mystical seediness of the Pacific Northwest at the time. *Streetwise*, a 1984 documentary by Martin Bell about homeless kids hustling on Seattle streets and squatting in empty warehouses, all while turning tricks and doing drugs, is probably the best representation of the geographic isolation and stark economic reality of pre-tech-boom Seattle. It would not change until the mid-1990s—not until companies like Amazon, Nintendo, and Microsoft took off and changed the landscape, investing millions in Seattle infrastructure. This would eventually lead to the gentrification of neighborhoods where the Rathouse and the Frontier Room were, but it is *that* gritty, working-class Seattle I remember.

Mia was the first of us Gits to find work. She walked into a combination dive bar and greasy spoon in the Belltown district called the Frontier Room and walked out with an apron in hand. The Frontier Room was on the corner of Blanchard and First, a neglected part of town just north of Pike Place Market. There were a few bars, some decrepit Section 8 housing units, and abandoned storefronts. The dark streets were mostly deserted except for drunks, crack dealers, and sex workers.

Each morning, Mia wrapped her apron around her twiggy, yellow dreadlocks and walked into the dark morning. On one occasion I was arriving home at the Rathouse after an all-night temp job, and I decided to walk to work with her. We caught a bus on Fifteenth Avenue that dropped us at Third and Pike and from there we walked seven blocks uptown to Belltown and the Frontier Room.

Mia said good morning to the homeless man curled up under a mess of wet newspaper as she unlocked the diner door in the rain and darkness. I pushed aside the vagrant's gear and some empty bottles of Robitussin. "Hit the road, Jack Kerouac," I said trying to sound tough, but instead I just sounded like a college guy. I hated sounding collegiate.

"The name's not Jack," he mumbled. "I know Mia."

Meanwhile, Mia turned on the lights and started the coffee machine. It seemed like an hour before the coffee was ready. She lit the pilot light on the grill and flipped on the kitchen radio, which was tuned to the oldies station. The rain outside blew sideways. At last Mia poured coffee into a Styrofoam cup, for which I thanked her profusely.

"You can wait," she told me before handing the cup to Jack Kerouac. In turn, Jack dug into his pockets and handed Mia a handful of sticky, lint-covered change. She accepted his payment and asked if he'd like anything else. Mia understood that by accepting the dirty pocket change she allowed the man some dignity. I hadn't even allowed him that.

"Keep the change, Mia," he said as he gathered up his soggy paper bedding and shoved it into an empty newspaper vending box out front.

"Oh, you know I will, Lumpy. Have a good day your own self," Mia replied, spinning around and tossing the coins into the empty tip jar on the counter. Sometimes that was the only cash in the jar at the end of the day.

"You too, Mia. Don't take any wooden nickels."

"Oh, you know I won't, Lumpy. Now get on outta here before I have my drummer break your skinny legs."

"Yeah, I'd like to see that," said Lumpy.

The Frontier Room opened at 8 a.m.—more or less—at which time a small group of men would begin to gather around the front door, alcoholics who passed the desperate hours between 2 and 8 a.m. drinking Lysol or Scope to stave off delirium tremens in those terrifying hours during which liquor could not be sold. They grumbled and twitched nervously waiting for their bar to open.

Physics-defying stains covered the thirty-foot ceiling of the Frontier Room like a faded mosaic of Depression glass. It was covered in grease and yellowed from a hundred years of unabated smoking, and . . . was that dried blood? Seattle was like that. The city was rife with dive bars, strip clubs, drugs, homeless people of all ages, and general seediness. There was as much filth and decay as there was youth and excitement. It was very dark on starless cloudy nights and the streets felt dangerous to me. I was mugged on two occasions, so I took to carrying a knife. I worried about Mia.

Homeless folks and chronic alcoholics composed the nucleus of the Frontier Room clientele, but they were certainly not all the regulars. Andy and I often made our way down the hill from the Rathouse to the Frontier Room to hang out with Mia and try to get some free food. Mia would amble over and take our order as if she didn't know us, and Andy ordered the same thing every time in a comedic ritual. It would go something like this but varied in theme and characters.

Andy: "I'll have eggs . . . any style!"

Mia: "Great. How would you like your eggs?"

Andy: "Any style!"

Mia: "Yes, sir, but how would you like them?"

Andy: "Any style, dammit! I want my gaddam eggs. Are you deaf, woman?!"

I didn't find the role-plays particularly funny, but somehow this back-and-forth was a metaphor for the ridiculousness of everything at the time. In order to play the straight man, I tried not to laugh, but I would eventually give up like a giggly schoolgirl and tears streamed down my cheeks. Hunger made the skits that much funnier as each morning new characters emerged with unique accents. We were bored and broke and it made us hungrier to make something happen for The Gits. I put my head down on the table and closed my eyes, famished.

Maybe the grill wasn't hot enough to fry an egg properly, or maybe Mia was just a hopeless short-order cook. I can't remember a single time that the eggs I ordered were not runny and undercooked. I tried sunny side up, over medium, scrambled, even any-style eggs. The eggs were always runny, and I could never eat them. Andy agreed that the eggs were inedible and that the soup du jour was a safer bet. "Very well," Mia replied, "the gentleman shall enjoy today's special, Owl of Soup!" The menu on the wall had lost the B from the word "Bowl" so it simply read "owl of Soup $4.10."

"Indeed, it'll have to do," Andy responded reluctantly.

When it came time to pay for breakfast. Mia took my money and returned the same amount in change and I'd tip her the $4.25 back again. I still don't get how that worked. Mia would not intentionally steal a penny from an employer, or anyone else for that matter. Looking over at my untouched food, Mia would ask in her best saucy serving-wench voice, "What's the matter, fat boy, don't like your eggs?" and then she would take my plate, sometimes serving it to a middle-aged woman named Colleen who spent much of her day seated at the lunch counter, quietly mumbling.

Above the Frontier Room were Section 8 subsidized housing apartments assigned to disabled people and the severely mentally ill. Colleen lived in one of the units and treated the diner and bar as her own dining and living room. Mia loved to listen to Colleen and gain access to her inner world.

Colleen did not drink at the bar, as liquor would not have blended well with her Thorazine and Haldol. Mia told me that Colleen held hushed conferences with an array of imaginary associates such as Dear Abby, John F. Kennedy, and Jesus Christ. I often saw Colleen animatedly chuckling, nodding in conversations with these imaginary luminaries. Other times she sat quietly sipping a coffee, adding sugar and chain smoking but saying nothing. She simply stared, disassociated, until she suddenly sat up straight and cackled maniacally while rolling her eyes. To Colleen, Mia was a personal secretary or assistant, assigned the task of making Colleen's imaginary guests feel both welcome and real. Mia would sometimes even pour coffee for Colleen's guests.

"Oh, thank you Mia, but Jesus would prefer tea," Colleen requested.

Putting on a demure Southern-belle voice, Mia replied, "Right away, Ms. Colleen."

The two had an understanding, a symbiotic greasy-spoon sisterhood. If a customer's order went wrong, Mia would slip the club sandwich with too much mayonnaise, or the burnt chicken-fried steak, to Colleen, who was happy to accept. Colleen could be either gracious to or dismissive of Mia, her tone depending on the discussion with the dignitaries with whom she held court. Refilling her cup of coffee, Mia waited on Colleen with all the formality and respect that was due to a woman so seemingly casual yet so important and worldly. Mia's kindness was not lost on Colleen. In exchange for her thoughtfulness and confidence, Mia was allowed access to Colleen's psychotic insight.

Mia said Colleen had children and, when they were young, Colleen liked to lie on the kitchen floor and pretend she was dead. She waited for her little ones to come home from elementary school to find their mother cold "dead" on the floor. Then she would just sit up and laugh because apparently, she thought this was hilarious.

Colleen sat up straight in her seat then leaned over the counter, her bottom too clearly visible through her threadbare house dress. Colleen then whispered in hushed tones, "I know that you know, Mia."

Mia told me that she had always wanted to work with the mentally ill. "My people," Mia remarked, as she made the rounds hitting her customers' coffee cups with a freshly burned pot of Farmer Brothers. I mentioned that I thought psychologists make more than four dollars an hour. But Mia liked what she did and, anyhow, school could not teach her about crazy people the way dealing with Colleen could. The stories she told of Colleen seemed implausible, if not impossible; however, there were witnesses who repeatedly verified Mia's retellings. I soon discovered that Mia's versions were tepid when set against the actual truth of the matters she recounted. Mia passed on these tales as we drove to gigs or while seated on the porch of the Rathouse, impersonating Colleen with crippling accuracy.

On the road to a gig at the Satyricon in Portland, Andy and Matt were having a heated discussion about one thing or another. That in and of itself was unusual because the two rarely argued; Matt was almost always in agreement with Andy. We had picked up Mia from work at 4 p.m. and were rushing the three-to-four-hour drive to make our eight o'clock soundcheck.

Wishing to distract from the argument, I asked, "Mia, how is your pal, Colleen?"

Mia got the clue and spoke up from the back of the van so she could be heard. "Oh, Colleen, that poor thing. She disappeared for a couple weeks, and I started to worry but she came in this morning. She was all fucked up with bandages on her face and arms. Her hair and eyebrows were burnt off. But she was her usual self, giggling like a little ol' girl, but she looked a mess."

"Why a mess?" I asked.

Mia explained, "Well, she swore to God to quit smoking."

"Good for Colleen! See? You can do it too, Matt," I teased.

Mia continued, "Yeah, one day she told me she was gonna quit smoking cigarettes. She crossed her heart and swore to God that she would quit smoking. Since she talks to Jesus all the time, I figured she was serious. Colleen don't use the Lord's name in vain . . . but I do, Goddammit!" Mia giggled. "Jus' kiddin," she added, giggling again.

"But what happened to her?" Andy asked.

Mia motioned with her hands around her face and hair. "She got all burned up. Her hair was all gone, and her eyelids and brows were burnt clean off. She looked like she put her face on the grill at work. So, I asked her why she was all fucked up like that and all she said was that she swore to quit smoking."

M99
GITS
TREE HOUSE
BLACK ANGEL'S DEATH SONG
SATYRICON
FRI. OCT. 16

"Yeah, so?" I pleaded for more details.

Mia could do uncanny impressions of the Frontier Room regulars. Mia imitated Colleen's overmedicated, flat, nasal voice without expressing shock, regret, or self-pity. She was a good listener and could parrot the inflections and accents in people's voices remarkably well. Mia cracked her voice, rolled her eyes skyward, and smiled just as I had seen Colleen do when she was talking to her voices. "'I swore to God to stop smoking, Mia. But I made a terrible, terrible mistake, Mia, I smoked a cigarette . . . I swore to quit smoking, but I smoked a cigarette. So, I set myself on fire.'"

To Colleen, and, I dare say, Mia, this was simply a matter of logic. Of course, if you swear to God to do something, and you mess up, then you set yourself on fire. Obviously!

"'I set myself on fire to punish myself for Jesus. Everything is fine again, though. I can smoke now and it's all fine!' Colleen just smiled and ordered coffee as usual," said Mia.

I nodded, trying not to express shock or disbelief. Mia couldn't make this up. "'Oh, thanks to you, Mia darling. I knew you would understand . . . I know that you would do exactly the same thing if you swore to Jesus, Mia.'"

"'I do, Colleen. And I'm sure I would do exactly the same thing.'"

Imitating Colleen or her southern belle routine weren't the only accents Mia affected. On more than one occasion she used her racist Mad Asian Doctor voice to diagnose me with "Exacaly-lika" Disease. "Oh my God, Mia! What is that?" I queried, and thus she explained, "Yo arse look exacaly-lika yo face." (I walked right into it every time. She tried it on stage. Nobody got it.) She also said I had been struck with a case of acute "ridiculopathy," a disease she made up to describe the ridiculous nature of our humor. Acute ridiculopathy was endemic at the Frontier Room and with booze, helped infect others.

The Gits at the legendary Portland venue Satyricon in October 1990. From author's archive.

HERE COMES A REGULAR

13

Sailor Scott was another one of the characters who earned the esteemed title of a Frontier Room Bar Regular. He had been homeless since the 24-foot catamaran he claimed to have sailed from Hawaii to Seattle earlier that summer had sunk in shallow waters after colliding into Seattle Aquarium's new sea-otter exhibition at Pier 58. It lay there in 40 feet of water and all Scott needed was enough money to hire a crane, drain her hull, and patch her up for his return voyage to Hawaii.

While hunting for a job at Pike Place Market, I saw Sailor Scott leaning over the railing along the seawall, craning his neck to catch a glimpse of his vessel and his ticket out of there. I seriously doubted that there was a boat down there, but I told him that I could see it . . . sorta.

One night I happened to be walking home from work with Mia when Mia noticed Sailor Scott uncomfortably drunk, crumpled amidst the embrace of the man-sized

Mia holding a postcard in April of 1992. Photo by author.

galvanized steel petals of the tulip sculpture outside the old Seafirst Bank tower at Third and Madison. He was dead asleep, and his head was wedged in an area that was filling rapidly with rainwater. Mia banged the cold metal with the side of her fist and shouted over the traffic and the pouring rain, “Hey, dipshit! Get your drunken bum’s head outta that stupid flower. You’re about to die, Sailor Dumbass. Hurry up and get outta that flower or I’m leavin’ you here to die . . . again!”

Waking from his stupor, Sailor Scott untangled his body and stumbled out. He believed Mia had saved his life and was loyal to her thenceforth. She became his Guinevere. Sailor Scott began to follow Mia and, by extension, The Gits. His home was underwater so he sorta moved into the Rathouse and slept on the sofa as Mia’s houseguest. He was respectful and I liked him. He fell in love with Mia, of course, but she was not interested.

Washington State’s liquor laws at that time required establishments to serve food in order to maintain a liquor license, so the Frontier Room food service was a legal formality that simply needed to exist on premises. This was reflected in the menu options but not in the service offered by Mia. She loved her job and did her best to present herself as a legitimate diner waitress, the gold standard. She never learned to tie her apron properly, carry multiple plates with one hand, or do two things at once, but Mia was adept at the language of a classic rural American truck stop. She mastered the dialect by simply employing her Southern charm and Kentucky drawl with great effect.

If you walked past the Frontier Room diner counter and through the swinging double doors there was a much larger bar room. The bar had only twelve stools and they were off-limits to Frontier Room non-regulars. Scattered about the room were a half-dozen small, sticky tables with unmatched chairs, and larger, red pleather booths in the corners. A modern CD jukebox took paper money: five songs for a dollar. Mia dreamed of one day seeing a Gits CD in the jukebox. We would make it happen.

The Frontier Room bar was a subcultural Mecca for the human gristle trimmed from better cuts of Seattle society. Few ate in the filthy diner where Mia worked; it was dead most of the time, but the bar room was lively and seemed dangerous to me. It would simmer to life in waves throughout the day as various musicians and artists stopped in and as zombies and vampires emerged from their offices and crypts at night. The place was also popular with “alternative” people who played “alternative music.” I did not know the alternative to music— some horrible noise, perhaps? I recall meeting fake vampires with real fangs embedded in their jaws, a guy with a completely tattooed face who swallowed swords, a cowboy heroin dealer, a car thief, a disgraced Seahawks fullback, and other punk bands. These were real people who made up The Gits’ first fan base in Seattle, and they seemed to feel Mia was one of them.

Nina was an indomitable bartender and manager of the Frontier Room. Standing 6′4″ in her size-12 O. J. Dingo boots, she was equally revered and feared by the regulars. A beautiful Cherokee woman with high cheekbones, shining dark shoulder-length hair, narrow hips, flat chest, and a business-like smile that was both friendly and disinterested, Nina was tough and carried a gun in her front pocket. I could see it in her Levi's 501s accentuating her crotch like Robert Plant's cucumber. She easily inhabited her butch identity. I liked to sit in the corner of the bar and watch Nina take care of business, even as she scared me. Few dared to cross Nina, according to Mia. Occasionally a drunk would start something or complain about a drink, but if the tone of his voice was wrong, or if Nina sensed disrespect, there could be trouble.

It was early December of 1991. It was raining. It was always raining that winter. Mia had asked me to stop by the Frontier Room and pick her up for band practice. Some dude had been showing up and hitting on Mia after her shifts, saying he wanted to make her a star and generally trying to get in her pants. She didn't want to be left alone with the guy. "He just sits there and stares at my chest with his mouth open. No matter what I do, he won't get a clue and leave me alone," Mia explained, quite upset. "The guy will not take no for an answer."

I showed up a little early and Mia insisted on buying me a beer. It was a Friday night, and I took a seat alone in the red pleather booth closest to the bar exit. I was reading a day-old paper when Mia signaled with hand gestures that I should wait for just a couple more minutes. The bar was crowded for 6 p.m. and the diner was reaching a fever pitch. It was happy hour, but I was feeling depressed and anxious; I didn't want to be there. Some sort of rock power ballad came on the jukebox. It was a slow song and there was so much reverb on the snare drum that it sounded like the band was playing in a cave or in a faraway stadium arena. The vocals came in and the chorus repeated so many times that I could sing it word for word by the end of the first listen. "I-I-I-I'm still alive. I-I-I-I'm still alive, ohhhh . . . " and so on. Then there was a guitar solo that seemed to go on forever. It reminded me of REO Speedwagon, who I had loved as a kid. Later I learned this was Pearl Jam, and it was being played everywhere all the time. I started to observe Pearl Jam graffiti popping up on overpasses and bridges around the city. It was a publicity campaign designed to mimic an underground revolutionary movement. It was corny to me. The Pearl Jam underground, risking freedom and life itself for the free grassroots promotion of a soon-to-be-top-40 rock band being built from the ground up by the biggest record company in the world.

The major labels were trying to emulate the DIY punk music scene by pretending that the bands they promoted were underground grassroots musical phenomena. Once properly watered down and mainstreamed, Seattle music could be manufactured and packaged to order by the corporation that brought you Backstreet Boys and Milli Vanilli. A&R scouts from all the major record labels now descended on Seattle like Avon ladies, selling their label to that week's next big band that sounded somewhat like Pearl Jam or had the right look. That was not The Gits.

Labels' "street teams" created a buzz and generated press by paying publicists to solicit writers from different music publications to write stories and invent hype about the bands. J.C. Penney and Target marketed cheap flannel shirts made in Bangladesh and called it Grunge Fashion. Everybody could get on board and certainly did.

The regulars at the Frontier Room didn't care what was on the jukebox. They occasionally unplugged the thing en route to the men's room. The bar was more crowded than I had ever seen. There was a crush of screeching female office workers and football fans to see the Seahawks game televised in the bar. They ordered daiquiris and cosmopolitans. Loudmouth football tourists tried to pay for drinks with traveler's checks. They lit cigars and wore Bill Cosby sweaters. They were "slumming" at the Frontier Room; this was not their scene. When the Pearl Jam song came on, some frat boys started high fiving as though they had scored a touchdown.

I listened to men in suits and Seahawks caps talk about their winning stock portfolios under ten years of Republican trickle-down economics. "Poverty sucks!" one declared as he toasted his good fortune. Were these my straight-world contemporaries? They glared at women's breasts and yelled thinly veiled rape epithets at women minding their own business: "I'll tap that dyke ass," and "She'd blow me for a ride in the Jag." This, followed by chuckles, more drinks, longer glares, and a debate about who would go first and who would get "sloppy seconds."

They smoked cigars and blew the acrid blue smoke above their heads. It reached the ceiling and fanned outward, enveloping the entire bar in a foggy blue haze. They blew smoke rings and violated the fluttering "O"s with the cherry-red tips of their stogies. The huddle of idiots thought this was just hilarious.

I was getting extremely uncomfortable and wished Mia would hurry up so we could go to practice. My bottle of Rolling Rock drained, I waited another ten minutes. It was getting louder and louder. I was bored. Where was Mia?

A drunk trio of female office workers with enormous handbags were already making themselves welcome in my booth. Shoving and sliding their asses between the slippery horseshoe booth and the sticky table, they edged me to the opposite side. The combination of the overapplied sickly perfume with the smell of mall-acquired new leather, Madonna lip gloss, and musky breeding hormones was nauseating. I wanted to be left alone.

"Hey baaaby, there enough room for me and my girlfriends? We are Forty-Niners fans, ya know. Don't haaate on us. Can't we all just get along? We are totally bi . . . coastal"—wink!— "if you know what I mean. Can we sit with you?"

I didn't bother to tell her that San Francisco and Seattle were on the same coast.

The combination of their perfumes was overwhelming. Feeling defeated, I avoided eye contact and relinquished the booth.

Standing, I craned my neck to see over the drunks, searching for Mia. Maybe she got another ride, I reckoned. I wrapped my black-and-white checkered Yasser Arafat commando scarf around my throat twice and fumbled for the keys to my Dodge Colt and headed to the door. Mia wouldn't wait for me in the same situation. She always did her own thing. She worked, she can get a cab.

Over at the bar, Nina continued to take orders and pour drinks—chatting casually about the Seahawks or boats—all the while aware of every interaction between every group in the room. I noticed that the suits I had seen earlier now had a young woman cornered against the wall by the jukebox. Pearl Jam was being played again, something about Jeremy. The woman struggled to get some distance as one suit or another kept blocking her ability to get away. By the lights in the machine, I could see one of them reaching up her skirt to his elbow.

At that exact moment, Nina one-hand-vaulted over the bar, grabbed the harasser by the throat, pulled his face so close that her teeth were against his ear and said something so frightening that the man dropped his glass. Nina, grabbing his throat and clutching the rear end of his underwear in a distinct bully's "wedgie" lift, simply said, "Intercepted!"

The Frontier Room regulars also had a few tricks up their sleeves. Tonight, they had lined up in a battle-tested, defensive phalanx, parting just enough to allow Nina to do her job, then they closed ranks and went back to their drinking straws and lamentations. They had seen this all before—the phalanx served a role in the choreography, blocking anyone from throwing a cheap shot at Nina's turned head. It happened so fast that no one in the bar seemed to even notice.

With the agility and power of a tight end, Nina escorted the offender on his tippy toes through the diner and onto the street—but not before delivering a combination to the jaw and nose that left a mess for Mia to clean up. She hadn't abandoned me to the suburban horde.

"The old bum's bush," Mia observed casually after wandering over to watch the eviction.

"The old bum's *rush*," I corrected.

"What?"

"Let's get the hell outta here, man."

"Yeah, this dump is boring. And I don't hang out at no dumps," she proclaimed.

"What?"

"Hee hee, I jus' wanna get the fuck outta this dump," she laughed nervously.

I loved Mia's throaty little chuckle. She would squeak, growl, and giggle in a burst of childlike excitement. No doubt some people who heard this judged Mia to be one of the upstairs Section 8 neighbors of the bar. Nina turned to go inside but stopped and, over her shoulder, she said, "The lamb is sure to follow . . . "

And out scrambled the other suit. He hailed a cab as he quickly crossed First Avenue. He abandoned his chum on the curb with a bloody nose and quickly hailed a cab, not once looking back.

Mia snatched a mop from inside the kitchen to clean the piss and blood from the floor inside the door of the Frontier Room. But Nina cleaned up her own messes and therefore took the mop from Mia unceremoniously before looking me square in the eye and saying, "Y'all have a good practice and a good night, hear? Mia, I'll see you at 7:30 sharp tomorrow."

I hated violence and fighting; I couldn't find a reason for it. I grew up being bullied. I was the only white kid in my elementary school. I knew that fighting always made things worse and I learned to avoid trouble with alacrity. However, nonviolence did not preclude me from feelings of anger and injustice when people were responsible for my suffering or for the suffering of my friends. I understood that egos bruise more deeply and painfully than flesh. I also knew that, anywhere I went with The Gits, our combined street wisdom served to avoid most violence. We did not talk tough, nor did we talk about our own band very much. We knew that we had something special, but self-assurance and humility did not help us get gigs or articles written about us. Unfortunately, narcissism and self-aggrandizement are needed to make it in the rock-and-roll business.

One day, I sat in the lobby of the *Rocket* magazine office waiting to speak with an advertising representative who didn't appear. I waited quietly, invisible, and was duly ignored by the receptionist. We were having a tough time getting any press for our shows, and we decided to spend $42 and buy ourselves a one-sixteenth-page print ad in the weekly music magazine the *Rocket* to publicize an upcoming gig. I was there to give them money and reserve the ad space. It had become clear that, if we were to compete with record companies and the established Seattle bands, we would have to do more than write good songs, play them well, and make records; we needed to be proactive and play the game.

Being a starving artist was part of the struggle, I thought, as I looked down at the envelope of cash tucked in the fold of a tiny 2-by-2-inch inch print ad. It was so small, I could barely read the date we were playing. We would never gain any exposure or attention if we were forced to pay for it. We were paying our dues in the rehearsal space and on the road, but we didn't have the hard currency that could increase the visibility of The Gits outside of Seattle.

Forty-two dollars would not be enough, I lamented. I decided to leave the *Rocket* office and return the money to the van gasoline fund. I rose to split as a frantic blonde woman with far too much makeup, smelling of Swedish Fish and wearing a baby-doll dress, burst into the *Rocket* office. Following behind were two guys I reckoned to be bandmates. She stomped her feet and yelled at the patient receptionist, just trying to do her job, "I wanna be on the cover of the *Rocket*. Right now, goddammit! You're gonna put my band, Hole, on the cover. Where is Charles Cross? I wanna talk to your boss right now! I am gonna be on the cover of the fuckin' *Rocket*! Do you know who I am?" she demanded.

What I didn't know I soon found out. But I guessed it must be a big deal for her to be on the cover, so I excused myself and left the building. I exited onto Third Avenue and looked for the bus stop. If I hurried, I would make it back to the Rathouse in time for band practice. Three weeks later, Courtney Love's band Hole was on the cover of the *Rocket*. Later that week I heard on the local news that she had married Kurt Cobain. "That's gonna be fun for him," I thought to myself.

Mia wearing Subvert T-shirt on stage, c. 1990.
Photographer unknown, from the author's collection.

SUBVERT

Mia and Matt in the spotlight filming *Hype!* at RCKNDY in Seattle, c. 1992.
Photo by and courtesy of Charles Peterson.

ANOTHER SHOT OF WHISKEY 14

Practice went well and Mia sat on the floor of our little practice space that Hoagie, the new drummer for D.C. Beggars, had built out of scrap drywall and two-by-fours within the cellar of the Rathouse. I had found two Mason jars of white powder in the cellar earlier that day while cleaning out the area for gear. I noted faded labels on the side of the jars indicated “Sodium Chloryde,” misspelled with a “y.” I thought the salt must be there to melt the ice on the walkway to the house. I was from Indiana, and it was always a chore to keep the snow and ice clear from the roads and walkways. The pressure was dropping, and it felt cold enough to snow, so I tossed the jars under the front porch stoop.

There we worked on “Another Shot of Whiskey.” Andy was concentrating on the arpeggiated picking at the beginning while Matt and I played the first sixteen bars over and over in a loop so that Andy could get it just right. Mia was trying to get her lyric journal positioned on a music stand, but the cardboard cover was so soft from being handled so much that the book kept falling over. She disappeared a moment and returned with two big Mason jars full of rock salt to prop up the book so she could read her lyrics. We finished the practice on high note because we could tell that this was going to be a great song. We seemed to know immediately if a tune would be a great one. This would be one of the greatest, I reckoned.

Mia needed more time to work out the lyrics. She was mad at herself for taking so long. She left practice mumbling something in her phony Spanish cursing words and went up to her little room to continue writing. She left the lyric book opened next to the Mason jars. I picked up the book to return it to her along with the Mason jars. With the lights now on, I realized I had misread the labels on the jars: "Sodium C-y-a-n-i-d-e." I held two full Mason jars of sodium cyanide!

I reasoned there could be some danger involved with keeping such a lethal element in our basement. Rent was due, so I called Frank, our warlock landlord, who had lived in the house prior to renting it to us.

"Oh yes," he said joyfully. "It is cyanide. Took forever to get all that together. It's enough cyanide to, if dumped in the reservoir, wipe out 75% of the residents of Seattle and 40% of Tacoma. But no worries, I just use it to extract gold from iron ore."

Sure enough, there was a pile of rocks by the cellar door that could serve no other purpose.

"Okay, Frank. Can you just pick it up and get it out of here?"

Frank sounded annoyed but said he would pick up the jars and use the contents to extract gold from TVs or something. He showed up with his wife, who looked extremely nervous. "You didn't call or tell anyone about the little chemistry set you found in the basement, did you?" she queried.

"Just the warlock," I said.

Imagine our good luck when the warlock's wife declared we didn't have to pay rent that month in return for handing over the poison stuff we didn't want anyway. I gave Mia's journal back to her and added that the song looked really good. "Why not just leave it as is?" I suggested.

Since so many bands used the Rathouse to practice, our time to rehearse could be limited, so we had to make the best use of it. When the vibe was right and our collective pistons were firing in sync, we could turn out a song in an hour. "Second Skin" was written during one of these prolific sessions and just before police showed up to close down our rehearsal.

Andy's room was upstairs, just on the other side of the wall from the room Valerie and I shared. Mia, Julian, Carla, and whoever was staying on the couch at the time slept downstairs.

Mia often came upstairs and spent hours writing songs with Andy in his room. I listened to the two strumming his cheap Kay acoustic guitar while Mia hummed a vocal melody, slowly replacing the hums with words to go along with Andy's guitar notes. Andy made gentle suggestions and helped Mia to streamline her lyrics. It was an intimate process, and I would have been intruding on them if I had entered. Our songs "Seaweed," "While You're Twisting I'm Still Breathing," "Another Shot of Whiskey," and many more of our repertoire were conceived of and written in Andy's tiny bedroom. The two of them sat on a single mattress on the floor surrounded by Andy's books, records, tapes, and the same little boombox he had had at college. I wished I could have contributed in some way to the melodies or a word, but I did not interrupt. Instead, I admired the creative constructive interaction simmering between the two geniuses. Soon I would have an opportunity to hear what they were working on and contribute rhythm. It was just a matter of time—time which could not be rushed.

We held parties at the Rathouse and hosted numerous touring bands. There seemed to be dozens of bands arriving in Seattle, just as we had. We were just the first wave of immigrants. To release some music on vinyl and have the record in stores like Tower Records was a badge of legitimacy for a band. A seven-inch vinyl single was enough. Most bands released a few singles and then combined the singles along with additional music to release a full-length album on vinyl, cassette, and CD.

It wasn't easy and it wasn't cheap, so only a few bands had the wherewithal to pull it off. Recording was all analog and tracks were limited. Depending on the budget, one could record on eight, sixteen, or twenty-four tracks. There were also very few qualified studio engineers who could capture the tones and timbre faithfully enough to record a rock band well. The art design was next and then the pressing. Once pressed, records had to get into stores, and there were very few distributors of independent music. Lastly, marketing and sales and, finally, distributing royalties to the musicians.

If I had known any of this, I would never have launched Rathouse Records. In the early '90s there were very few women playing in rock bands. Seattle was a boys' club where there wasn't much interest in bands that wavered from a midtempo, hard-rock style with a male lead singer.

Matt devised a plan to send a dollar to each club booker to symbolically bribe the agents into giving us a gig. We had been in Seattle nearly six months and had only played one local show, a warehouse party. We needed a club date, and there were two venues in town: a Goth club frequented by the queer and underground drug and arts community called the Vogue, and a tiny beer joint on Pike and Tenth called Squid Row. Matt put four songs on a dozen cassette tapes and invested a dollar for each envelope. The letter read:

> Dear Band Booking Agent,
>
> Our band The Sniveling Little Rat-Faced Gits (aka The Gits) is booking shows. We think your club,[insert your club name here], is the best club in town!
>
> We are including one dollar so that you might give us a gig at [insert club name again]. Thank you very much for your time and have a nice day.
>
> Signed,
>
> SNIVELING LITTLE RAT-FACED GITS

The trick worked and the Vogue asked us to play a show with a popular Portland band, the Obituaries, who had a powerful female front person named Monica. We took the stage and tuned up, despite the grumbling soundman mumbling "amateurs" and "hicks" under his breath. We took the stage like seasoned professionals and blasted through a set of fourteen songs without a single pause between them. The soundman was speechless. The members of the Obituaries were standing in the front admiringly and everyone in the club was drawn to the edge of the stage. Mia, possessed by the spirit of Kali, destroyed that night at the Vogue. She exuded the confidence and talent of a much older singer, I thought. We played our first Seattle encore before relinquishing the stage to the Obituaries.

A small group of people queued up to speak with us after the show, and several of the people we met that night became longtime friends and supporters. There was Selene Vigil, who would become singer for the band 7 Year Bitch. There was her boyfriend Eric Greenwalt, singer for the anarchist hardcore thrash band Subvert. Eric stood six feet, four inches and wore a Battle of Stalingrad-era Russian fur hat. There was a brewer named Bones, recognizable because of his ample handlebar mustache. A huge Black cowboy wearing a black hat, dark glasses, and engineer boots with spurs carried a brief case and laid out his drug wares on the bar for the bartender and the insiders to numb their faces. There was an Iranian exile named Mohammad Ali. A bubbly woman with pink and black dreads and a gold tooth that peeked through blood-red lip gloss and a lit cigarette when she smiled introduced herself as Friday from San Francisco.

"I'm really just Stefanie Sargent. In San Fran everybody calls me Sargent Friday from that old TV show." She introduced herself, already making herself at home on Matt's lap.

Stefanie had recently moved back to Seattle from San Francisco to get clean from heroin and play guitar and stay at her mother's home. She was only nineteen. Stefanie fell in love with The Gits that night. She was so impressed with Mia that she could barely speak when Mia introduced herself after the show.

"I love you! I want to be in your band—I mean, help you guys out. I can be your manager or agent or whatever," she stammered. Stefanie, who would later join Selene and Valerie in 7 Year Bitch on guitar, was adorable and kind. Her infectious smile made it impossible not to like her. She was young, but she had already lived some tough years. She had been a teenage runaway, and she had recently cleaned up. Within a week, she was staying on the Rathouse sofa. Matt was defenseless against her undeniable charms, and soon they were dating.

A formidable severe older man with a square jaw and blond dreadlocks introduced himself to Andy. "I admire your work," he said, as if addressing a dignitary.

"Pardon me?" asked Andy, a bit unsettled by the older, grim-looking man offering his hand.

"Your work. Your guitar playing. It's very unusual. I enjoyed the show very much, sir. Thank you for playing. I'm Robert."

Andy shook Robert's hand and thanked him for coming.

Robert, Eric, Selene, Stefanie, and our new friends in the Obituaries came over to the

Rathouse that night for a cocktail or two, and we all became pals. Robert was infatuated with Mia, and this time, the feeling was mutual. I rarely saw them apart after that night.

Mia was a perfectionist in two things: writing emotive song lyrics and, sadly, drinking, getting loaded, which was why "Another Shot of Whiskey" was such a perfect song for The Gits. The song is largely about Robert, who was now her boyfriend. He was the strong silent type, "like a statue full of vengeance," as Mia so brilliantly wrote.

Robert came from the original generation of rock-and-roll conscripts. After surviving the nightmare of being part of an invading force in Vietnam, he and other young Americans like him came home to derision, with nothing but physical and psychological scars to show for their serving the good old US of A. Conscription quashed the lives of many young would-be artists, musicians, radicals, and rabble-rousers. Those who weren't killed on the battlefields were finished by post-traumatic stress disorder, forever chained to their traumas by overexcited amygdala.

Robert was, in fact, a mild-mannered and soft-spoken guy, but that changed on the anniversary of the Tet holiday offensive of 1968, when Robert had violent flashbacks.

It was February 8th, my twenty-fourth birthday, and I waited for Valerie to return from work for a dinner date. I could hear Mia trying to calm Robert, who seemed to be crying in her room. Crying, then shouting and glass breaking. Mia exited her room and walked past me without saying hello—very uncharacteristically. Robert followed but stopped when he saw me standing dumbly in the Rathouse kitchen. He did not appear to recognize me. "Hi, Robert, what's happenin,' are you going out tonight?" I offered.

Robert looked my way with cold blue-grey eyes that did not focus. "I don't go anywhere. It's Tet."

I knew just enough to put my boot squarely into my mouth. "Oh, Vietnam," I blurted, in search of an icebreaker. "What was it like?"

Robert shrugged. "It was cool. Good tent parties."

"Lots of free Army beer?" He shook his head glumly yet smiled, as if explaining to a five-year-old why the sky is blue. "When your commanding officer or sergeant, who is by nature an asshole, is getting you killed by sending you out on useless patrols so the Viet Cong can rip your guts out, you have a little tent party. One guy'd radio another guy from a different command post and say we are under attack. Then everybody in the platoon gets their weapon and fires like mad into the commander's tent. All of us at the same time. That way nobody knows who did it; no guilt, no one to blame. The commander dies, and we got to live another day. Like I said, good tent parties."

I did not ask Robert about Vietnam again. Robert's deep suffering hid in the depths of his eyes and in the lines of his worry-worn face. Mia saw the pain, and she fell in love with him for it. The two were inseparable for years. Robert had a band called Hell's Smells, a "horror country rock band" that rehearsed in Robert's own movie-set dungeon basement. Mia and two friends joined as backup singers.

Squat show in Holland, c. 1991. Unknown photographer, from the author's archive.

Steve drumming with intention with The Gits, Yellow Springs, Ohio, c. 1988.
Photo by Lynn Peterson, from the author's archive.

JUST TO GET AWAY

15

Following the unprecedented success of Pearl Jam, Nirvana, Soundgarden, and Sup Pop Records, record companies flocked to Seattle to sign the next big-selling grunge band, and dozens of bands signed top-dollar contracts in hopes of following in Nirvana's bootsteps.

Major record labels were not approaching us. We were not particularly approachable. We speculated that we were too old, too surly, too independent, or too wary of being taken advantage of by the music industry. We weren't very social, and our sound was atypical for a Seattle band, but the clear answer was that we had a female front person. And not just any front person. It was Mia. Mia, who stood up against sexism when she saw it and didn't fit into the narrow definitions of how a "girl singer" was supposed to look and behave. Virtually everyone in the bands that were to become synonymous with the "Seattle sound," and especially those on the Sub Pop label, were dudes. There was blatant sexist exclusion and stereotyping within the growing local music industry as in the industry at large, which was mostly based in L.A. and New York.

The only Sub Pop band with women was an all-female band called Dickless. They were a good band and as sincere as all the rest, but their label marketed them as a novelty or a sort of burlesque "girl band." The simple fact that The Gits had a female singer and lyricist made us an empowering anomaly to fans and female musicians. Mia inspired outsiders wherever we played. Her charisma and innate musical talent prompted women to start and join bands. The riot grrrl scene was unfolding in Olympia and the result slowly crept into Seattle clubs. Women began to show up on stage and not just fronting bands. "I decided to sing because of Mia Zapata of The Gits" is something I often overheard.

I constantly thought of ways to garner more attention for The Gits. I studied how other bands advertised their shows on posters, how often they played, and how they released their music. We needed consistent, powerful, and compelling artwork. I approached another recent immigrant to Seattle, Jeff Klinesmith, whose artwork I'd seen on posters for a band called Hammerbox. Jeff designed a logo for The Gits and went on to create art for dozens of our show posters. He went on to become Senior Art Director for Sub Pop Records.

There were too few places to play in Seattle, so we concentrated on playing nearby towns and cities. Nearly every weekend, we drove to a different city or town—Portland, Olympia, Tacoma, Eugene, Bellingham, Vancouver (Washington), Salem, Chico, Sacramento, San Jose, San Francisco—to play to different audiences. We played high-school gyms, house parties, Moose Lodges, warehouse rent-parties, cable-access shows, strip clubs, colleges, tourist bars, county fairs, Oktoberfests, metal fests, VFW Halls, bowling alleys, cafés, and after-hours clubs. I once had to set up the drums in the bathroom with the toilet for a drum throne while playing a basement kegger party.

Any show we could get outside of Seattle was a good one. None of us was shy about speaking our minds. That could, at times, be a deal-breaking combination. Seattle was very self-important, with three weekly newspapers that focused on music, and there were even Northwest album charts. Seattle was also insulated from the rest of the world's music scene. Many local bands drew bigger audiences than national touring acts.

The Gits were different in several ways from the most popular bands labeled Grunge or Emo or Pop. Of course, we had an exceptional singer who was female. We drew inspiration from the melodic English punk bands like the Damned, the Jam, the Clash, Stiff Little Fingers, etc., but Andy's interest in more aggressive hardcore music exemplified by Portland's Poison Idea is evident in Gits songs such as "Wingo Lamo," "Spear and Magic Helmet," and "Sign of the Crab." Our tunes were laden with humor and were about everyday subjects that reflected Mia's actual life and her friends. The grunge bands didn't tune down to D on guitars instead of customary E. It is a tuning style that slackens the tension on strings and creates a deeper and heavier overall guitar sound. Most of the grunge bands such as, Soundgarden, Nirvana, and Alice in Chains tuned down to D or even C. The Gits played in traditional E tuning and allowed Andy to move more adeptly on the guitar fret board. Our songs were faster, yet we also drew on other styles to spice up the Gits mélange of influence like jazz, classical guitar, marches, samba, and tribal African drumming. "Absynthe," the lead song on our first album *Frenching the Bully,* uses a variety of styles. A typical forty-minute Gits set might include a ballad like "Precious Blood" and an anthem such as "Second Skin," followed by a midtempo pop song like "Seaweed" or "Another Shot of Whiskey." We played an R&B cover by Sam Cooke or an Iggy Pop song like "Loose."

We had no stage outfits or anything distracting on stage. For the most part, we wore whatever we put on that morning. The recorded music and the way in which we performed represented The Gits entirely. In the era of MTV, The Gits didn't bother to produce a video. Relentless touring and playing live shows were the method behind the mission. There was limited promotion; we depended on word of mouth to win over new fans one fan at a time. This was a grassroots approach to developing a music career. It was all we knew, but doing it ourselves kept us copacetic with a growing community of underground artists and activists who rejected corporate music. If it was on a major label, it automatically sucked. Since we drew from styles other than punk rock, we attracted supporters from various alternative or underground arts communities. The Gits' willingness to play virtually anywhere and do our own booking, recording, and performing independent of corporate influence earned us a loyal and fiercely partisan fan base.

We toured up and down the western half of North America, from Albuquerque to San Diego to Vancouver to Anchorage. We shared bills with act after act that blew up and became rock stars in the wake of the "Seattle scene": Hole, Alice in Chains, Tad, Everclear, Beck, Nirvana, Death Cab for Cutie, Modest Mouse, Elliott Smith, Soundgarden, Bikini Kill, Sleater-Kinney, Queensrÿche, the Decemberists, the Flaming Lips, our pals 7 Year Bitch, and many more.

Without a manager, we had no choice but to handle the marketing, booking, and networking. Although we considered one another family and were a creative force together, we were four opinionated and eccentric artists with different understandings of the music business. We had different definitions of band success and the means for achieving it. Somehow, we formed a consensus on most subjects, although it could take time and many discussions. We noticed that audiences could not always hear Mia well enough and the music sounded muddy and, well, grungy, like the other bands. We needed the help of a professional sound engineer to mix The Gits live.

We agreed to ask Julian Gibson, our Rathouse roommate and D.C. Beggars guitarist, who had become a top-notch live sound engineer. Despite his own projects, Julian began traveling with us as our sound engineer and tour manager. He was incredibly helpful. With his expert ear and advocacy at front of house, we became a better band. We were more comfortable on stage—and we sounded better. His kind and beautiful nature kept us in good spirits, and he went on to develop a brilliant career as a tour manager.

At the beginning of 1992, we were writing songs, recording singles, working on an album, and playing live as much as possible. It felt as if our peers were flying by us in the fast lane and we were stuck in first gear, without gas money. Our peers were signing record contracts, buying homes, and going on permanent music sabbaticals to the places I had always dreamed of playing.

I borrowed $600 from my family to buy (used) a better drum set. It was a bright orange '77 Rogers XP8—the same kind of kit played by Roger Taylor of Queen, Paul Cook of the Sex Pistols, Rick Buckler of the Jam, and Gina Schock of the Go-Go's, and it had been state of the art in the early '70s. Multiple eight-ply deep maple tom-toms—five in all—allowed me to create monstrous rock drum fills. I paired the kit with my piece-of-junk thirty-year-old snare, which I'd learned to tune so that it sounded like the crack of a shot from a handgun—for the first three or four songs anyway. It was held together with broken guitar strings and a dead nine-volt battery. I loved that old drum set and she garnered the nickname Pumpkin Patch.

Sitting on my drum throne onstage, I could feel the bass tones rattling the drum riser. It felt like raw power. Andy's amp cut through the tonal mid-range, leaving just enough audio space for Mia's voice to occupy the mid and upper sound registers. Bass, guitar, drums, and vocals all occupied a unique sonic level—we were a nimble and well-tuned machine. No matter what the venue or the state of our equipment, we always sounded like pros because we had Julian doing our live sound.

We often opened our shows with "Absynthe." Matt and I came up with the intro of the song. It had a driving swing beat played at an extremely fast 120 beats per minute. I clicked off the song and began the hard swing beat on top of a backbeat to create a kind of jazz-punk intro. Matt came in with a simmering, jazz-tinged walking bass solo line, and Andy dropped broad power chords at the top of each bar, then dripped into a staccato picking melody with palm-muted strings, raising the tension and drawing the crowd closer to the stage.

Then it was Mia's turn. She began singing just above a whisper, "There are these people that use you for their own need for deception . . . " Her voice rose to meet the blazing tempos and the climbing intensity of the music and her words. The audience didn't have time to get comfortable with the song structure before we slipped into a new part, then, without warning and without a musical bridge, I dove into a jungle drum solo. Matt liked to throw up his hands and dance during the solo, which always cracked me up. The song then dropped a key, and the rhythm changed to a syncopated hardcore flourish with accents like punches of a bare fist against a brick wall. Mia sang about struggling for recognition in the music scene and the many opportunistic bottom-feeders and unscrupulous music-business people we encountered.

I think I've had enough
Wonder why I don't just go off
Don't like to be a violent woman
But I know I have it in me . . .

The song ends with a chord progression first played one way, then played again in reverse, accented with syncopated tom and bass-drum triplets in perfect sync with guitar and bass and, just as the song changes direction for a third time, we all stop on a dime. Perfect, every time. That was just the first song of a typical fourteen-song, forty-two-minute set. Each song defined another truth about our band, our mission, and each one of us. Then came "Insecurities," "Twisting Breathing," "Beauty of the Rose," "Guilt Within Your Head," "It All Dies Anyway," "Ain't Got No Right," "Insecurities," and "Precious Blood." And we ended with the anthemic "Second Skin."

Our music drew from various musical styles, including English punk and American hardcore and blues, but it was difficult to classify. We didn't fit the description of those obsessed with grunge bands—young men who related to the dark, heavy, metal side of traditional rock-and-roll themes of sex, drug-fueled depression, and Generation X alienation. The big, anthemic, big-budget arena rock of Pearl Jam, Alice in Chains, and Soundgarden appealed to kids raised on bigger-than-life super groups and arena-rock bands like Supertramp, Foreigner, Kansas, and Rush.

The Gits were not influenced by pop-rock music or MTV. Andy's original guitar style, my jazz training, Mia's love of the blues, and Matt's complete lack of formal training meant that the band was ostensibly self-influenced. We drew inspiration and ideas from each other.

A growing cadre of music critics and musicians was singing our praises. Ann Powers, who is now the Senior Music Critic for National Public Radio, was then writing for *Spin, Rolling Stone,* the *New York Times,* and the *Village Voice* and reviewed our records favorably. So did Neva Chonin of *SF Weekly,* Steve Albini, Mark Arm, Tim Sommer, and Danny Goldberg.

John F. Kennedy, Jr., the son of the late president, started a glossy arts and politics magazine called *George*. The little kid in shorts holding Jackie's hand and waving bye-bye to his daddy in the horse-drawn carriage was apparently a fan of The Gits. We appeared in the inaugural issue of the magazine. There was a beautiful full-page color picture of Mia pouring her heart into a song, clutching the mic, eyes closed, lost in a profound moment of connection with the audience and her band. Seattle's rock-and-roll culture of sound, fashion, art, entertainment, and community had risen to the forefront in the international media. *Rolling Stone, Spin, GQ,* the *Village Voice,*

Melody Maker, *New Music Express*, *Alternative Press*, *Circus*, and MTV mentioned our records and shows, but we never made a video or toured with an arena act. Any recognition we got was hard won by the music itself without any gimmicks.

The fairness we strove to practice in our lives was evident in the division of labor within our band. We each excelled in a particular area vital to our success. Andy was the musical director and taskmaster at practice. He was always on time and always willing to put in extra hours to get it right. Mia wrote the lyrics and came up with her vocal melodies. She was a perfectionist in two things: writing brilliant, emotive song lyrics and hosting cocktail parties for two or twenty, which was why "Another Shot of Whiskey" was such a perfect song. Matt owned the van and drove almost 100% of the time on tour and between regional gigs. He was quick to learn songs, and he came up with strange and perfect bass parts. I was good at arranging the rhythm parts of the songs and organizing our shows. I worked at clubs in Seattle, which helped us get a foot in the door at the venues. Everything I did was focused on the long-term interest of the band.

I considered my playing to be the musical anchor and engine for the Gits machine. I respected music as a legitimate occupation, and I expected respect and to get paid. I felt strongly that musicians should be paid for their hard work. I never played drums as a hobby or pastime. Like a blacksmith or an electrician, one practices and studies music for years prior to performing, like any skilled worker. I insisted that we see the receipts and ticket sales after our shows.

I pushed myself physically to play harder and faster. I needed strength and endurance to be able to overcome childhood asthma, a thin frame, and exhaustion from working as a landscaper between tours. I wanted to set our sound apart with unique styles of drumming and rhythms. We captured the attention of audiences beyond the boundaries of punk with our unusual beats and unbridled energy.

Mia at Avast Recording, Seattle, c. 1992. Photo by author.

ASUW Productions Presents
NIRVANA
TAD GITS
with
CRUNCHBIRD
Saturday, January 6, 1990 8p.m.
HUB East Ballroom
University of Washington
FOUR BANDS.
FOUR BUCKS.
$4/University of Washington
students w/student ID
$6/General Public

16

FOUR BANDS, FOUR BUCKS

We'd each made friends and music-scene connections, but we were still having trouble getting local gigs, which was making us impatient and frustrated. There were too few clubs that featured live music in Seattle, and even fewer had bands on weekend nights, when more people went out.

The city was not yet on board with our burgeoning yet struggling music scene, even with the breakout success of the grunge bands. The state liquor board could show up anywhere at any time, day or night, and they always patrolled in plain clothes. They could fine an individual or an establishment for an offense such as not checking the IDs of everyone in the bar, no matter their age. They could revoke a liquor license if a bar had noise complaints, or if it was over capacity. They could charge an unlicensed establishment for having a poetry reading. The rules seemed arbitrary and their enforcement even more so.

Nirvana and The Gits show poster for January 6, 1990, show at the University of Washington, HUB East Ballroom.

One summer night in '93, The Gits played in Tacoma at a small bar that allowed smoking and had little ventilation. The bar used 1500-watt "Licos"—hot, antiquated stage lights. The bulbs were covered with colored gels that could catch fire. The temperature in the venue was around 100° when we went on. If my hands became wet with sweat, my stick often went flying across the stage, sometimes nailing an innocent bystander in the back.

After the second song, I was dying. I took a long swig of beer and took off my T-shirt, already soaked with sweat. I counted off the third in the set of fourteen songs. A minute into the song, a bouncer began yelling at me from the side of the stage. I couldn't understand him, so I nodded politely and went into the next song. When that song ended, the bouncer strode toward me aggressively and said, "Put your shirt on! You can't be topless on the stage!"

If the look on his face wasn't so deadly serious, I might have thought he was joking. I was a skinny dude with nary a boob bulge in sight. "Fuck you!" I yelled back.

We normally transitioned from one song to another without so much as a breath in between, so I was already counting off the next song when he turned and stomped off the stage. Moments later, I saw through the corner of an eye that he'd returned with black gaffer tape. I was drumming when he shamelessly slapped sticky pieces of tape over my nipples. What the fuck, dude?!

After the show, I apologized to the bouncer on tape duty. I hated to be rude to people working in clubs. He was just doing his job, like all of us. I learned that I'd violated the Tacoma cabaret "nipple ordinance," whose language didn't specify gender, but it was a law to limit topless bars from getting too racy for the Liquor Board members' underserved libidos. In the bouncer's defense, I was breaking the law. So I acknowledged my transgressions, made peace with my god, and copped to the violation. My scarlet letter, I wore the tape on my nipples for a week (at least during the time between showers).

If there was to be a future for live music in Seattle, more cooperation from the city was needed. A cadre of club owners, booking agents, managers, youth advocates, and musicians met to find a legal precedent to get rid of the litany of oppressive codes. They recruited sympathetic City Council candidates and publicly challenged the laws. The scandals eventually came to light and, by then, the success of bands like Pearl Jam and Nirvana were generating undeniable revenue for the city and helping grow the Seattle music scene in ways that led to the eventual downfall of the Board and to a rewriting of the city and state ordinances governing liquor, live music, and promotion.

The Vogue allowed bands to play only on Tuesday and Wednesday nights. Located in the touristy Pioneer Square district, the Central Tavern had music Saturday nights, but they usually booked blues bands in Hawaiian shirts or the occasional touring jazz group. Another spot, closer to home, was Squid Row, which held about forty people and hosted "garage bands" on Fridays. It was next on Matt's dollar list of possible Gits-friendly venues.

* * *

None of us was prepared for the cold. It rained all the time, but most Seattle natives said that it never snowed, and the temperatures rarely dropped below freezing. Yet that year snow fell in clumps and blanketed Seattle, and that night the temperature dropped to 10° Fahrenheit. The snow started falling during the wee hours after a party we hosted at the Rathouse with D.C. Beggars, and, in their first show, 7 Year Bitch. It was a great party. Ben London came up with the name 7 Year Bitch during a night of drinking with Valerie, Selene, Stefanie, and their new bassist Liz Davis at the Comet, a long-standing dive bar and live music venue. The band's original name, Barbie's Dream Car, was too light, too cute, and no longer seemed apropos given the increasingly hostile conservative environment.

It was 3 a.m., and the party was winding down. Several people I didn't know were crashed in the living room. Mia had retreated into her little room and locked the door. Valerie was asleep upstairs, so I turned off the porch light and headed to bed too. I needed water. In the upstairs bathroom I opened the tap and the water came out in a trickle. Then it stopped flowing altogether. I rightly guessed that the pipes were frozen. One more hassle—I would call the warlock landlord in the morning. I passed Julian in the hallway and in passing I mentioned the pipes.

Julian's eyes widened, and he said simply, "The gear!"

I pulled my boots on and out we scrambled into the night to the cellar door leading to the basement rehearsal studio where we had left our equipment set up. The two of us scooped the snow away from the cellar door and pried it open. We peered down the stairs to the practice space below. The entire cellar was flooded. The pipes had burst and ice-cold water had reached halfway up the stairs. When Valerie came out to help, she looked down the stairs behind me and gasped.

"Steve, don't do it. You'll be electrocuted!" she warned.

That was the last thing I heard before I jumped feet-first into the waist-deep ice water. I reasoned that, since the lights were still on, the water hadn't shorted the electricity. My first stroke of luck came when I wasn't fried like a pork rind. Then I noticed that the water was potable, not sewage. I wouldn't die of cholera.

My drums were floating like big fishing bobbers, and all the amps were completely submerged, totally out of sight. I squatted down and stretched my arms out to either side in the black water until I touched Andy's amp. I pulled the amps out one by one, water streaming out as we laid them out on the snow, which was still falling. Valerie,

Julian, Carla, Andy, Stefanie, Mia, and Robert formed a bucket brigade to bail out the water. We were frantic and we worked until dawn. Robert shut off the water main and it took hours to drain.

Later that morning, we sat around the big gas heater in the common room, staring blankly at the waterlogged gear resting on dozens of towels, rags, and band-merch shirts. None of us had slept. Selene and Eric trudged through snow to the liquor store and returned with a bottle of Stolichnaya vodka.

Selene and Valerie each poured a shot into a glass of juice and handed the bottle to Robert, who took a deep pull before passing the bottle down the line.

"It's too bad the cellar wasn't flooded with vodka," Robert joked. "The alcohol would have cleaned the amps."

"Don't turn 'em on!" Matt shouted as he rushed through the Rathouse door. "That'll kill the amps. Don't turn 'em on!"

Nobody wanted to touch anything for fear of tipping the scale and accidentally murdering one or all the amps. The guitars hadn't been down there because Matt and Andy always kept them close at hand. But everything else we needed for a band—drums, amps, PA system, microphones, speakers, effects pedals, cables—had drowned in the flood. None of us had extra gear or extra money to replace or fix anything. We'd all been in Seattle less than a year before our gear had been destroyed by someone else's cruel and vengeful God.

Stefanie was unperturbed. She walked into the room with Matt, and she was already acting like our agent.

"Oh, hey, I forgot to mention last night that my friend who works with Sub Pop loved your show at the Vogue, and she wants to know if you can open for some big band next month at the University of Washington Hub Ballroom," she casually announced. "You guys should definitely do it."

It sounded promising, except that we had no gear. It was less than a month before the show, and none of us had wealthy families to bail us out.

A week passed, but none of us dared try the amps. We took turns blow-drying them, and we prayed to the rock gods. The drums still seemed round, and the only damage I could detect was a small crack in the bass drum's shell, which I fixed with Elmer's glue and gaffer's tape.

Our spirits should have been rising as the temperature increased, but we only had two weeks until the show.

We drew straws to determine who would flip the switch on the Fender Bassman amp. Julian won the honors. He sighed as he studied the amp, searching for clues that would argue against turning it on. But then he suddenly reached for the toggle on the back of the amp head and clicked it on. A light flicked on. Tubes slowly warmed. We heard no fizzing, and we didn't smell any shorts. When it was warm, Julian plugged one end of his curly-cue cable into his guitar and the other into the amp.

We held our collective breath as he flipped off the standby and turned up the gain. He struck a G chord on the guitar, and it rang out loud and clear. It was probably my imagination, but somehow it sounded even better than before. Next, Andy clicked on his Fender amp. No problems. Andy played scales, smiling, and shaking his head in disbelief. "Fuck," was all he could muster.

Matt clicked on the bass amp, and the hum that had pestered him for months was gone. It was fine. We theorized that the ice-cold water had cleaned the inside of the amps and rinsed off the capacitors, connections, and pots, making the amps essentially as clean as new. I don't recommend submerging your dirty gear in ice-cold bath water, but it somehow worked miracles for us.

On January 6, 1990, the night we were opening for a "big band" as arranged by Stefanie's friend at Sub Pop, snow was again falling on Seattle. I put chains on my car just to drive across the University of Washington campus to the show at the Hub Ballroom. It sounded grand but, on arrival, we saw it was no more than two large conference rooms with accordion room-dividers opened up to create a single, enormous, low-ceilinged lunchroom—not a proper ballroom by any means, yet it held about 800 people shoulder to shoulder. At one end of the room was a hastily constructed stage that stood about twenty inches off the floor. Fluorescent tube lights flickered above, supplementing the basic red and blue stage lighting.

Behind the stage, a door led to a small classroom that served as a dressing room for all the bands. The desks had been pushed to the middle. Atop the desks was a restaurant bus-tub filled with sodas and bottled water on ice—plus a bag of chips. I was glad Mia had remembered to pick up a pint of tequila on the way to the show.

Crunchbird was the opening band, the first of the four on the bill. Mia was helping their drummer move his gear onto the stage as people were starting to file into the lunchroom after coughing up four bucks for a ticket. One dollar for each band, I supposed.

Mia always made it a point to help me with my drums. It was very thoughtful, because we often had less than five minutes to set up, then we had another five minutes to clear the stage after we played our set. Mia only brought a single Shure SM58 microphone to shows, and she figured that she should help the guy who had the most gear to load on and off stage.

That night she was helping "Batcave" Sean Anderson, the drummer from Crunchbird. He was having trouble setting up. His face was bandaged, and his shirt was covered in blood and iodine from cleaning wounds. He had great difficulty speaking yet explained that he'd been jumped and robbed earlier that night by some gangsters in Belltown. They had beaten him badly and broken his jaw. He refused to turn over his snare drum, and the thugs hit him with a baseball bat. He had just left the hospital, against medical advice, to join his band on stage. His jaw had been wired shut just an hour earlier. He looked a mess, and I was amazed by his grit. The show must go on.

"You okay, man? Can you play?" I asked him.

He spoke through clenched teeth. "I'm fine, brother. I just have to make sure I get through the set before the Demerol wears off."

"That's why I'm helping him right now and not you," Mia explained.

She put one end of a straw into the bottle of Cuervo and the other between her new friend's lips.

"Much better. Thanks," he mumbled.

"Have a good show, man! Don't break a leg!" she yelled at him as she hurried off stage.

Then came the "one, two, three, four" from the stage, and Crunchbird was up and playing.

"I like that guy, Steve," Mia told me. "He's cool."

"Me too."

Back in the "dressing room," I sat on the floor with the band, passing a bottle around to Matt and Mia. Nirvana's bassist, Krist Novoselic, was chasing Kurt Cobain around the room with the tub of ice, threatening to soak him. Kurt scrambled around the desks while upending chairs to slow Krist's attack. When they were worn out, Kurt plopped down on the floor next to Mia and me and lit a cigarette. Krist threatened to drench us all, but he hesitated, probably because he didn't know what we would do. Krist was a huge guy—six foot five or so—but for whatever reasons, we'd developed a reputation as tough punk rockers. We dressed differently from other bands (not consciously—we just wore what we liked): Andy had tattoo sleeves on both arms, Mia had nuts and bolts braided into long blonde dreads, and I was wearing a "Fuck Bush" T-shirt and combat boots. We looked out of place among college kids in flannel shirts.

"Hey," said Kurt.

"Hey," I said back, passing him the tequila.

"I like your band," said Mia. "We're The Gits."

Kurt looked at Mia intently for a moment, then said, "Yeah, saw you at the Vogue one time. You're a great fucking singer!"

Krist resumed his assault on Kurt, who shot to his feet and ran two circles around the desk chairs before counterattacking with a barrage of erasers he'd found on the ledge of the whiteboard above our heads. An eraser popped Krist in the ear. Kurt's eyes widened in renewed terror, then he ran for his life. Desk chairs flew and tumbled, and journalists got wet.

The tub of ice went flying again. The freezing water and ice sloshed against the whiteboard and covered the professor's desk at the head of the classroom. Bystanders giggled and whispered, as if they were witnessing a rare rock-star mating ritual.

Matt reentered the room and shouted, "Let's go. We're starting in five minutes. The place is packed."

Minutes later, as we were getting ready to walk onto the stage, a fire alarm rang, and an adult got on the microphone to announce the immediate evacuation of the building.

"What the fuck?! Just our luck," Andy grumbled.

We were foiled by a stupid fire minutes before show time.

Kurt, still dry, ambled over and leaned toward us. "Don't worry. It's not a fire. The promoter just pulled the alarm to clear the place out 'cause it's over capacity. He'll let more people in the front door as these people go out the back. You guys will just start a little later."

The room was full again in minutes. We'd never played for so many people before. They said it was about two thousand, but it looked like a lot more to me. When we got the word from the stage manager, we rushed onto stage and set up our gear in a well-practiced dance of musicians and instruments. We could load our gear (including the drum set) onto the stage, fire up amps, check tuning, and hit the downbeat of the first song in less than fifteen minutes. We were used to playing hardcore punk shows that jammed three to eight bands onto a single bill, so we knew how to get on, make an impression, and then get off to allow the next band to do its thing.

Andy winced as he checked his tuning, chiming the harmonics of E, A, D. Then he reached up the neck of his heavy Les Paul to tune, detune, and retune the D string. He'd been playing his guitar for years, and it needed adjustments, but he didn't have the money to work on it. Andy decided that imperfect tuning would have to do that night, and he strummed a power chord to signal that it was go time. Andy glanced at Matt to his left and at me over his right shoulder. Mia was already leaning on the mic stand center stage, looking down at her feet, rocking slowly back and forth, waiting to explode.

"One, two, three, four, five, six," I counted off while smacking the sticks on each count. We blasted into "Here's to Your Fuck." I played at a tempo of 120 beats per minute, standard for "hardcore punk" bands like Bad Brains and Dead Kennedys. It amounts to roughly two snare strikes per second and four thumps on the bass drum.

We played the set as we'd rehearsed it hundreds of times over the previous several years—one song into the next without a pause. By the third song, we were in our groove. Kids in flannel shirts and leather jackets jumped on stage to dance, then jumped off before the bouncers could get their hands on them. The monitors rocked back and forth until one of them fell off the stage and smashed onto the dance floor. Dead.

The soundman ran onto the stage and told us to stop playing. He began shouting at the bouncers, and the crowd shouted at the soundman. I stood up, walked downstage, and unplugged the monitor. No problem. We could play without monitors.

It felt as though our set was over before it started. Our pal Ben London served as guitar tech for Andy and general support for us as we played. It was the largest crowd we had played to date, and I suppose we should have been nervous, but we had become unflappable after years of intermittent touring. When we finished our last song, we exited the stage as efficiently as we had entered, leaving it empty for the following band.

Tad, a trio fronted by the band's namesake, Tad Doyle, casually took the stage. Tad worked as a butcher by day, and his band had a record deal with Sub Pop Records, as did Nirvana. They recently returned from a European tour where they had played parties to celebrate the falling of the Berlin Wall. Tad lived near the Rathouse, and he often walked by en route to his girlfriend's place. Occasionally he stopped in for a beer and a chat. To me, Tad's sound was the epitome of what would come to be known as grunge. He tuned his guitar down a step to the key of D and growled into the mic like an angry bear. Through the low rumble of Tad's wall of sound, I heard catchy melodies that sounded almost Beatles-esque. There was always something more to his songs. Tad's lower-pitched tuning created a deeper, heavier guitar sound that gave the songs a sonically menacing, dark tone.

Finally, Nirvana hit the stage. Like The Gits, Nirvana was onstage tuning their guitars in a matter of minutes after Tad was done. Nirvana was extremely well rehearsed. Without so much as a "Hello, Cleveland," Kurt opened with the song "Scoff" and then segued into "Floyd the Barber." Unlike The Gits, Kurt took his time between songs. He and Krist were relaxed and continued to horse around on stage as they worked through a sixteen-song set list. The drummer, Chad Channing, played a bizarre-looking North brand drum set that had dead white tom-toms that curved at the bottom like exhaust pipes and reminded me of the Matterhorns on stands. Chad looked small behind the big drum set. As Nirvana finished their final song, Krist tossed his Precision bass high up in the air and caught it before it could crash on the stage. Kurt began to knock over the mic stands and swing his vintage Fender Jaguar like a tetherball on a maypole. He knocked over his amp and kicked the broken monitor. His amp was on the ground, causing terrible feedback. Chad kicked the oversized tom-toms of his drum set. These antics appeared well rehearsed to me. I noticed that Chad was not altogether on board with this schtick. He was careful not to damage the drums too much. Drum stuff was expensive.

Kurt fell over one of the tom-toms, but he held on to his guitar as a photographer crawled on the stage and shot a roll of 35mm film, the repeating flash eliciting more excitement from the crowd. The destruction of the gear and the stage made an encore impossible. I thought it was an inventive way to leave work early. They seemed to have fun, and the audience was riveted.

The next day, we discovered that Nirvana, Tad, Crunchbird, and The Gits were banned from playing on the University of Washington campus—"for life." Apparently, the professor whose classroom had become our dressing room did not appreciate arriving to

Nirvana and The Gits show poster for January 6, 1990, show at the University of Washington, HUB East Ballroom.

discover the mess—the broken chairs, deli tray leftovers, beer-bottle glass, and potato chips. The ban contributed to The Gits' notoriety, and people recognized us from the show and commented on it for years. We played well, and I believed that wonderful things were on the horizon. I was right. Great things were on the horizon, just not for us, not yet.

I had read an article in the *Seattle Weekly* about Nirvana and Tad's European tour, just as the Berlin Wall was falling. They were in the right place at the right time, I thought. Huge concerts were hastily organized with dozens of bands playing on stages throughout Berlin to celebrate the momentous political shift spawned by *glasnost*. The German people were fed up with totalitarianism, oppression, and separation. Muralists and renowned artists like Keith Haring and Andy Warhol created pieces of art-as-commentary on the wall itself. The forty-year-old symbol of Communist oppression and control was graffitied with images of love and peace. It was said to be the largest outdoor art museum and longest continuous public art display in the world. It was reportedly the greatest party ever, and it lasted for days, and Nirvana, Mudhoney, and Tad got to be there! The guys in the bands were interviewed about what it was like to be playing in Berlin at such a monumental historical geopolitical moment.

"Uh, the beer was really strong, and we got trashed. Everybody got trashed. Somebody crapped their pants." Or something to that effect.

I read the article, and I felt my ears burn. I was indignant. How could these guys, with the best gig imaginable, not get it? History was right in front of them. Could they not even appreciate the fact that the Berlin Wall was being torn down, brick by brick, by people who had been separated by politics and ideology for the past forty years? I was envious and indignant. I wanted to be a witness to history! These guys had played in Berlin during the most significant historical event of my lifetime, and they didn't even notice! Their responses pissed me off no end, and I had to do something.

"Class War" graffiti in Nijmegen, Netherlands, c. 1991. Photographer unknown, from author's collection.

17 EUROPEAN SQUAT TOUR

I went to work to try to book a tour of Europe. I was able to gather contacts from various bands I met who had toured Europe. I made up twenty-five promo kits containing our "Precious Blood" seven-inch single, a handmade, then Xeroxed, 11x17 poster, and a letter asking for a gig. To my utter surprise, a pair of Dutch squatters Valerie and I had met during our "Road Scholar" travels responded to my letters and offered to book the shows for The Gits. They loved the music and set up sixteen shows in twelve cities from Amsterdam to Oslo. They arranged a tour van, driver, guitar amps, and drums, and we would stay at community centers and squats in the towns we played.

In October 1991, Andy, Matt, Mia, and I boarded a plane to Amsterdam with a minimal amount of gear. We stuffed my drum shells with T-shirts and cassettes to sell in hopes of breaking even. We heard stories of bands being fined or losing money paying excise tax to each country for sold or unsold merchandise. We planned to traverse eleven borders and play in nine countries. We had no contracts or guarantees, but we put faith in the tenacity of our friends.

We had no dollar guarantees and booking shows was still in progress when we arrived in Amsterdam. A Dutch bassist named Scheet ("fart" in Dutch) and a young squatter named Erna (nicknamed Nasty) were our hosts. We stayed in a mammoth three-story Archer-Daniels-Midland distribution compound which was mothballed and then squatted by punks. The squatters had equipped the place with a few apartments, a repair garage for bicycles and motorcycles, a recording studio, rehearsal rooms, and a concert hall for shows. The police had tried to evict the squatters several times, once even bringing a wrecking ball on a crane. They began to smash away at the side of the building, but the squatters resisted en masse, wearing motorcycle helmets, armed with cricket bats, bricks, and cobblestones. The ADM squatters used the security gates installed by the original tenants to keep the police at bay. The occupiers lived off the grid and were part of a loosely organized movement across Europe. They were overtly antiauthoritarian anarchists and communists. They were well-intentioned and tough as nails, and their movement was fueled by punk rock music. They had established an international network of venues for touring bands they supported.

We played shows with some American touring bands like Big Chief, Big Drill Car, and False Profits but usually the bills were made up of one or two European bands or sometimes, to our surprise, we were the only band and were expected to play two to three sets. The names of the bands were unusual, and many owned our records and were excited to meet us. Our reputation had somehow preceded our arrival in Europe. The political, anti-fascist nature of the punks and squatters made them targets for both local police and skinhead gangs. The kids had to stick together and, in a pre-Web world, they communicated their ideas across borders through fanzines, international "info centers," and sharing music. Somehow, The Gits were one of the bands that the anarchist squatters supported, and they were fierce and loyal.

Our European tour lasted about six weeks and we played all manner of venues. After Amsterdam, we played Nijmegen, Berlin, Cologne, Oslo, Copenhagen, Bern, and a dozen cities in between. We played at government youth centers, anarchist squatter compounds, and info centers and at concerts sponsored by city governments. We were offered a welcome and given the respect we had not encountered in the States.

In the stunning Swiss capital, Bern, we performed in a gigantic, round nineteenth-century warhorse training center with a couple American bands. We played very well, and, despite closing the van's cargo door on my index finger during load-in, we had a great show.

Mia and I found ourselves in a bit of trouble after the show. We "borrowed" the tour van after Matt and Andy had crashed. We thought it would be nice to have one more drink to cap off a great night. We drove around and could not find anything open. I looked at my watch and it was approaching 4 a.m. Then we saw lights on at a restaurant.

The place was just opening for the early breakfast crowd. It was a traditional Swiss place. Mia and I would have a proper nightcap, then go back and crash, waking up with the guys so we could be off to the next show. Between the two of us, we had pockets full of cash—red money from Holland, Swiss francs, blue stuff from Germany, and tens of thousands of lire from Italy.

We had gotten paid out in krone in both Denmark and Norway. We were flush at last. We ordered a cocktail pack, a bottle of apple schnapps, dumplings, and strudel. We had a lovely chat and reminisced about our hard work and good fortune.

The server, dressed in traditional Swiss attire with a colorful dress and maiden's cap and adornments, presented us with the bill. It came to a little over 75 Swiss francs. Surely, they accepted other currencies. We only had about 12 francs. No problem. We had plenty of other monies. I pulled out a small green note worth ten thousand lire. Surely, that would be enough.

We could get change in francs and fill the tank to make up for stealing the van. All would be forgiven, remarked Mia.

I had a currency exchange-rate booklet. Ten thousand lire only came to twelve cents. No worry. We could use the krone, and that would bring us up to about fourteen bucks. I emptied my pockets and separated the bills from change on the table.

"Mia," I commanded, "give me all your money!"

Mia did as I said until a rather large mountain of beautifully colored notes and silvery coins was piled up in the middle of our table.

The sun was rising over the majestic Alps as truckers and loggers began to occupy adjacent tables and order coffee. This distracted the small klatsch of servers in traditional Swiss Miss–type costumes who had been eyeing us suspiciously and observing our money-counting.

I felt responsible. I had to think quickly. I hatched a plan and shared it with Mia, leaning over the table and whispering loudly with a splattering of secret pidgin Spanish I'd picked up from Mia.

"We leave all the money on the table. Mia, you go to the ladies' room and count to seventy. I will go warm up the van. At seventy seconds, leave the ladies' room and meet me out front. I'll get us outta here. Don't worry. Besides, we didn't mean to fuck up. We just thought we had more money. If we get busted, we don't get to finish the tour and the guys will be so pissed at us."

Mia went along with the plan and slowly rose and exclaimed she would be right back after "powdering her nose."

I gave her my watch and then made an obvious gesture of checking my watch. But the watch was no longer attached to my wrist, which may have been the fatal mistake in the execution of the plan. I began counting: one one-thousand, two one thousand . . . I got up and zipped my coat, leaving the leftovers on the table with the colorful mound of cash and coins we amassed on the table.

Thirty-one one thousand, thirty-two one thousand . . . The old diesel Mercedes mini-van was nearly warm.

Fifty-two one thousand, fifty-three one thousand, fifty-four . . . I slowly rolled the van up over the slush and snow melting in the car park. Seventy-one thousand . . . I was waiting in front of the restaurant with the passenger door ajar. Where was Mia? The seconds clicked away on the dashboard clock. Two minutes had passed. Three minutes. Six minutes. Where the hell was she? I was beginning to panic. "Where the hell are you, Zapata?" I said out loud.

I pounded my palms on the steering wheel. "How could I have been so stupid? Fuck me!" Just then, the front door of the chalet slammed open against the building and out came Mia. Her coat dangling from one arm. In her haste, she nearly slipped on the ice on the steps leading down to the lot where I waited nervously. In her other hand, Mia was holding fast to a big one-liter bottle of apple schnapps. In hot pursuit was one of the servers. She was shouting in German at Mia and waving her fist. "*Halt, halt!*"

Behind the Swiss Miss were three others, all dressed identically and irate. One held a large knife above her head. The other had what looked like a leg of lamb. Mia slipped and nearly fell on the ice. She looked tiny compared to the Swiss women on the attack. A split second and just an arm's length out of reach, Mia scrambled into the passenger door with the bottle in hand. The first and fastest Swiss Miss got hold of Mia's jacket arm and nearly pulled her from the vehicle. But Mia released her jacket just in time to send her pursuer tumbling to the hard ground, shouting obscenities in Swiss German. It sounded like the devil's own curse. Another Swiss she-devil shouted, "Give me za bottle. Give us za bottles!" The van was a diesel and had very poor pick up, especially when loaded with gear. I stomped on the accelerator and the getaway van nearly stalled.

The second pursuer was already on Mia and she grabbed at the bottle.

"Give her the fucking bottle, Mia. It's not worth it!" I screamed.

Mia's fear turned to rage and she placed her Vietnam War issue combat boot dead center between the enormous bosoms of the enraged Swiss Miss. Mia yelled as she kicked with both feet like a Kentucky jackrabbit, sending the mad Swiss Miss flying backward into the third Miss and onto the ice with an audible thud.

"*Schreckliche Frau. Verdammt. Dafür wirst du bezahlen!*" she yelled at Mia.

"Fuck you, bitch!" Mia shouted.

I floored it out of the icy lot, the back tires finally received the message, and they were spinning as we fishtailed our way onto the open road.

"What did she say?" Mia asked finally.

"Have a good tour. See you next time!" I replied matter-of-factly.

"Really?" Mia followed.

"I doubt it," I said.

We sat shaking in silence for several miles before the van warmed up at all. Neither of us was sure whose fault it was, who had started it, or what had happened. We were too exhausted to care, and the sun reflected on the snowbanks piled high along the road and the amazing Swiss Alps emerged pink and orange on the horizon.

"Well," I muttered solemnly as we parked in relative safety round the corner at the band house, hidden by some overgrown shrubbery by the place we were staying. "What's next, Zapata—we knock off a bank?" I teased.

Mia didn't answer. We walked up the steps to the kitchen where Matt was making coffee and Andy was restringing his guitar. "Good morning, gentlemen," Mia said. "Sleep well? I slept great, man."

Mia sat in a chair and rolled a joint to smoke for breakfast. She didn't speak to me for a full day after that.

Our Swiss host appeared and offered to take us all out to breakfast. We were all starving, especially Mia and I. We loaded into the van and Matt commented that van must still be warm from the night before.

Our host was excited to take us to a traditional Swiss breakfast restaurant. "It's in an old Swiss Chalet just a few kilometers down the road. You will love the place," he said proudly.

"Oh, shit."

In all we did about eighteen shows in twenty-six days around western Europe. It was the experience that we needed to inject life into our struggle. We were treated very well in Europe and paid for our effort. The people often would not physically allow us to leave the stage without playing an encore, sometimes three. We had made some wonderful friends and met great bands from Germany, Holland, Norway, and elsewhere. Before we touched down in Seattle, we were already plotting a return to Europe. The Portland band Dead Moon, arguably the best band in the Northwest, would later invite us to tour Europe the following year. Dead Moon was an underground rock phenomenon in Europe, and we would be playing for hundreds or thousands of fans, not dozens like the first time. It would be a perfect musical pairing and I couldn't wait.

We played a homecoming gig at the OK Hotel and sold it out. From that point onward, The Gits' star began to rise, albeit slowly. It was steady, nearly imperceptible, but gears were beginning to turn as the word got out. Our friends in 7 Year Bitch were fierce advocates for The Gits. They generously shared opportunities offered them by their comparatively meteoric success, but it was limited. Important music-industry creatives and executives, who had elevated the careers of Nirvana, Patti Smith, Sonic Youth, Hole, and others got wind of The Gits (as I would discover in the months to follow).

Meantime, we went about our lives in Seattle. We looked for work and housing; we worked on our relationships and played locally. We began work on our second record, the completion of which would fulfill our contract for two albums with C/Z Records and make The Gits free agents for some better labels that we had our eyes on. We hired our friend Scott Benson to record and produce the album, and I insisted that we get Jack Endino to consult, especially for the recording of the drums. Endino was a master of analog budget recording of heavy sounding rock music. He had discovered Nirvana and connected the band with their record label, Sub Pop. He had worked with Mudhoney, Soundgarden, Tad, and nearly all the successful "Seattle sound" or "grunge" bands. Endino was low key and brilliant and in very high demand, but he made time for us, and the results are evident on the recordings of the drums and, later, the mastering of the final record. Not long after returning from the previous tour, I began work organizing another.

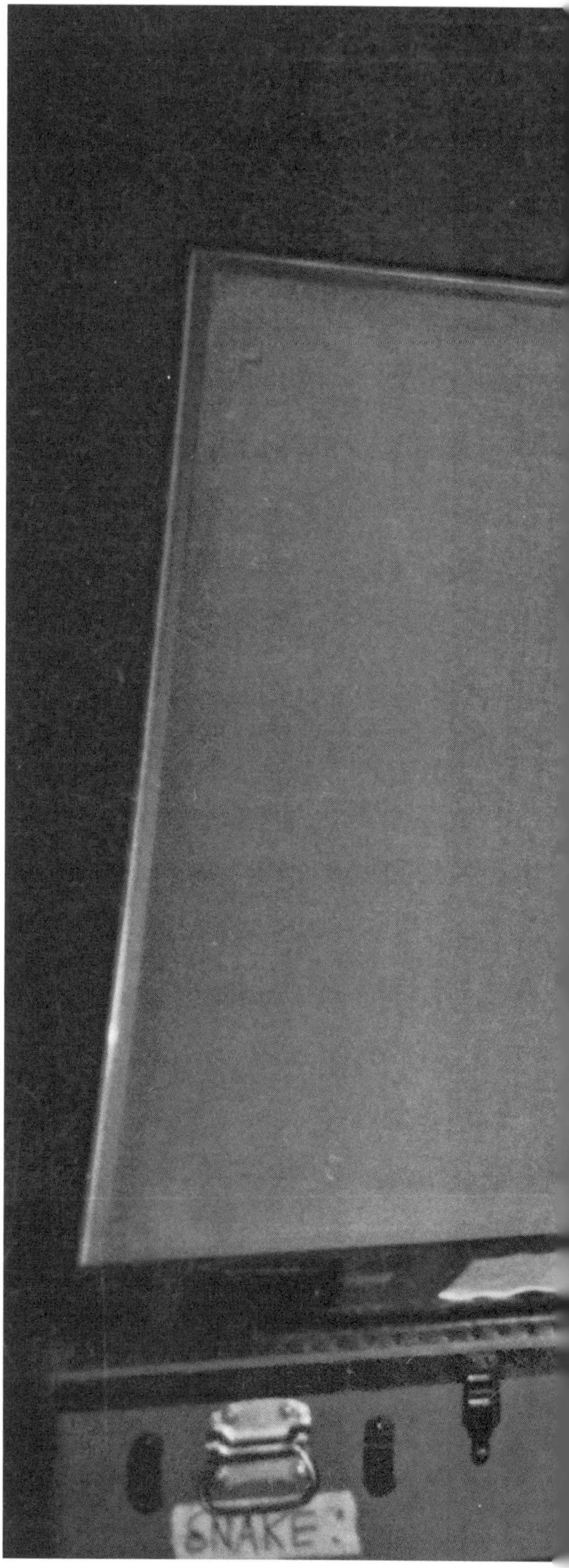

Mia grinning in vocal booth during recording session at Soundhouse Recording, Seattle, 1993. Photographer unknown, courtesy of Scott Crane and Scott Benson.

18 BARBIE'S DREAM CAR CRASHES

Valerie and Selene worked together at an independent grocery store in Pike Place Market. They had similar tastes in music. In fact, they had met at the first Seattle Gits show at the Vogue. Inspired by what they saw on stage, they recruited Stefanie to play guitar and decided to form a band. The artist Lisa Orth worked at Sub Pop part time and the band she envisioned was named Barbie's Dream Car.

Valerie, Selene, and Stefanie found their bass player working at another market stall. Liz Davis was the most accomplished musician of the four. She spearheaded the songwriting for 7 Year Bitch and essentially led the band. The four women began rehearsing in the Rathouse cellar. Sometimes I could hear them pounding out the same song, for hours, over and over again, trying to get it right. We encouraged them to stay with it and never to give up on the dream.

Promotional band photo of 7 Year Bitch, c. 1992. (From left to right: Valerie Agnew, Selene Vigil, Elizabeth Davis, Stephenie Sargent.) Courtesy of C/Z Records.

Liz was raised in a strict Christian family and educated in excellent schools. She spoke several languages and had music training. She left her community and worked on dangerous fishing vessels in the Bering Sea off Alaska. Not a gig for the faint of heart. Liz and Valerie became fast friends. They both had a knack for partying, as did we all. Liz was especially enthralled with the life of sex, drugs, and rock and roll, the very sins her parent's religion had vehemently forbidden. Valerie didn't know how to play the drums, so I began teaching her in earnest through focused drum lessons between various band practices. Mia coached and encouraged Selene to sing and to trust herself on stage. Stefanie knew a few guitar chords, just enough, and the foursome was off to the races.

In a matter of months, 7 Year Bitch was putting out its first single on Rathouse Records. Shortly after that, they signed a deal with C/Z Records to record an album. In no time they were negotiating with major record companies. The pace of their success and popularity in Seattle and elsewhere was remarkable. It was in no small part due to their enthusiasm, sociability, and hard work. It was great news. One for our team. It felt strange that we had worked so hard in The Gits for so long for more measured successes.

I drove my car to Pike Place market almost before dawn. Valerie had played a gig the night before and went straight to work without even going home to change clothes. I didn't know where she had been all night, and I was confused. Instead of showing my concern, I denied my jealousies and suspicions and planned to surprise her at work with a nice coffee. She received it but refused me a kiss goodbye. "We have to talk," I insisted.

"Not here, in the food court."

There she told me she was breaking up. She wanted to see other people and she didn't care if I did. I could move out of the apartment any time. It was over. The four years we had spent traveling, building the Rathouse collective, and living a dream together were simply a wash. No looking back and no discussion. I was blindsided by the news. She had grown aloof and distant since forming her band. I was stunned. I'm sure I muttered something, but I don't know what I could have said. I got up and turned to go. I could see the meter cop giving me a ticket for double-parking to drop off the coffee. It couldn't get any worse.

"Hey, you forgot your sunglasses," Valerie called after. I couldn't speak and I left the sunglasses to her. "They look better on you," I said over my shoulder. "You keep 'em." I shrugged and went to the car. I left the ticket under the wiper and started the little Dodge Colt. I popped the clutch to scuttle up the hill on Pike Street with tears and intense morning sun burning my eyes. I did not see the light ahead turn yellow. I was in third gear, but I jumped on the gas to make it through the light. The car stuttered. I looked to my left and saw a Ford F150 barreling down Third Avenue on a collision course with my subcompact. I tried to punch the gas again and the thing stalled just in time for the bumper of the F150 to crush my driver's-side window, destroying the door and bending the right wheel so far it broke free of the axle. That was enough.

The man in the truck jumped out of the cab and started yelling obscenities. Traffic was stacking up in all directions. I heard more honking horns and more obscenities. I moved to the passenger side of the twisted mangle of cheap metal and plastics and used two legs to kick the passenger side door open. I felt the emptiness that is known by those who know the grip of freezing cold rejection. I felt utterly worthless and unlovable. I was gutted like a bass in a bathtub. I left the car there and walked away.

I left my keys, stick bag, jacket, and cassette tapes in the wreck of the Dodge Colt and left the car in the intersection of Pike and Third. It was a crossroads for me. I was caught between light and darkness, but the bright light had blinded me. I believed in being with Valerie forever. I should have seen the signs. She would be out all night with guys I thought were jerks. She hadn't wanted to take my calls on tour. She stopped caring, but the more one suffers in love the tighter one hangs on. Believing in the miracle of unconditional love led to the belief that love can be revived when on life support.

I walked the streets alone. I wandered by Lake Union and through an old, abandoned warehouse. I had no place to return. We were not touring enough to stay on the road full time. I had to maintain a rental. I had started at the Rathouse; I could return there—maybe hide out until the police stop looking for the lunatic who left the car in the road and ruined the morning commute for Seattle's upwardly mobile rising young tech professionals.

Valerie preferred having a fandom to being a fan of her boyfriend's band. I understood. She broke my heart anyway, and the winter of '91 was especially long and cold, even by Seattle standards. There were weeks between glimpses of the sun. Mudslides and floods made homes slip off foundations and slide into the streets. My way of coping was to walk. Dejected, I shuffled over Pill Hill, across Pike and Pine, then over Capitol Hill to the Rathouse. Before I'd left to tour Europe earlier that fall, Val had insisted we move out of the Rathouse, vowing to find a place for us to live before I returned from tour. But she found a small apartment with Selene, and on my return I found I was not welcome. Maybe it was premeditated or maybe it was just an innocent act of callousness; I never knew for sure. But the darkness was closing in on me again, as it had in Ann Arbor. Every day I woke up, I had to fight to keep from falling back into crippling depression. I busied myself with booking shows at the OK Hotel and organizing events and fundraisers for nonprofits. It was a long, frigid winter that felt like it would never end.

OK HOTEL
CAFE
Live Arts & Entertainment

Entrance to the legendary OK Hotel, Seattle. Courtesy of Steve and Tia Freeborn.

19

FRENCHING THE BULLY

It was 9 a.m., and the temperature was already approaching 90°, unusually hot for Seattle.

The front door of the Rathouse was unlocked, so I entered. I knocked on Mia's door and called her name softly a couple of times. No response. Then I removed the needle from a Mission of Burma record whose innermost groove had been popping and cracking, probably all night. I poked my head into Mia's room.

The heat had forced Mia out of her tiny room, attached to the Rathouse like a little caboose. She was on the little porch in a bathing suit. She had an open beer.

Mia still did not look up. It wasn't like her to neglect manners. She only moved her face closer to the page, like an elementary school student learning to "draw" her letters.

I looked at Mia and my eyes betrayed my attempt at stoicism. My arms dropped to my side, and I started to cry. I hated Valerie and I hated myself. I hated music. I hated Seattle. I couldn't eat, and in that moment I couldn't find words to articulate the heartache that was crushing me.

Mia stood and looked at me. She handed me a warm Old Milwaukee. It tasted horrible in every other instance but tasted good coming from Mia.

Andy and Mia in costume for St. Patrick's Day show, 1993.
Photo presumed to be by Chris Sievanen, from author's archive.

"It's too hot. Let's go to the beach!" I said, half joking.

Unbeknownst to me, there was already a plan afoot. Somehow Julian had corralled Carla, Stefanie, Maria, Mia, Robert, Julian, Andy, and Mia into going to a little beach park on the shore of Lake Washington. I had shown up at just the right time. We got towels, a couple old golf umbrellas from a dumpster, and a half-rack of beer. We loaded into the van and drove over the hill to a little dirt patch that lay between houses on the lake. The little park was popular with lesbian families with young children.

I saw the faces of sun-loving, peaceful same-sex couples and loving parents turn sour when our crew of broken, tattooed, pale, drunken punks pulled up in the rumbling Dodge window van. We had the cooler full of beer, a Weber grill, books, a boombox, and torn umbrellas that we stuck into the dirt for shade. We dressed in our bathing attire consisting of old bras, underwear, cutoffs, and band T-shirts. We set up camp and spread out on the makeshift beach. Just behind and above us on the hillside sat a large cedar-shake-roofed mansion with a matching detached garage adjacent to the big house. A public tennis court was nestled in the lush hillside just below the garage.

"I think that's the house Cobain just bought. We should go see if he feels like swimming," Mia said to me.

She was disappearing into her notebook, but when Stefanie accidentally spilled Mia's beer Stefanie made a run toward the water for her life. Mia shrieked in real anger and ran after Stefanie into the water. Maria ran after them, and they splashed and screamed like madwomen. Andy and I watched from shore and laughed out loud. It was nice seeing someone having some fun for a change.

Imagine the sight—several half-dressed, tattooed women in tattered swimwear made of rags, splashing gleefully in the shimmering lake. Young parents corralled their children to keep them from the crazy women wrestling, playfighting, and rubbing mud and seaweed in each other's hair. Looking like monsters from the deep, the trio waved their arms skyward, giggling and screaming at the top of their lungs. Andy's laugh was deep and utterly unhinged, and I couldn't help but laugh too. It felt as if I hadn't laughed at all for years.

These fools were like family to me, and I felt hopeful again among my trusted, flawed comrades. I accepted them for who they were, and they accepted me. They made me feel valued and respected. I couldn't imagine a life without my friends. They gave me permission to fail and a path to succeed. They allowed me to be broken and to struggle onward. My friends saved my life every day.

Mia, Maria, and Stefanie returned to dry land coughing, looking like swamp creatures—seaweed hanging from their hair, dripping water on the topless sunbathers. Curious babies wearing Pampers and sailor hats cried. An exhausted Mia changed into dry clothes, and she accidentally exposed herself to the young families whose peace we had invaded. All were aghast at the band of loud, dirty punk kids drinking beer, cursing, and laughing out loud.

“Wait a minute. Nobody move,” Mia declared, her face deadly serious. “Where is it?” “Where’s what?” asked Maria.

Mia knocked over the cooler and tossed towels and blankets into the air, as if searching for lost drugs.

“My book. My journal. It’s not here. Who took my book?!” she yelled.

“Don’t worry. It’s right here, Mia,” Andy said calmly. “I didn’t want it to get wet, so I put it out of the way.”

Mia calmed down, but she didn’t thank Andy for his courtesy, or say anything for that matter. She snatched the tattered essay book and flipped to a particular page. With a tiny golf pencil, she wrote something with great concentration. She was wrestling her muse. During the next hour, she jotted notes in the lined composition book despite the intense sunshine. She didn’t look up, ignoring the sweat that dripped from her furrowed brow.

Mia shared her world in her lyrics, but, unlike a mystic or a *curandera,* she didn’t speak in riddles. She existed in the real world of emotion, dreams, and the inertia of her feelings and empathy. She could articulate her feelings in poetry and conversation. I admired the honesty of her words. She possessed the ability to express herself in personal interactions as effortlessly as she did in the songs—always from the heart and almost always with a sense of humor. On stage, Mia could make every person in a crowded club believe that she was speaking directly, intimately to them. Her voice gave others power and the belief in self-determination. She could imbue total strangers with a sense of comradery. To some she offered a reason to live or to go on living . . . and she had no idea.

The warmth of the afternoon was beginning to fade when Mia finally closed her book, looked up, and asked if there was any more beer. Andy handed her one.

“It’s my lucky day, Andy,” she said as she screwed off the bottle cap. “This one’s gonna be really good, man. I can feel it. It’s called ‘Seaweed.’”

“Cool.” Andy nodded. “Can’t wait to hear it.”

“Let’s get outta here. I don’t hang in no dumps,” said Mia.

“Let’s git, then,” I quipped.

At our shows, our fans often yelled out to us between songs, “When does the album come out?” We had been a band for nearly five years, and we had not released an album on a label, only tapes we released ourselves.

* * *

If we wanted to keep up with the bands we were helping, we needed to focus on our own productivity. We needed to find money and be proactive about the business of music, not just the art of it. At a band meeting around this time, we talked about searching for a record label, dropping “Sniveling Little Rat Faced” from the band name to officially be called The Gits. We'd get on the road more frequently to build our draw. We were slow to adapt to the rapidly changing music environment. It was unbelievable how long it took for us to change anything about how we approached getting ourselves and our music out into the world.

We released three singles and a compilation album on our Rathouse label. Ten songs had been allocated to projects that could have made up a full album. We booked time at the Avast! Recording Company studio to record enough songs to complete a debut album. We hired as producer Steve Fisk, known for albums by Portishead and Screaming Trees and for Nirvana's first EP. Fisk recorded the songs and coaxed excellent performances from Mia. Scott Benson mixed and mastered the recordings. We had been playing most of our songs for years, so the tracking went quickly. We were quite pleased with Benson's work. In a hastily organized Rathouse porch meeting, we decided to call the album *Frenching the Bully*. It's a great title, but I can't recall how we arrived at such an odd phrase. The creative process can be mysterious.

We opened the album with a new song full of twists and turns called "Absynthe" and we closed the thirty-seven-minute, twelve-song album with "Second Skin," a song we had released as a single and well loved by our fans. We decided to shop the album around with record companies, hoping to license the recordings to the highest bidder. That could mean cash or a commitment to publicize the album and support our mission, which now included recording and releasing music.

We made fifty cassettes to send to labels as demos. We needed a label to press vinyl records and make CDs and then distribute them worldwide. We handwrote witty letters and sent the demo tapes to labels we'd heard of or who had put out records by bands we liked—Sub Pop, Frontier Records, Twin/Tone Records, Alternative Tentacles, Epitaph Records, Sympathy for the Record Industry, Empty Records, Epitaph Records, C/Z Records, and Broken Rekids.

After we mailed the demos, we waited expectantly for a letter to arrive or for the Rathouse phone to ring with good news. But there were no responses at all. I later discovered that the cassettes we paid to have duplicated for demos had not been duplicated properly. All were totally blank. I can only speculate about what the record companies thought when, after opening an envelope from a band called the Sniveling Little Rat-Faced Gits (as we were still known officially), they found a ridiculous note and a blank cassette. Were we taking a piss, as the English say? It was no wonder we didn't get a single reply. It wasn't even funny.

Still, our live performances and the touring helped us gain attention. Our audiences grew show after show, and our following was loyal. That helped us make many new friends along the way. Musicians from better known bands began to show up to see us play. By '92, Seattle was all the rage around the world, but we didn't notice. We were too busy writing, playing, and recording.

The Gits in the basement of Club Chameleon in San Francisco, c. 1993.
Photo by Jennifer Miko, courtesy of The Rocket.

TAMA.

SEAWEED

20

Mia spent endless hours writing in her journals. She learned to weave her words and thoughts into lyrics that were rich with feeling and color—deeply personal but also universal. Someone once wrote that the Gits' most important song, "Second Skin," was penned in half an hour at one of our rehearsals in Matt's garage in 1990. But that's not exactly right. The truth is that Mia had been poring over her personal diaries and journals for weeks, even months. Like a careful collagist, she clipped a word here, another there, or she moved a whole phrase that answered another phrase in a different song.

I often saw her writing in her room or on the porch at the Rathouse or in the corner booth at the Frontier Room. Slumped over her graph-paper notebook, eyes three inches from the page, she scribbled words while chewing her nails. Those who

On stage in Anchorage, Alaska, at 10:00pm in August of 1992.
Photo by James Atkins, from the author's archive.

knew Mia well knew to leave her alone at these moments because no sensible person would dare deprive the world of the imaginings of such a beautiful thinker. Sometimes I found Mia wrapped in the cocoon of her thoughts, seated in an impossibly twisted ball, holding a fountain pen. Her mind was far from the Rathouse or the Frontier Room or the back of the van. She was in conversation with her muse, who was generous but who also exacted a pound of flesh for each song. Her lyrics were salvation for others but were born of her own suffering. She valued hard times as a means for people to understand one another and to find common ground. Empathy, community, and resilience were themes common to her songs and were her most cherished values.

The songs could be about troubling thoughts or the challenges that her friends faced. The lyrics often told a compact story that included an introduction, a conflict, rising tension, and a resolution. The songs usually ended on a note of hope and resilience in the face of staggering odds. "Guilt Within Your Head" is an example.

"Second Skin" is a dark personal ballad about the longing for love and partnership. "Spear and Magic Helmet" cries for justice for a friend who was victim of a sexual assault. It was impossible to know the direction a song might take, but we could always be sure that, whatever subject Mia chose to explore in her lyrics, it would be lyrically brilliant, fit perfectly with the music, and be devastatingly honest.

A couple months after making one of our cassette demos, a small local indie label called Empty Records invited us to record a split single with a band also known for being more punk than grunge. I supposed that was the idea of the pairing. The guys from the other band lived near the Rathouse and often showed up at our parties. On one such occasion, the singer and guitarist got in an argument. Words became blows, and the two were soon on the floor, wrestling and punching one another. They did this a lot.

Mia had invited them and took responsibility for their behavior. She asked them nicely to stop fighting several times. When that did not work, she warned them gravely, saying, "Stop it right now, or I'll make you stop fightin'! I'll take this pan to your heads!" They ignored her threat, but Mia did not bluff. She grabbed an iron frying skillet from the stovetop and banged them both over the head. That put a quick end to their fight. Eric and I threw the drunker of the two out, and peace once again settled upon our noisy little punk house.

One of Mia's unusual friends from the Frontier Room was a tall young woman with long blonde hair. I often saw the woman walking around Seattle, her eyes down, reading a book, rain or shine. I would often say hi, but she rarely looked up and she never seemed to speak—to me, anyway. She spoke to Mia, but the two kept the details of their conversations a secret. One day, Mia was upset because the young bookworm confided in Mia that she had been raped in an alley by a "band guy." Mia wouldn't tell me who had done it, but she admitted that she knew the guy. He was in a band, and she planned to do something about it.

Around this time, Andy wanted to write a parody of a "thrash" song, which Matt later named "Spear and Magic Helmet," while on a Bugs Bunny cartoon binge. Andy broke the song formula down into three basic elements: verse, fast part, and mosh part. We added an intro and an outro because Andy found it impossible to write a bad song. When Matt and I added the bass and drum parts, the arrangement was complete. At our next practice, rather than contributing lyrics on par with the songs we had parodied, Mia described the assault of her friend and told of what she planned to do to the perpetrator.

Not long after we wrote the song, the band with whom we were to share the 7-inch single dropped out of the project. Their singer had suddenly left town to live with his mother in another state. Someone must have told him that the Gits song intended for the record was about him raping Mia's friend. Mia's subversive sense of justice had prevailed. She rid the Seattle music scene of a rapist by threatening to expose his crime on the very record he was to share with her band. Her activism also freed up the B side of the record for two more original Gits songs, "While You're Twisting, I'm Still Breathing" and "Running."

* * *

We wrote songs, practiced, and played locally and traveled to Portland, Olympia, Tacoma, Bellingham, Vancouver (B.C.), Edmonds, Eugene, and elsewhere. We played gigs with just about every band of note of that era. We flew to Alaska to play a show in Anchorage. We played live on college radio shows. We played cable access video shows, house parties, high schools . . . anything. When we didn't have offers to play outside of Seattle, I booked The Gits locally at the OK Hotel, where I was now working pretty much full time. I didn't get paid an hourly wage, but I did get a nominal cut of the cover charge. More importantly, I met agents, promoters, managers, and band members. Being able to help touring bands with a Seattle gig put me in a position to ask favors for The Gits in other cities.

The OK Hotel was one of the few all-ages punk venues on the West Coast, therefore notable bands wanted to play there. During a two-week stretch in '92, the calendar featured Babes in Toyland (Minneapolis), the Brian Jonestown Massacre (San Francisco), Neurosis (Oakland), Agent Orange (Los Angeles), DOA (B.C.), Superchunk (Ashville), MDC (San Francisco), Poison Idea (Portland), Toad the Wet Sprocket (Santa Barbara), Subhumans (England), Sublime (Long Beach), and Green Day (Berkeley), and Nirvana played a show to pay for gas to get to L.A. to record their 1992 release *Nevermind.*

The OK Hotel became famous—or infamous—because it was ground zero for Seattle music. There was no bar, therefore the audience couldn't spend their money on drinks. They spent their money on the band's merchandise, which the bands needed to pay for gas and travel expenses. A band could also develop its sound at the OK Hotel while earning much-needed cash for recording projects. Word about the OK Hotel spread around the country as agents and record labels clamored for bookings. The demo-tape box overflowed with cassettes from around the world. Everybody wanted to play the little all-ages venue. I tried to listen to every single cassette.

In addition to the bands booked during the summer of '92, other bands that played the OK Hotel read like a history of '90s music. Soundgarden, Mother Love Bone, Pearl Jam, Screaming Trees, Tad, NOFX, Lagwagon, Face to Face, the Dayglo Abortions, No Means No, SNFU, Hole, Fitz of Depression, No Doubt, Sublime, Stone Temple Pilots, Alice in Chains, Poison Idea, Jawbreaker, Bill Frissell, Jawbox, Shudder to Think, Ween, Mudhoney, Blood Circus, Melvins, Supersuckers, Bikini Kill, Bratmobile, Elliott Smith, Beat Happening, and Queens of the Stone Age —we hosted all of them and more at the OK Hotel. MTV sent a news crew to do a story about us, and journalists called the office daily. I used the contacts I gathered while booking and organizing the shows to book tours for The Gits.

Hammerbox, The Gits, and 7 Year Bitch at the Off Ramp, Seattle, January 17, 1993. Poster by Jeff Klinesmith, from author's archive.

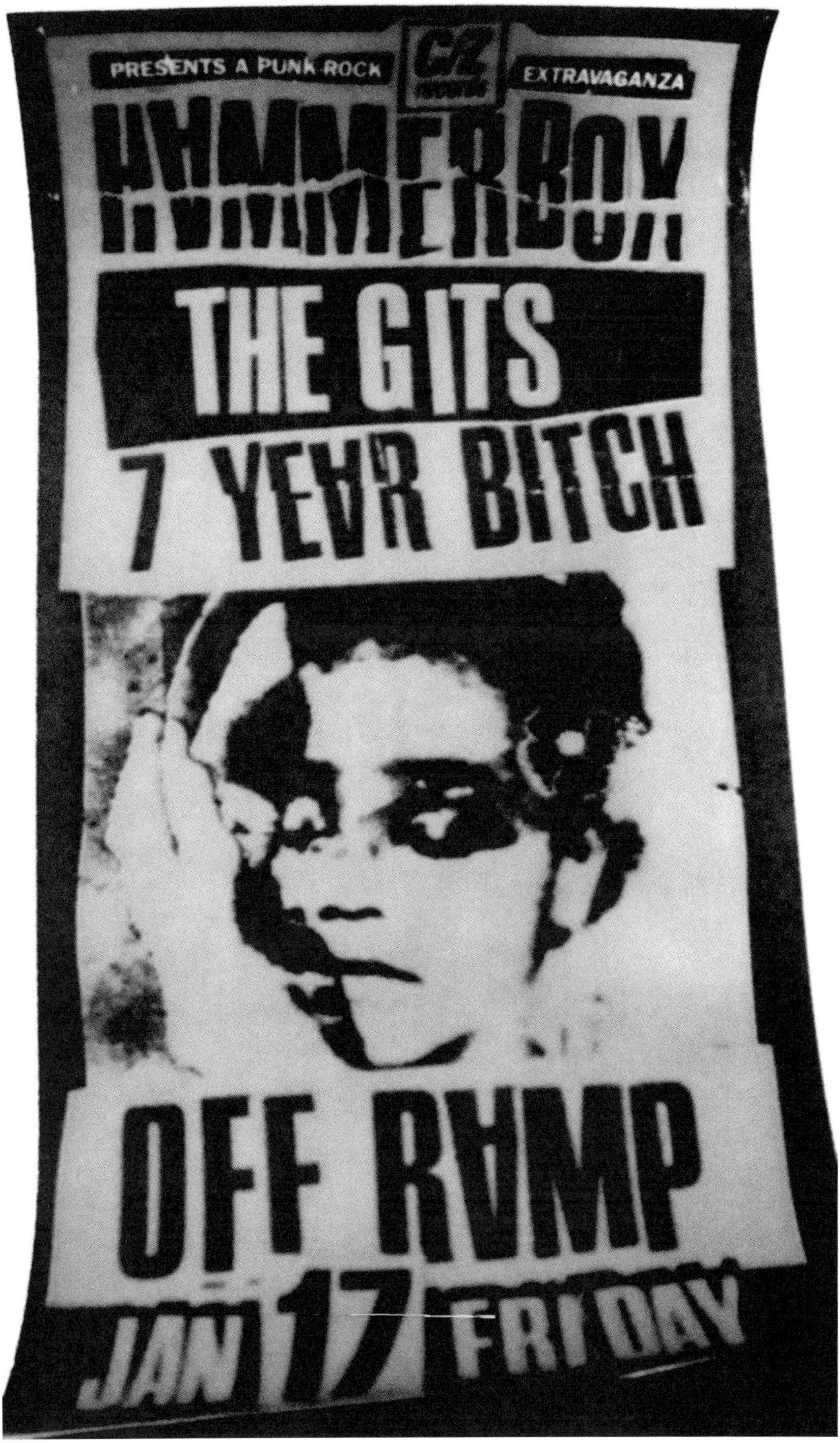
PRESENTS A PUNK ROCK
EXTRAVAGANZA
HAMMERBOX
THE GITS
7 YEAR BITCH
OFF RAMP
JAN 17 FRIDAY

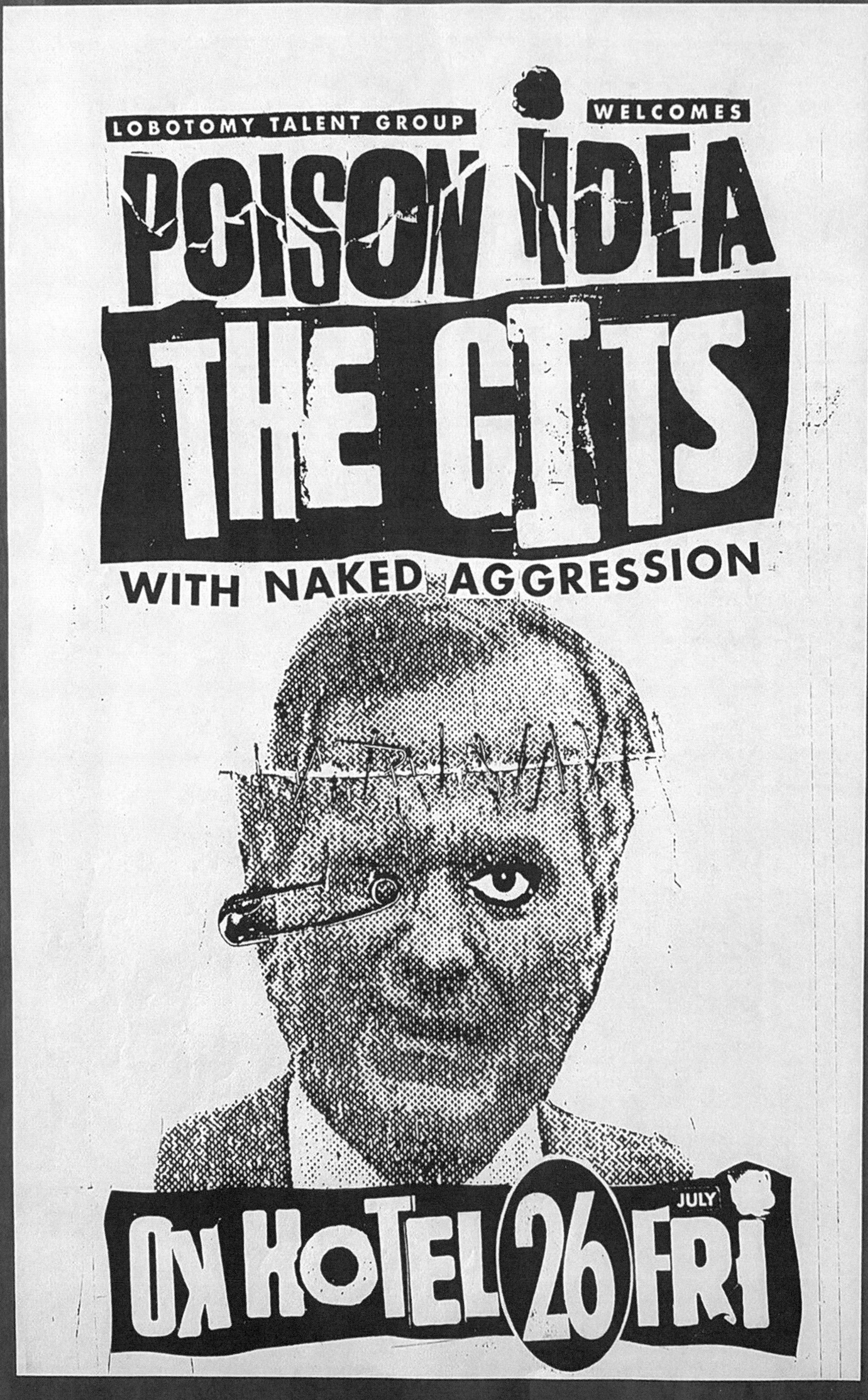
LOBOTOMY TALENT GROUP
WELCOMES
POISON IDEA
THE GITS
WITH NAKED AGGRESSION
OK HOTEL
26
JULY
FRI

PRESS DARLINGS 21

I was seated on the Rathouse stoop drinking with Julian when Valerie pulled up in a vintage Ford Mustang Fastback she had bought with her cash advance after 7 Year Bitch signed a deal with a major record company. Seeing her, I felt nauseated, but I tried not to let it show.

The sick feeling wasn't rooted in jealousy. I was genuinely happy for her and her band. I loved their sound, and I was proud of having taught Valerie to play the drums. I felt sick because . . . honestly, I'm not sure. Maybe it was exasperation or exhaustion or self-pity. I was tired of The Gits' relative lack of success. We generously shared what we could with other musicians and bands, but we could never seem to catch a break.

"Yo, Steve—what's up?" Valerie shouted from her window. "Yeah, we got in this rad bidding war with Rick Rubin from American Records, Slash, and Atlantic Records. Three record deals. Gonna open for the Chili Peppers, Rage, and Pearl Jam. I'll be on tour for a year at least. Damn, I haven't slept in three days, dude. So cool. Later."

It was as if we had never been lovers—or even friends, for that matter. I was still in love with her, but I could not let on. It hurt to be reduced to a 7 Year Bitch fanboy. I was not green with envy. I was not jealous of her success. I was heartbroken, and it would be years before I could move on from Valerie.

Poison Idea and The Gits with Naked Aggression at the OK Hotel, Seattle, c. 1992. Poster by Jeff Klinesmith, from author's archive.

I must stay focused on the mission, I thought. I never cried. I wish I could have, but I never did. I began to wonder if The Gits were just too much for people. Was Mia too deep? Were her lyrics too mature for people who seemed to relate to the lyrics of popular bands that sang gems like, "Fuck you, I won't do what you tell me!" "Fuck me I'm rich," "I want to fuck, fuck, fuck, fuck you!" Maybe these groups were geniuses, as some seemed to believe. I thought not.

But who was I to judge?

In an interview with a writer for a Seattle fanzine, an exasperated Mia said, "I don't think people take music as seriously as we do. We work real hard at what we do, and we don't play simple music. We put thought and time and heart into every word, every chord. And we want people to feel connected. Connected to us, to their friends, and to themselves. We all gotta live through shit every day, and we're all the same that way. We're serious, and we ought to be taken seriously, man!"

I couldn't agree more. We just needed to get to work on an album to prove once and for all that our band was incomparable.

A writer from *Rolling Stone* was interviewing me about the club but, upon discovering that I played in The Gits, she shifted gears and started asking questions about the band. The writer was quite young, even next to my twenty-four years. Her name was Ann Powers, who would go on to champion us and other women-lead bands in national outlets.

Although The Gits were becoming press darlings, we were still treated as outsiders in our adopted hometown. But after we returned from our home-made European tour that began to change. During a homecoming show, we played with Poison Idea (remember the poster in Andy's room?) at the OK Hotel. The sold-out crowd of four hundred went mad for The Gits.

They pushed us to play two encores, but we had to refuse a third so that Poison Idea could take the stage. Jerry A., Poison Idea's singer, thanked us from the stage and asked the crowd to cheer for us once more.

After the show, crowds of kids wanted our autographs. They asked us to sign their records, T-shirts, and bodies with Sharpie pens. It felt as though we'd finally won over Seattle.

It had taken years and much work, but we could now be selective about the venues we played and ask for dollar guarantees instead of begging promoters for money after the show. While I took care of bookings and dealt with much of the band business and promotion, Matt managed the bookkeeping. But we really needed a manager, or at least a dedicated lawyer to help us from time to time. The prevailing wisdom among bands was that major labels were corrupt by nature and cared little about the bands and artists they were supposed to represent. We needed someone in our corner to protect us from the unscrupulous takers who wanted a piece of everything they saw.

Photo shoot for C/Z Records at the OK Hotel (Seattle), 1992. Photo by Jackie Ransier, from the author's archive.

DIRTY HANDS 22

On Saturday, June 27, 1992, I had my hands full running the Sublime show at the OK Hotel when Valerie came running into the club.

"Steve, I need a ride to Stefanie's house! Something's wrong!" she blurted, her face drained of its color.

Just a week before, I had overheard Stefanie telling Mia that she didn't feel like she was ready for so much attention. She didn't feel like the band was ready. Everyone from Drew Barrymore to Rick Rubin was clamoring to meet 7 Year Bitch. They were in films, flying all over the world, and doing lavish photo shoots. They had offers to do festival tours with the biggest bands in the country, Rage Against the Machine, the Red Hot Chili Peppers, and Pearl Jam. Stefanie hadn't been playing very long and didn't think that 7 Year Bitch was musically prepared for the commitments they were making. That might have been true in the first couple months they were a band, but after a year of practice and so many live shows, they were fast becoming a very good band. The fact that a band made up of four women could rise above the rest in Seattle's male-dominated rock scene said much about their abilities and their gumption.

Mia and Stefanie Sargent. Date and photographer unknown, from author's archive.

I think she felt guilty, like she was an imposter, but I don't think she was right. 7 Year Bitch, in their relative simplicity, wrote powerful songs that challenged the bullshit they encountered and had unapologetically feminist themes. They associated more with bands like Motörhead and The Gits than the nascent riot grrrl movement that was emerging from Olympia at the time.

Selene became a commanding and cool presence on stage. Liz, already an excellent all-around rock musician, was the musical force of the band, and Valerie developed remarkably solid time as a drummer. The Gits could easily claim that we gave 7 Year Bitch their start, but they were a great band of their own accord. They easily reached the goals we'd struggled for years to achieve. All we could do was watch their star rise and wonder what we were doing wrong.

So, on this June night at the OK Hotel, I was surprised to see Valerie. I was shocked that she was asking me for help. 7 Year Bitch had been in Vancouver, British Columbia, playing shows with the Red Hot Chili Peppers, partying with Drew Barrymore, and flying high on their success. Since my car was totaled, I called a taxi and Valerie and I arrived at Stefanie's shared flat in Seattle's Central District. We arrived in time to see Stefanie being wheeled out by paramedics. She was on her back, one of her engineer's boots hanging on one foot. She had scored heroin and shot up. She slipped into a drug-induced sleep and did not wake up when she began to vomit while on her back. She choked and died in her sleep. Same as Jimi Hendrix. She was only twenty-four years old. I could only stand there, transfixed by Stefanie's dangling boot. I wanted it to be a bad dream, but it wasn't, and I couldn't sleep for weeks.

Our hearts were torn apart by the loss of the sweet and humble Stefanie. The rifts that had festered between our bands and tested our friendships faded into the ether. We came together to remember Stefanie and to remember our shared values and goals and renew the bonds of our friendship. The Gits honored our friend by dedicating our first album, *Frenching the Bully*, to her. Stefanie's death was a bomb that shook us all to the core. It was the first of several waves of human tragedy to follow.

Only a few weeks had passed since Stefanie's death, and again I was working at the OK Hotel when Valerie called me sobbing and choking on her words.

"My dad's dead. Can you come with me to my parents' house in Queen Anne?" My chest burned at her words and at the memory of the last time she'd come to me at work.

Valerie's folks lived in a beautiful hilltop apartment in the Queen Anne neighborhood, overlooking Seattle's Space Needle and the Seattle Center. Her mother and stepfather's presence in Seattle were one of the reasons Valerie had decided to drop out of college and move to Seattle with me. Valerie and her mother were very close. They were more like friends than mother and daughter. It was a weird energy, not what I was used to, but it was natural for Valerie and I missed spending time with them.

Her stepfather, Ron, was a jet pilot who had dropped napalm on Vietnam during the war. He was a gregarious man who loved to be the center of attention, but his eyes spoke of something haunted in his soul. He was generous, often treating people to lavish dinner and drinks, and he was often the life of his own party. He could be boorish and sexist, but he had raised Valerie and her younger brother as if they were his own. He was damaged and complicated, but I liked him.

A second death in a matter of weeks and the intensity of it all made the world wobble on its axis. I could feel something inside me hardening, closing off. I felt the downward tug of depression, and the only thing that saved me from complete despair was the band and our ongoing mission to conquer the music world and succeed. Remember the mission, I reminded myself. I said it repeatedly; it was my mantra. We wanted to touch people's souls with our music, to let them know that we understood their pain. We wanted to inspire and empower and entertain.

We often did interviews for small fanzines and radio shows. A tape sent to me by a photographer and writer for one such zine included a microcassette of a taped interview with us from 1992. Most was inaudible non sequiturs and absurdist banter among us, however Mia said something at one point that shut us up: "Yes, life is terrifying, and the world can feel like a shithole at times, but there are people out there who care, who are trying to make life less scary and the world less shitty. That's why we're doing it, man, and we take it seriously. Other bands don't take it so seriously, but we do and we want you all to know it. That's our mission."

Despite the personal losses, I was confident that The Gits would be successful one day. Yet so much death had me feeling tired and unhinged. I was waiting for the other shoe to drop.

In the weeks following, Mia struggled in the aftermath of Stefanie's death. Mia had adored Stefanie, and her death cut Mia to the core. She became less joyful and more reclusive. Her mourning also contributed to squabbles with her boyfriend, Robert, and increased their drinking. We saw less of Mia, and it was troubling. She missed rehearsals and, when she was there, she was often too drunk to sing.

One of the hardest parts of the death of a close friend or family member is how little it matters to the rest of the world. Stefanie was well loved by a relatively small circle in Seattle and in the music community. No one seemed to notice except those of us who adored her. For the rest of the world, it was just another heroin-related death, one of several that summer, and there would be more to come. We rallied to support the women in her band. Stefanie's passing had an enormous impact on Valerie, and I was glad to be able to mend fences and support her during that time. It also hit Mia especially hard, affecting her ability to manage her life.

My personal financial situation was quickly becoming desperate. Matt worked full time at a brewery, but Andy, Mia, and I didn't have regular jobs. *Frenching the*

Bully was getting stellar reviews, and attendance at our shows grew. Word was getting around about the fiery little punk band with the scruffy female singer with the incredible voice and the undeniable stage presence. The press was taking notice of The Gits. But critical acclaim was not translating into revenue to pay rent.

It was confusing and frustrating to see so many less committed, generic sounding "grunge" bands signing lucrative record contracts. Nirvana had blown the lid off the Seattle scene, and every record company in the world was courting "Seattle bands" in hopes of cashing in on the multimillion-dollar appeal of Nirvana's hugely successful debut album, *Nevermind.*

In spite of our collective malaise, we pushed on. 7 Year Bitch auditioned guitarists and, after passing on Carrie Brownstein (who went on to co-found Sleater-Kinney), hired Roisin Dunne to take over as guitarist for their band.

We hit the road as much as Matt's brewing job would allow. But a bigger problem was also becoming known: Mia's grief over Stefanie's death was driving her to the bottom of one bottle after another.

There were, however, high points for The Gits during those dark days. I got a deal on the rental of four unwashed costumes formerly used for a Shakespeare festival. We were approaching the peak of our powers as a band. We invited D.C. Beggars to play a show, as well as a kindred punk outfit, Zipgun. By the close of the opening band, the venue was sold out. We took the stage wearing the moth-eaten old costumes. We looked like something from a punkified *Lord of the Rings* cosplay convention or a Renaissance fair. The crowd chanted, "Gits! Gits! Gits!" until we were introduced by our roadie Mikey Nichols dressed as the Bard himself. Julian put on a CD of the epic opening of Beethoven's Ninth Symphony and blasted it through the PA. Fog enveloped the room as we launched into our set. Mia took the stage last, dressed in a green, yellow, and red jester outfit and cap. She banged her head to the beat and whipped the crowd into a fever before taking the mic and mesmerizing the audience, and us, with her powerful voice and brilliant delivery. We played fifteen songs, one after the other, barely a single-second break between the songs. During the instrumental part of a song, Mia launched her body off the end of the stage in a terrific stage dive into the mosh pit. Her slender body was held aloft by the adoring crowd, like the angel atop Mrs. Carson's gravestone in that Ann Arbor cemetery. She rode on the hands of the adoring crowd until, as if on cue, she was placed, boots first, back on the stage to start the next song. I was astounded by how good The Gits had become. We had surpassed our own expectations. By the spring of 1993, we were, without a doubt, one of the most dynamic, engaging, and crushing bands in Seattle.

Mia had struggled with alcohol for longer than I'd known her. Just as The Gits were starting to gain traction in, Mia's drinking became heavier than ever. She wasn't writing, and her voice sounded wrecked from lack of sleep and from screeching at the top of her lungs at her boyfriend Robert. An added stressor arose when our warlock landlord put the Rathouse on the market and told us that we had a week to find another place to live.

Mia in jester's outfit at the Weathered Wall Club, Seattle, in spring of 1993. Still taken from live performance video.

I happened to be in the Rathouse kitchen, just outside Mia's door, while she was trying to break up with Robert over the phone. They'd been having serious troubles. His PTSD symptoms were severe, and she was in no position to help him. He experienced night terrors, and the sound of fireworks or jet planes could, in a flash, send his tortured soul back to the Tet Offensive of '68. Robert drank whiskey every day, which only caused Mia to drink more.

Wiping away tears, she spelled out in detail the ways that he had failed to support her emotionally. Mia didn't raise her voice or rant irrationally. She spoke calmly, respectfully, as she broke off the relationship with Robert. But after she hung up she slammed her door and sobbed in great heaves into her pillow. It hurt her to hurt him. It was difficult for Mia to live with such acute empathy. Sometimes she drank to be social, but I think she drank to mute her sense of empathy and concern for people. While the alcohol numbed her to the torments, it was also poisoning her body.

Mia's innate social intelligence kept her lucid in dark times. She was not one to dwell on pain. For most of us—including Robert—we learn to protect ourselves from the worst by denying our losses or excusing wrongdoing. This often ends up just allowing a traumatic experience to eat us from the inside out. Mia understood that, to get through hard times, one must process the past—the good, the bad, and the horrific. Mia diffused her traumas through her art.

She understood that, by facing difficult memories and allowing emotions to develop and manifest, one can move ahead with power in the present. But Stefanie's death and the break-up with Robert proved to be so painful Mia was struggling to make sense of the losses.

We were coming up with new songs for our second album, but Mia struggled to write lyrics. She was also forgetting lyrics to songs that she'd sung a thousand times. She disappeared right before show times. We took turns keeping an eye on her, so she would be present to take the stage on time or board the van for the next show. Her drinking was becoming a burden to the band as much as it was destructive to her health. It became clear that we couldn't continue The Gits' mission unless she got help.

Steve and Mia getting back in the van in Albuquerque, New Mexico, 1993.
Photo by Mikey Nichols, from author's archive.

22

MY ONLY WAR (NOW I AM)

Thinking that we could somehow manage Mia's drinking, we loaded our gear into our 1976 GMC window van and hit the road for a gig in L.A. Operating on autopilot, we fell back into our familiar tour roles. Matt kept the van running and drove. I booked the shows and collected whatever money the venue was paying at the end of the night. Andy kept his eye on Mia. She could become dissociated and wander off, lost in her thoughts, her internal GPS badly miscalibrated. When alcohol was available, Mia might follow her craving and somehow get drunk in a matter of minutes. She sometimes took the stage drunk—if she could find the stage at all—and she sometimes forgot her lyrics mid-song. This uncertainty made for stressful shows. I could see Andy's expression sour as Mia tried to act sober while stumbling around the stage.

Sometimes the roar of the amps and the thump of the bass drum brought Mia to her senses and she could sing well, even though she was nowhere near her top form. Occasionally she couldn't pull it off and it was embarrassing for her.

Andy was the band's musical-compliance officer, and after a disastrous gig he might take Mia aside and suggest that she not drink so much prior to the shows. But it was hard for him to be a disciplinarian because he knew what she was going through, what we were all going through. Mia wanted to do her part and perform well, but she just couldn't get through the day without a drink. Alcohol quieted some of the demons that tormented her, but it created others.

She wanted to slow down or stop drinking, but her addiction, fueled by grief, was more powerful than her will to resist.

We began our spring '93 tour in Portland, where we played at a little all-ages DIY club and bookstore called the X-Ray Cafe, which served coffee and held punk shows on weekends. The X-Ray's emcee, Trey, asked if he could record our set on his eight-track tape recorder. It proved to be an excellent decision because it would be one of our best live recordings.

The place was full of pimply artsy youth and pre-teens with cool parents. We were the grownups in the room. I set up on the floor of the tiny bookshop between the travel and self-help sections. The space was barely big enough to move in without getting poked in the face with a guitar headstock. Both of my twenty-inch Zildjian K heavy crash cymbals were inches from Mia's ears, so I had to be careful not to smash them when she was close. There were no real stage monitors because there was no real stage. We stood face-to-face with the audience—no separation whatsoever between the band and the crowd. The way it should be. We were no more important than the kids who came to see us. We were a little older—and jaded perhaps—but the nose-to-nose synergy in that setting was the essence of punk rock. No rock stars, no idols, no difference between the band and the audience.

Trey handed Mia four little bottles of water and a hand towel. It was 100° inside. In return, I gave him a pair of beat-up drumsticks. Then I gave him the signal that we were ready to begin. Trey introduced us with a hint of punk sarcasm, saying, "Ladies and gentlemen, this is a wonderful, wonderful band. All the way from Seattle . . . to play the X-Ray Cafe . . . and the drummer gave me his drumsticks! He gave me his drumsticks, man!" He pretended to choke up. "So, let's give a warm welcome to The Gits!" He sounded like Kermit the Frog introducing Barbra Streisand on *The Muppet Show*. Then he flapped his arms above his head like Kermit. "Yeaaaahhh!"

Andy jumped right in with a guitar slide as we kicked off the set with "Absynthe." It was one of the most challenging songs to play on drums because it included several complete changes and bass and drum solos, all at a blazing tempo. Then the song switched keys, rhythm, and tempo. Mia's lyrics are about the booking agents and the self-important industry creeps who promised the world but delivered nothing. Bass and guitar descended the fret board, and I went to a double-time syncopated hardcore beat that played out to the end. "I see you walking around, Just like hogs / rollin' in the mud. / It's a dyin' shame / That's where you find your truth . . . "

As soon as we finished, I counted off "Another Shot of Whiskey." Like Dead Kennedys, we played one song after another for forty-five minutes—an entire set of fourteen songs without so much as a pause for a sip of water.

Mia developed as a performer and our audiences grew. She engaged with them in new ways as she sang. Sometimes she locked eyes with someone in the crowd—a friend or a stranger—and sang to that person, the way an actor sings to a love interest on a Broadway stage.

During other shows, she pumped her fist and stomped her foot in time with my snare drum. During a ballad, she might focus her attention on a wallflower standing alone stage left to sing "Social Love." I noticed people in the audience singing along, which seemed crazy to me given the album had only been out for a few weeks.

Gits fans weren't fanatics or groupies—to me those were belittling terms used to describe those who consider musicians bigger-than-life rock stars or heroes of pop culture. Something in our songs spoke to them. We were "a band of the people," as Andy once said. I loved and respected most of our fans and (in many cases) considered them friends and supporters, not simply consumers.

Mia would sometimes get distracted by an admirer or an old friend. She was incapable of being inauthentic with fans and she could get into deep conversations. She might slip out for a drink at a bar next door to the venue, or to share a joint on the street. Sometimes she would go missing. This was happening with ever greater frequency. Her behavior became stressful. "Where's Mia? We go on in ten minutes!" or "Where's Mia? We have to get on the road." Her drinking was back to pre-rehab levels.

After Portland, we played in Olympia with SNFU and the Melvins. Then we headed south to play for eight fans, a bartender, a couple of other bands, and a booking agent in Eugene, Oregon. Next show was in San Francisco, where we played at a collectively run music venue, recording studio, and art gallery called Klub Komotion. There was no place like it in Seattle, and for the first time we were headlining a show in San Francisco. Strawman and J Church opened for us. We gave two encores and debuted our cover of Sam Cooke's 1966 civil rights anthem "A Change Is Gonna Come." The poster featuring the calendar of shows read, "NOFX, Sublime, No Doubt, Lagwagon, Jawbreaker, MDC, and The Gits."

After the show we sat for an interview with the international punk zine *Maximum Rocknroll*. Lance Hahn, of J Church and Cringer, and Michael Millet, founder of the punk record label Broken Rekids, were the interviewers. They introduced us to the publisher, Tim Yohannan, the man responsible for forging the unique San Francisco and Berkeley punk scenes of the '80s and '90s.

Unlike Seattle, the Bay Area music scene was decidedly political. Yohannan launched what would become the most complete archive of punk music records in the world. He founded the international punk music publication and record label *Maximum Rocknroll*, which gave a voice to music fans and activists in small towns and cities all over the world.

From San Francisco, we drove to Los Angeles, where Mia was a bit anxious about seeing her older brother Eric, who owned a successful hair salon on Sunset Boulevard. During the five-hour drive, Mia entertained us with more of her father's stories about his grandfather, Emiliano Zapata.

A mi estimado
amigo el Sr. Gral. Miguel
C. Zamora dedico el presente.
Tlaltizapan 27 de Mayo de 1915.
Emiliano Zapata.
GRAL. EMILIANO ZAPATA.
PROP. ASEGURADA.
H. S. GUTIERREZ
FOTO. MEXICO. D.F.

Photo of Emiliano Zapata, c. 1915. Photo by Gutierrez, Foto Mexico, D.F., courtesy of the National Archives of Mexico.

24 CUT MY SKIN, IT MAKES ME HUMAN

From the front seat of the Gits van, Andy said, "Mia, that story's incredible! Your father told you all that at lunchtime?"

"Yeah, man. Well, maybe over a few lunchtimes, and I might not remember it perfect, but somethin' like that. And I know for sure that he once said, 'Strong like bull for revolution!'"

Andy busted out laughing. "Oh my god, Mia. That's funny stuff. 'Strong like bull for revolution!'" he said in imitation of her imitation of her father's voice.

Mia nodded and smiled. "Yeah, man. My dad has a letter or a medal or somethin' that proves he was related. He's, like, very proud of it. He's totally into bein' like Mexican Revolution royalty. My mom is Scottish or English. So, what does that make me? A chicken-bone knapsack. A cat-eating freak?"

"So that makes us two Hebes, a Mick, and a Spic," Matt added gleefully.

Mia affected a Southern inflection that sounded like it came from farther south than

Mia singing at the Off Ramp, Seattle, c. 1992. Photo by Zannah Noe, courtesy of Zannah Noe.

her home in Louisville, Kentucky. "Cheekin bohon nap-sack. Cahut-eatin' fawr-eek."

Matt turned halfway around in the driver's seat and said to no one in particular, "Cat-eating freak!" Then he turned his attention back to the highway and pressed his foot on the gas, closing fast on the VW microbus putting along in the passing lane. A Grateful Dead dancing bear bumper sticker and Dead skull curtains dangling jollily in the passenger windows told us everything we needed to know about the people inside.

"Punish!" cried Matt. "Punish!"

The mighty 76 GMC window van roared to ramming speed, and in seconds we were three inches from the bumper of the minibus.

"Not in the fast lane! Not in the fast lane!" yelled Matt, hoping to scare the living shit out of the Deadhead dipshits. It was a punk mandate to tease Deadheads. The Grateful Dead's music was long-winded, self-indulgent, repetitive, and mind-numbingly boring.

"Oh my God. We're gonna die!" I said, genuinely terrified.

Mia hid under the blanket on top of the equipment loft in the back of the van.

"Punish!" said Matt, seeming blinded by his rage.

"Matt, what the fuck, man?! Slow down!" Andy yelled.

"Fuckers!" Matt was genuinely pissed. He was on a mission to get to the next show on time, but he slowed the van and allowed the trembling minibus to totter over to the right lane. Matt turned up the Minutemen side of the home-dubbed cassette tape stuck in the player, *Double Nickels on the Dime*. He stepped on the gas pedal again and blasted past the Deadheads, our speed approaching a hundred miles an hour.

"Ah-ha!" cried Andy. "Strong like bull for revolution, ah ha! But, uh . . . maybe you should slow down now, Matt?"

"Why?" asked Matt.

"Well, Matt, it's very hard to play the guitar when your body is splattered all over the fucking highway alongside a busful of hippies!"

Matt finally got the message and slowed from ninety-five to eighty-five, then to seventy-four. He lit another Camel, exhaling smoke into the cabin.

Mia crawled out from under the blanket and pulled her journal from her bag. She crossed her legs and opened it across her lap. "I love that smell," she said before diving into her notebook.

"You don't even smoke," I replied.

"Of course not. Disgusting habit." She made a blech face.

"I'm glad you don't smoke, Mia, because then you might have to quit and set yourself on fire," I said, smiling, hoping she'd pick up on the Colleen reference.

"Uh-huh," she grunted, already lost in her thoughts.

We were still at ramming speed on the freeway when I opened my eyes to blue lights flashing from a Highway Patrol motorcycle, cruising at a respectful distance from our back bumper, on which hung a bumper sticker that said, "KILL A BIKER." Why the hell had Matt put that sticker on there? I wondered. Andy and I had urged him to remove the sticker before the tour, but he refused, saying, "No one is stupid enough to not get that the sticker is a joke." We were about to put that theory to the test.

"Fuck!" spat Matt as he slowed the van and made his way across three lanes of traffic to the shoulder of the highway. Mia fumbled frantically through her bag. When she located a small baggie of weed, she shoved it into the side panel of the van. Andy shook his head and sighed. I worried about the ticket, which could seriously eat into our food and gas fund. The cassette tape reached its end and clicked over to the other side, then it began playing the sound of an ignition turning over, just as our van stopped and Matt powered down the engine.

The cop—decked out in polished helmet, mirrored sunglasses, and knee-high motorcycle boots—sauntered up to the rear of the van, a tiny notebook in hand. He scrutinized our license plate and bumper for too long. Then he turned, walked back to his bike, and called something in on the radio.

Mia was hiding under a blanket, whimpering softly.

"Mia?" I called in a loud whisper. "What?" she answered.

"Don't worry. He's not gonna arrest you and take you back to L.A. County jail on the back of his motorcycle."

"Strong like bull for revolution!" Mia whispered before going quiet again.

The cop moseyed up to the driver's-side window, where Matt was waiting with his license and registration at the ready before he was asked for them. I didn't say a word.

The cop examined the vehicle documents, then removed his sunglasses to peer inside the van. "There's a lot of people in there. What's in the back, under the platform back there, Mr. Dresdner?"

Matt blurted out, "It's our gear—guitars, drums, bass cabinet. We're a band from Seattle, on tour."

When I heard the words "band" and "tour," my chest tightened. I was convinced that we were doomed. I glanced down to my right, where Mia had stashed her pot, and I shoved it farther into the crack in the door panel. The cop craned his neck to make eye contact with Andy and then with me, sitting in the rear bench seat. I tried to smile a little. "It's not like we're a real band or anything," I said stupidly.

The cop asked to have a look under the loft. We were on I-5, a smuggling route for guns, drugs, and people traveling from Mexico to Northern California. Matt nodded and pulled his door handle to exit the van so he could unlock the back for the inspection.

"Whoa there! Stay inside the vehicle, sir." The cop held a hand in the air. "Are there any more people traveling with you in the vehicle?"

"No, sir," said Matt.

"Okay then," replied the officer. "You know how fast you were going?"

"Yes, sir. Eighty-five or so. I think," Matt mumbled.

The cop shook his head. "I clocked you at 102 miles per hour in a sixty zone. I gotta write you a ticket."

"Of course," said Matt, who seemed to have the situation under control.

The cop began writing the ticket, but then he stopped and tapped his ballpoint pen twice on the flip pad. Looking at Matt, he said, "I gotta ask you all one more question." He paused, as if preparing to cast his final judgment. "What kind of music do you all play?"

"We're a punk rock band," said Matt proudly.

"Damnit, Matt," I muttered. I thought he was being defiant, and my heart sank. I was convinced that he'd blown it.

The officer sort of smiled, then went back to filling out the ticket. He lifted the pad and ripped the ticket from the booklet, just like they always did on *CHiPs*. He handed it to Matt and said, "Well, that's a good thing. Because if you were a country band, I'd have written it for 102 and reckless driving. But since you play punk rock, I'll give you a warning. Watch your speed, and drive safely, Mr. Dresdner. Have a good concert." He handed Matt the warning ticket, and just before he turned on his boot heel he said, "'Kill a biker'—that's hilarious, dude."

Before we had a chance to take it in, he mounted his bike and zoomed past the driver's-side door to pull over another speeding vehicle.

"What just happened?" I asked Matt.

Matt shrugged. "Let's go."

The worn out mixtape stuck in the cassette deck played on. We listened to the last song on the tape, Minutemen's "Tour-Spiel," for the seventh time that day. The chorus mimicked our life on the road.

At the gig that night, the music moved through Mia, who was a conduit for everything she and the audience held inside. For just a moment, time, sound, the song, the show—it all seemed to disappear. I hit the drums harder on the down beat, slamming the snare drum a hair behind the beat for more of a blues feel. Mia leaned into the mic, her eyes pressed shut, tears streaming down her cheeks, her left fist clenched against her gut.

Mia created a powerful emotional coalescence among herself, us, and her audience. Few if any punk rock singers can claim that distinction. Whether her medium was a painting, a letter, or the stage, Mia's authenticity and emotional intelligence shone through. There was nothing shallow about Mia's lyrics or Mia herself.

It was a gift to be able to accompany Mia, to share a juvenile sense of wonder, to seek adventure, to take risks. We knew that when we were playing music—especially when we were playing with The Gits—we were doing exactly what we were born to do. We were made for The Gits.

I was Mia's drummer and her devotee. She was like a sister I'd suffered in poverty with, or like the good Samaritan who had saved my life. I felt something unconditional for her, and I think she felt the same about me. I would have taken a bullet for her.

Dawn came too quickly after our late-night gig in L.A. Bleary-eyed and grumpy, we dragged ourselves off of a friend's floor to drive to another gig that day. Mia's brother Eric had attended our show the previous night, and he planned to meet us at a Texaco station in West Hollywood to say goodbye. We had to fill up and add oil to the engine or we wouldn't make it through the California desert.

We took turns checking the fluids and clearing the insects from the windshield. Mia jumped out of the van and grabbed the squeegee from a bucket to clean the windows. She was doing a thorough job, and a man in a gold Jaguar convertible at another pump asked Mia if she would clean his windows. Mia was wearing an old coat that looked like a gas-station attendant's jacket. Annoyed, she ignored the man's request. When he raised his English-accented voice and asked her to fetch him a pack of "fags" from the shop, Mia got angry.

"Get your own fucking 'fags,' and wash your own damn windows. And fuck you for assuming I work at a gas station. I'm on tour with my band, in fact!"

Indignant, Mia turned to get back in the van.

Her bother Eric had been chatting with Andy and me in the passenger seat and witnessed his sister's altercation. Eric's salon was right on Sunset Avenue in Hollywood. He cut the hair of famous people all the time. The show biz world was important to him.

He looked agitated and raised his voice to scold his sister. "Mia, don't you know who that is? That's David Bowie, you asshole. You just cussed out David Bowie! He lives nearby and he could have helped your band, but you screwed it up Mia."

Mia stood mute for a moment. She turned to look over her shoulder. Bowie had become dejected, and possibly a bit frightened. He was pulling away from the pump to leave the Texaco. He stopped to wait for oncoming traffic. Mia made her move. She reached into the van, behind the seat, and pulled out the box containing the merch. She extracted a handful of 7-inch singles and a Gits T-shirt and took off to make amends to Bowie.

Mia ran across the lot after Bowie, but he saw her coming and roared out into traffic, just missing a U-Haul truck and a Volkswagen Beetle. Mia was determined and nearly ran down the street after him.

Standing there watching the drama unfold, we were left speechless. Mia finally turned and walked back to the van with her head held low with shame.

"I'm sorry I screwed up everything with David Bowie. I'm so sorry, guys."

"Mia, there was nothing to screw up. He happened to be at the gas station. It's no big deal. Really." I spoke.

"Good to see you sis," Eric added. "I'll see if I can get your record to David Bowie anyway. I know a guy who knows a guy."

"Thanks Eric. Okay, see ya later, bro," Mia said.

We loaded ourselves into position in the van and we were off to the next show.

Wrapped in a blanket, Mia continued her father's incredible story about the Zapata brothers.

Mia's made-up Spanish and bizarre colloquialisms were always good for a laugh.

"Yeah, the dictator heard about General Zapata beating the Golden Fifth, and the Mexican dictator, Díaz, immediately left his country for exile in France," said Mia.

"He escaped to Texas. Is that all true?" I asked.

"That's what my father told me anyway," Mia mumbled as she curled into a feline ball in the back of the van.

The purpose of touring is to promote the band to people in the record industry, introduce music to new people in new cities, generate press about the band, and sell merchandise, thereby creating individual living, breathing, walking advertisements for the band. Several people approached to compliment us on our performance or to ask us to sign their records. Although we were playing venues that were unconventional and underground, something was starting to happen that we were unaware of at the time. The people who turned up to see us tended to be involved in the music industry in some way, or else they played in other bands—music insiders checking out the music outsiders. Some record label representatives were showing up too. They weren't hard to identify in business-casual attire and strapped with pagers. They looked particularly important when they paid for drinks with credit cards. They seemed to know each other, and they knew the cool musicians. We couldn't be bothered. We had another show to play.

We drove through the boiling California desert and then over freezing snow-capped mountains, then back to the heat in Albuquerque, New Mexico. It was incredibly hot, especially inside the club. My hands were sweating so much that I had trouble holding on to my sticks. A tall, drunk guy in a Germs T-shirt started spitting at me while I was playing from behind the stage. Yellow balls of throat mucus landed on my cymbals and on my head and neck. "What the hell are you doing?!" I yelled. "Why are you spitting on me?"

"Because you rock!" he yelled.

"Do it again, and I'll put my drumstick in your fucking eye and dig out your eyeball!" I hollered over the music. He was a big guy who looked a little crazy, but I didn't care. When I was on stage in the heat of a frantic Gits show, nothing could diminish my sense of purpose and potency. The mission was to be defended at any cost.

He spat again. I sent a Promark 5B oak wooden tipped drumstick flying over my shoulder. The projectile, easily doing ninety miles per hour, clipped his right ear. It must have severed an earring, because blood immediately spurted from his ear and dyed his T-shirt, which was white with a blue circle design, red. I expected to be attacked from behind and I made note of the mic stand with a heavy leaded base next to my drum throne. The song ended, I turned to engage the assault, and the guy was gone. He took the stick I threw and disappeared, at least for a few minutes. I started the next song of the set. I looked down to see him standing in front of the stage, spitting, grabbing Mia's legs and reaching for her crotch.

"Motherfucker," I yelled as I chucked a second *broken* drumstick at him. I missed the guy but nailed an innocent young Goth woman square in her eye. What had I done?!

The guy in the bloody T-shirt continued harassing Mia, who somehow maintained her composure. Matt and Andy were aware of the scene and were prepared to stop the show and manage the situation once and for all when our host and booking agent, a six-foot-six monster of a man called "Uncle Al," took matters into large and capable hands. There seemed to be guardian angels looking out for The Gits, although sometimes the angels were from hell.

The next time I saw the spitter, he was spitting blood on the curb in front of the club as we loaded out gear. He had two black eyes, and blood poured from his nose. Spitting wasn't considered proper punk etiquette in 1992, as it had been in 1977. We later got word that he spat at the bands at every show he attended, and the result was always the same. He must have gotten some sort of masochistic jolly from getting his ass kicked. Who am I to judge? Each to their own.

He looked up at me through swollen eyes and said, "Great show, man. You guys were awesome! Can I buy a T-shirt?" I gave him one for free and he used it to wipe blood from his nose before putting it on.

"Glad you liked it."

The section of I-5 that cuts north from Grapevine, California, runs right through a desolate landscape pocked with craters full of muddy water and rusty machinery. Farther north is an infamous feedlot with tens of thousands of imprisoned cattle. The sea of walking meat extends as far as the eye can see, for miles on both sides of the freeway—a shit-ton of cows making tons and tons of shit.

It was nearing 100° F. The van was in danger of overheating and, because the van didn't have air conditioning, we had the windows down to cool ourselves. The smell made it hard to breathe. It was the fetid odor of death rot and American dietary corruption. These were the animals that supply Grade A beef to our supermarkets. I watched a particularly large steer lift his tail and expunge a brown mélange of fecal matter and urine.

"Yummy. Beef stroganoff!" I declared.

"Stephen, please shut the fuck up," said Mia. "Those cows are outstanding in their field."

Nobody laughed. It was too hot even for smiles, but the banter had begun.

"Those cows would be outstanding on a plate," countered Matt.

Andy's face twisted in disgust. "It's like fuckin' Cowschwitz."

"Da-cow," quipped Matt.

"Gits humor" ranged from the profane to the absurd. Non-sequiturs and simple word play were often at the root. I didn't always understand the humor, especially the paradoxically, absurdly antisemitic references made by Andy and Matt, who had both been raised Jewish.

Uncomfortable, Mia and I retreated from these exchanges.

I was never so glad that the Minutemen tape was stuck in the van's cassette deck as D. Boon shouted over a masterful guitar riff, saying, "My life, Jesus, and tequila! I'm satisfied, and I can't deny it . . . "

"Jesus and Cheetos?" I asked Matt, who, as usual, was in the driver's seat. We were only a quarter of the way through the killing fields.

"I don't fucking know. Look it up," Matt replied curtly. "You're just the drummer. Don't ask questions. Just drum."

"And how exactly do I do that, Matthew?" I asked.

"Do what?" Matt asked.

"Look it up." I said.

Matt didn't answer. He only lit a cigarette, the secondhand smoke wafting right back through the rear window and into my face.

"Matt?" I called. When he didn't reply, I raised my voice over the sounds of the Minutemen, now on their eighty-second rotation. "Matt!"

"We aren't stopping," he barked. "You should have pissed at the gas station with David Bowie."

Another cloud blew into the back of the van. Frustrated by the smell and hungering for a little salty revenge, I reached into my pack and pulled out a can of sardines. I pulled the top halfway off and nonchalantly slid the sardines under the driver's seat. Minutes passed.

Mia was the first to comment: "Smells like the woman's disease in here, and an unsanitary one at that. But that ain't me."

"My God," Andy said, covering his face.

I waited and waited for a response from my intended target of the sardine stink bomb.

Finally, Matt said, "The faster I drive, the less it stinks in here." He stomped on the gas pedal, the V-8 roared to life.

Andy and Mia express frustration on tour in Switzerland, c. 1991.
Photo by either Steve, Matt, or Scott (Benson, friend and studio engineer).

HERE'S TO YOUR FUCK 25

We made another stop in San Francisco, where we played a show with the bands Jawbreaker, White Trash Debutants (featuring Ginger Coyote), and Geraldine Fibbers. We took the stage and opened with "Social Love." The intro is a staccato drum build on the floor tom and the snare drum, played simultaneously with thirty-second notes in a crescendo for two bars. It's very fast, and I have to concentrate to get it tight. But in the middle of the intro the power in the decrepit little club went out completely. The amps died, and there was no P.A. The packed crowd of about two hundred "oohed" as if someone had peed their pants in third-grade gym class.

The sound person shouted out over the crowd, "Nobody go anywhere. It's the city again. The whole block is dark south of Market Street. Happens all the time. We'll be back up and running in a few minutes. The music will be back shortly. Don't leave!"

Mia consults Ben London prior to performance at the RCKNDY Club, Seattle, c. 1992. Photo by and courtesy of Charles Peterson.

The bartender said something to her, then she added, "And there will be free shots of Jägermeister at the bar. The Gits will continue soon. Free shots!"

I waited a bit before muscling my way to an open barstool, where the barkeep dropped a shot of Jäger in front of me. I downed the cold liqueur, which warmed my belly. It tasted soothing, like cough medicine. The bartender was flirty, and she gave me another. Then another. I made a point never to drink before playing. This was an exception. No one needed to know, I thought. It didn't taste very strong.

By candlelight, I noticed that the other Gits weren't drinking, so I had one for each of them. Then the lights flicked on.

The sound person shouted at the top of her lungs, "Thank you for sticking around. And now, The Gits!"

I hustled onstage and sat behind the drum set, a little unsteady on my heels. I counted off "Social Love" and began the intro drum build. Halfway into the intro, a stick slipped out of my hand and hit Matt square in the middle of his back. He turned around and handed it back to me. I counted off again and dropped the stick at the exact same point in the intro. This time the stick flew over Matt's shoulder and struck a grinning woman in the audience on the arm. Mia turned and shot me a confused, angry look.

"One more time," I yelled, "one, two, three, four!" and the stick went flying from my right hand yet again. This time, I was holding the stick tight. Was I being punished by God for drinking the shots?

Each time I began the song, I seemed to lose control of my hand. The more I tried, the harder it became to begin the song. I took a deep breath, dried my palms on my pant legs, and gave it one more try. I ripped a piece of gaffer tape that I used to dampen my snare drum and wrapped it around my right hand and the drumstick. I clicked four on the sticks and started the song one more time. I felt the stick slipping once again, but I squeezed my thumb and index finger and managed to make it into the chorus, then to the bridge, then into the outro. I did it.

As we made our way back to Seattle, we played a notable gig in Portland with Dead Moon, Sister Double Happiness featuring Gary Floyd, former lead singer of the Texas queer punk band the Dicks, and a slick-sounding new band called Everclear. We found ourselves co-headlining the bill with Dead Moon. The show was sold out.

Dead Moon's founders, Fred and Toody Cole, had been playing together since 1979. They played guitar and bass, respectively. They did everything themselves and were highly regarded among musicians and their fans in Portland. They made their records on analog tape machines and even pressed their own mono records. They had their kids design their posters, and when they were older their kids helped with band business and legal issues.

Fred and Toody were older than most in the scene, in their mid-forties in the early '90s. They both chain-smoked: as one of Fred's cigarettes was nearly finished,

Toody lit another for him, Fred did the same for Toody, and so on. They drank airplane bottles of Jack Daniel's in the same fashion; all night, never drunk and never exhausting the supply of whiskey. Fred had a waxing moon in the image of a skull tattooed on his right cheek, an unusual cosmetic feature in the early '90s, when tattoos were not commonplace, even in a rock and roll scene. Dead Moon's drummer was the garrulous yet shifty Andrew Loomis. (Loomis had a crush on Mia and made a nuisance of himself whenever she was around.) He put his head down as he played so his face couldn't be seen through his thick mop of hair. He bashed the drums like a hippie possessed and in a trance. Dead Moon was considered by the best bands in the Northwest to be the best band in the Northwest.

We were overjoyed when Dead Moon invited us to tour Europe with them during the coming fall of 1993. They toured frequently and were extremely popular in Europe, where they played in much bigger venues than we could. Touring Europe with Dead Moon meant we would be playing for four to five thousand people per night. Dead Moon had been courted by major record labels and producers, but they refused to relinquish any rights to record and release their music except in exactly the fashion they wished, and the labels lost interest. They had no illusion of rock stardom and were making a decent living from merch sales and tour revenue in Europe. They were masters of the craft of rock and roll, and The Gits and many other bands in the Northwest were both devotees and mentees of Dead Moon.

When we could afford it, we hired publicists to inform college radio DJs and journalists about The Gits. That investment paid dividends in the form of articles about us in the daily and weekly periodicals in the cities we played. Critics wrote previews and gave our records outstanding reviews. It was unbelievable to think that after such a long uphill struggle for validation we were being mentioned in mainstream music magazines like *Spin*, *Rolling Stone*, *Billboard*, and the *Village Voice*. The English press, known for their proclivity to eviscerate bands, hailed The Gits as the next big thing. *Melody Maker* and *New Music Express*, influential English music publications known for their serious—sometimes cynical—coverage of up-and-coming groups, wrote uncharacteristically positive reviews of our first singles. In fact, one of our earliest reviews in *Melody Maker* declared, "The Gits are like Billie Holiday meets the Sex Pistols."

The American music press was less journalistic than the English and had smaller, more regional readerships. *Maximum Rocknroll*, *Alternative Press*, *Flipside*, *Thrasher,* and dozens of small fanzines wrote reviews of our records or interviewed us for feature articles. We could roll into any city on tour, walk up to a newsstand or a bookshop, and find something written about The Gits. It became a kind of game, a scavenger hunt for articles about The Gits.

1980 Rogers XP8 Drum set with the Gits logo at the Off Ramp, Seattle, 1992. From the author's archive.

Mia on the East side of Berlin Wall looking at graffiti art in 1990. Photo by author.

26

PRECIOUS BLOOD

Being on tour felt like personal freedom and career progress. We would meet new people, read local news, and listen to the college radio stations. It felt like we were witness to history unfolding. Touring was never boring, whether in Europe bearing witness to the last days of the half-destroyed Berlin Wall or walking around the streets of San Francisco and Los Angeles. We made new friends in every city, and each day was an adventure. Coming home could be a depressing return to the real-world realities of unpaid rent, mindless temporary jobs, and struggling love relationships. It was difficult to maintain any of these life activities while touring what seemed like twenty months per year.

Back home, I had to scramble to find work for the few weeks between tours. We had to pay rent to have a place to return to. Businesses didn't want to hire musicians who planned to leave on two- or three-week tours every two or three months. It didn't help that we were often playing shows or rehearsing until early morning hours and looked unwashed, hungover, and exhausted in the morning.

I got a temp job in the basement of a Macy's department store, sticking tiny pins into designer shirts and underwear folded over cardboard. It was a mini-sweatshop, and I was on the folding and pinning assembly line with several dozen Chinese women who must have thought me a strange sight, standing there in my ripped jeans and earrings, towering over them. I stuck out like a sore thumb, but I needed a job so I could eat. It was one of countless dumb temp jobs I worked between tours.

Mia loved the idea of being on the road and away from Seattle for months. We had to move out of the Rathouse, and none of us felt quite settled with our new housing situation. Mia felt particularly unsettled in Seattle. She said on several occasions that she did not feel safe in Seattle, and she preferred living out of the van on the road. I figured that Stefanie's death was still weighing heavily on her. It weighed on all of us.

Mia was struggling to maintain her housing and meager income washing dishes at a pizza place. I didn't hang out with my bandmates much between projects. Living in the van with them was enough, but I heard rumors of Mia's after-hours drunken misadventures. One night, she accidentally took someone else's keys thinking they were hers. They happened to belong to the manager of Mudhoney. Mia nearly got in a fistfight with him when he demanded she return his keys. Another night, out drinking with her buddy Maria, the police suggested the two walk home and sleep it off. In response, Mia dropped her pants and simultaneously mooned and gave the middle finger to the officers. It was worrisome not knowing if Mia would wind up in jail or the emergency room during what seemed like nightly outings.

Mia was having trouble, and her new circle of fair-weather party friends were not positive influences. Some people wanted to be seen partying with The Gits' singer. Mia was always broke and appreciated the free drinks, but lately she did not look well. Her hair was dreaded, and she looked increasingly disheveled and broken in spirit and body. She was often sick with a cold or cough, affecting the sound and strength of her voice and her ability to hit the notes. We were concerned. We had work to do and we needed her to be well. We were due to begin recording our second album and we had a show booked headlining the Crocodile Cafe, the trendiest venue in Seattle at the time.

I was also booking another West Coast tour, our third in the space of a year. It seemed that the band's star was rising and we needed to keep up the momentum to be successful. I hated booking tours, but no one else would do it. We'd start on June 12, 1993, in Portland and end in eastern Washington at an all-ages venue in Richland. We would go back to Seattle and have a couple days off and Mia would finish up the vocal recording for the album.

I gathered my contacts from booking clubs and picked up the phone. I knew that a dedicated booking agent could book a better tour and demand more money, but there were only half a dozen decent booking agents in the whole country. We had approached at least four at various times, and they had all refused to help us. Fortunately for us, European bookings came more easily.

It was early spring 1993. I was seated alone at a little artist-run café in Belltown. I was typing the tour dates and calculating the distance between gigs and driving times. We would start in Olympia, then play Portland, Eugene, San Francisco, San Jose, Sacramento, Los Angeles, San Diego, and back up through San Francisco and Portland, ending in Richland, Washington.

I was sitting in a booth trying to calculate the cost of gas for the tour when a small entourage of hipsters sauntered into the café. They weren't locals, and their entry was causing a fuss amongst the servers and bussers on shift that day. At the center of the crew was a woman wrapped in a navy peacoat with a wool scarf wrapped round her throat. She took a seat with her friends.

She was engaged in a conversation with her friends, and I didn't want to interrupt. I would have told her that I was a longtime fan and that I admired her music very much. Joan Jett was one of the first rock stars that I latched onto as a preteen. I had followed her career for years. I saw her get pelted with cans and food items when she opened for the Police at Market Square Arena in Indianapolis when I was fourteen. I recognized her searing green eyes and jet-black Keith Richards hairdo.

I didn't say anything to Jett. I didn't want to bother her while she was eating. It was a random brush with celebrity. I didn't think of the encounter until two years later, when she appeared in my life as my friend and bandmate but then, I saw the encounter as a sign of good luck.

I left the café and made my way across the street to Kinko's. I knew some punks who worked there, ostensibly to make free copies for friends. I made copies of our tour itinerary and three hundred copies of a poster that the artist Jeff Klinesmith had created for an upcoming local show. At Kinko's our punk friend shot me devil horns and murmured approvingly under her breath, "The fuckin' Gits still DIY, still punk rock. You guys never sell out, man." I nodded knowingly at her devil-horned Ozzy salute.

I exited Kinko's wishing The Gits could sell out just enough to cover my rent while on tour. I was going to meet Andy and Matt at the Comet to go over tour dates. I didn't have enough money for the bus back to Capitol Hill. I walked up Boren Avenue, listening to Patti Smith's "Free Money" on my knockoff Panasonic cassette Walkman, fantasizing about how wonderful life would be with just a little cash for a taxi. After paying June rent, I had only $4.35 to my name and there was no food in the fridge. My darker thoughts were taking over my determined mood.

Andy was crafting brilliant riffs and writing songs that were radio-friendly and accessible without sounding too poppy or simplistic. The three of us were writing well together. We were bringing individual ideas into rehearsals and fanning the creative sparks. We decided from the beginning of the band that we would split royalties and band revenue equally, one quarter each. At that point, splitting band revenue was theoretical, because all the money we made went back into the van repairs and the gas tank. The agreement acknowledged each person's individual contributions to the band. We had different abilities and aptitudes that contributed. We each created our own musical parts, but we arranged the songs together. We all represented The Gits in the community, and we all looked around for band opportunities.

We were co-headlining the Crocodile Cafe show, and the house was packed. When Mia missed the sound check, we began to worry. I told myself that she was simply napping and she would come bouncing through the front door any minute. We were due to take the stage at midnight. Five to midnight and Mia was still nowhere to be found. The three of us exchanged not a word as we loaded our gear onto the stage to play. Julian set up the mics to run our sound. He tried to stall a little, but the house manager tapped her watch as a sign that we should start playing.

Andy's mouth was pressed into an angry line. Matt got on the microphone and asked if anyone had seen our singer. I intentionally knocked over my snare drum and dropped to my knees to fix it.

"Just stall," I said to Matt and Andy under my breath. "She has to be here somewhere."

The people standing in front of the stage started to whisper, and some peeled off to get drinks in the other barroom.

"Godammit, Mia!" I hissed under my breath.

Looking irritated, the house manager tapped again. Not good. I sat down behind the drums and adjusted a few things. I counted off the first song, "Slaughter of Bruce," which, fortunately, has an exceptionally long intro vamp before the vocals began. We couldn't play the songs instrumentally. We would have to face the audience and just apologize and leave the stage. Eight bars into the tune, I looked up from the drums to see Mia parting the delighted crowd and clumsily climbing onto the stage. She came in right on cue. She was a wreck, leaning heavily on the mic stand—fucked up, but she was there. "I was workin' in a shithole one day. Some fool came up to me and said, 'You'd make a star with that band.'"

Those were the only words that she got right that night. She repeated lyrics, forgot a verse, knocked over a mic stand, and spilled beer all over the people in the front row. Then she sat on the stage in a heap, mumbling words that had nothing to do with the songs we played.

We'd played about half the set when Andy turned abruptly and switched off his amp. He flipped his Les Paul into its case and left the stage without saying a word. Matt and I were left standing on stage and Mia was in a drunken heap on the side of the stage. It was utter humiliation. I tried not to make eye contact with friends in the crowd. I didn't know if I should apologize to the audience or pretend it didn't happen. Denial serves the function of protecting the ego from cold mean reality—at least for a little while.

To my surprise, the crowd was unperturbed by our failed performance. They weren't booing or leaving the room to get cocktails in the adjacent bar. People were cheering wildly, calling for an encore. "One more! One more!" they yelled. "Come on, one more!"

Mia seemed to come to her senses when she heard the applause. "All right," she said. "Let's go, guys. Let's start playin.' Everybody's here? Where's Andy?" She announced on the mic, "Will Joe Spleen please come to the stage and join The Gits!"

She was unaware that she had already played.

"Mia, we're done," I said. "Let's get outta here. We don't hang in no dumps, remember?" I led Mia past the hipsters and her fan club of admirers. Someone handed her a shot of tequila. "That was so awesome, Mia. It was great when you guys just left the stage like that! Like, fuck you, Seattle . . . so great!"

The audience wanted to join in the joke, as if it were all some kind of perverse punk rock act. They *wanted* to see Mia get fucked up and stumble around on stage. On-stage drinking had become a side show for the audience. Admittedly, we had drinking songs and a song called "Drunks." There were many drinking references in the lyrics, yet on stage we were all business. We toasted the audience during our shows, and, though people bought shots for us often—whiskey and tequila—we drank very little onstage, sometimes not at all. Drinking did not make us sound better. When the band was formed only one of us was old enough to legally drink. The novelty of drinking was exciting when we were twenty years old. At twenty-six years old, it's fair to say that each of us had experienced unwelcome interactions with the demon alcohol. Now there was a small group of devotees in our ever-growing fan base that delighted in seeing how trashed Mia would get on stage. People would ply her with drinks, and the other three of us to a lesser extent. It had become part of the show. I hadn't noticed before and I hated it.

The phone rang. "We need to have a meeting," said Andy. "We can't do this anymore. Mia's too sick to continue."

I decided to go by Mia's new place and check in. In addition to losing Stefanie and breaking up with her boyfriend, she had also been forced to move when the landlord kicked us out of the Rathouse to sell the house. Julian, Carla, and Mia rented a new, smaller house on the south edge of Seattle. I went up to Mia's bedroom. I heard her strumming a guitar with the TV on, *The Golden Girls*. It was the only time she seemed to laugh anymore. I knocked a couple times, softly.

"Come in," she crowed.

I walked in, smiling awkwardly.

"Hey, Steve. How ya doin'? You must feel terrible about the breakup," she said from the couch. (What breakup?)

"I mean, I do feel terrible about that, but . . . you know, mostly about Stefanie," I thrust my hands into my pockets.

"Me too," she replied.

She was nursing a can of beer. She didn't look well.

Patting the cushion beside her, she said, "Come sit. Steve, I been trying to put the pieces together and I just can't seem to make it work. It's all shaky and I feel like it's falling apart at the seams."

There was a wooden model of a Conestoga Wagon in broken pieces on the floor at her feet. It was a realistic scale model with little wooden wheels and a canvas cover. One of the wheels was missing, and Mia was trying to replace it with a top from a round oatmeal box. She stared at the thing, yet her gaze went miles beyond.

I plopped down on the floor across from her. Sighing, I said, "The show at the Crocodile was pretty bad. I mean, I played shitty too."

She shrugged and set the guitar in the corner of the couch. "Hey, man, it was just a bad night. We still crush every other band around here."

I stared at the four old ladies on the TV. They were making a fuss about cheesecake.

"They love cheesecake, and they always pull out the cheesecake when it's time for a talk.

"Do you want a beer, Stephen? It will have to do. No cheesecake."

I hate cheesecake.

"I don't know about that, Mia. We sucked pretty bad. Do you remember the show at all?"

She failed to reply. The shame on her face said it all. I wished I had brought a cheesecake.

She pulled on a pint bottle of Campbell & Cooper's finest Canadian whiskey blend, then handed it to me. I drank the cheap liquor, and it tasted surprisingly decent.

Handing the bottle back to her, I said, "Remember, we still gotta record in the studio next week. Maybe you should rest your voice and not drink so much."

Mia hugged me, squeezed me. "You and me together—we're gonna make it outta this dump and make something of ourselves." She spoke in an accent that was part Mae West and part Marlon Brando. "And don't give up. You know I ain't givin' up shit . . . 'cept for that crazy motherfuckin' boyfriend. See you at practice tomorrow, Esteban."

If she were capable of quitting drinking, Mia would have taken a cue from the terrible performance at the Crocodile. It was as if she didn't remember any of it. I worried that she would not be able to quit drinking. Drinking was a part of the beginning of The Gits, and it would be the undoing.

"Be strong like bull for revolution, Zapata!" I flexed my arms and she laughed. "I will see you at practice tomorrow, Mia."

Matt, Andy, and I met in our freezing practice space and decided that the band could not continue unless Mia got help. She was just too sick from the drink. No one felt like playing music that night, so we went our separate ways deep in thought. We will tell her at rehearsal tomorrow. I felt ill as I walked away from the meeting. What would I say? I knew that it was the right call, but I hated the thought of putting her on the spot.

Mia showed up on time to practice the following day, but I could smell the liquor oozing from her pores. She was trying ridiculously hard to be cheerful and to keep it together, but it was a front. Her hand trembled as she rummaged through her bag looking for her lyric book and microphone.

Andy, with characteristic bluntness, said something along these lines: "Mia, we've decided to take a break from playing. We can't go on like this. The drinking is too much. It's not helping you and it's hurting the band. We are gonna end the band unless you can quit drinking before the tour. We are worried about you, and we are gonna stop everything so you can get help. It's not a punishment. You are more important than the band."

Dumb, I just nodded. Anything I said would make it worse. Mia knew she was on thin ice. She was well educated about alcohol. She had attended rehab a few years earlier at the behest of her father. She knew about the night terrors, the shakes, the nausea, the dehydration, the depression, and the anxiety that would ensue if she quit cold turkey. There would be a few days of physical and psychiatric torment, followed by weeks and months of mood swings and anxiety.

We played in bars all the time—not the ideal setting for someone trying to quit drinking. The rock career would have to be abandoned. There was just too much temptation in that scene. It must have hurt Andy deeply to have to break the news to Mia. He is an empathetic man, and her pain hurt him. Andy was the only person who might get through to her. I was never more grateful for his honest, direct communication than I was at that moment.

Mia knew that we were sincere and that she was loved, but a tear slipped from an eye and slid down her cheek. She wiped it with the sleeve of her leather bomber jacket, as if to spare us her sadness.

We tried to play a couple songs, but Mia couldn't hold it in anymore. She looked down at the filthy carpet and wept. The sadness in the room was palpable, but so was the love.

Mia would have to use whatever skills she remembered from rehab to make it. It was obvious that her (ex-)boyfriend Robert would be no help and she finalized the split. She would have to distance herself from friends who drank to excess, which seemed like every person in her life, except Andy.

Andy hadn't had a drink for years. Even during the six weeks we toured through Europe, Andy didn't drink. He was routinely offered some of the finest beers in the world, and he didn't drink. He did not drink at the dozens of after-show parties in Seattle, San Francisco, and L.A. He was so nonchalant about it that I'd hardly noticed. Mia wouldn't be doing it alone. I declared that I would also remain sober on the coming tour.

Topless! C. 1991, eastern Berlin. From the author's archive. Photographer: Unknown

27

SECOND SKIN

Next day Mia showed up at rehearsal and appeared sober. I didn't expect her to show up.

While we hammered out a set list of new songs for the still-tentative West Coast tour, she was hunched over her notebook, working on lyrics. We played through some songs, then we launched into our cover of "A Change Is Gonna Come." Mia heard us play the intro and she sprang to her feet, tossed off her winter coat, and grabbed the mic like it was a fleeing soul. I held back the 6/8 beat to keep the drums in the pocket, and Andy transposed the guitar part to frame Mia's phrasing like a jazz accompanist. Mia's voice soared over the top. She had been living this song her whole life. "It's been a long / Been a long time comin,' / but I know change is gonna come . . . "

Mia put her whole heart into the cover song, which was originally by Sam Cooke and popularized by Otis Redding. The distorted crush of the guitar and bass and the crack of the snare drum lifted her up. The three of us provided her the wings. Mia could get sober and make this work. She had us and she had the music.

Mia and friend, c. 1992. Photographer unknown, from author's archive.

Without a pause, Andy went into the intro to "Precious Blood," the introspective ballad that Mia wrote with Andy, the same song that was on our first single. Then came "Beauty of the Rose," "Guilt," "Bob," "Drinking Song," "Kings and Queens," "Seaweed," "Social Love," "Cut My Skin," "It Makes Me Human," and, finally, "It All Dies Anyway." Mia never lost her resolve after that practice. She was determined to kick drinking, to shape up, and get on with the task at hand, The Gits.

As a band, we believed that our contributions were equally important but that we each had unique skills that we brought to The Gits. It made sense to evenly divide up the revenue from the band. U2, REM, Queen, Radiohead, Coldplay, and the Doors were known to split their royalties evenly. A Stanford study showed that bands who share equally are measurably more successful than those that do not. It seemed intuitive but is not customary practice. It was more common for one or two members to take the lion's share of royalties. That can amount to hundreds of times more earnings for one or two members of the group, despite the shared labor required to produce and market a song. It didn't matter if a band toured together for decades or played once a year, there would need to be in place a careful set of mathematical equations to figure a percentage to pay each member. Accounting could become so complicated that bands neglected the royalties or simply broke up. No wonder that fights among band members over money are so commonplace.

I took solace knowing that I wasn't the only one suffering money woes. Mia and Andy were also struggling to pay the bills, while putting 100% of their effort into the work of the band. (Matt's brewery job provided him some measure of stability.) I decided to completely refrain from drinking around Mia in support. That would certainly reduce my consumption and I could save money, I told myself.

We spent a week recording the second album, starting with the instrumentals. Matt, Andy, and I recorded thirteen songs without vocals. With the basic tracks recorded, Mia could take her time recording the vocals while singing along to the finished instrumental versions of the songs. Her writing process was delayed because she was still editing lyrics for songs that we had been playing for a year. By having extra time, Mia would feel less pressure and perform better.

She was clearly cutting back on her drinking but, like me, she was unable to piece together more than a couple of sober days. In the studio she sat with her head an inch from the page of her notebook. She was still working on lyrics. She scribbled notes in the margins and crossed out whole sections and replaced them with a word or two. When it was left to Mia to record her parts, she sang through three or four songs quite well, then started losing her voice. She put too much into those songs, and by the end of the first day of recording she had blown out her vocal cords. After several attempts at singing "A Change Is Gonna Come," Mia's voice was shot. Her words sounded raspy and so strained and gravelly that we decided to call it quits until she recovered.

A few days prior to the start of the upcoming tour, we again called a band meeting. We decided to proceed with the three-week tour. We would have two days off in Seattle before the next tour with Dead Moon in Europe. The plan was for Mia to return to the studio to finish her vocal track, hopefully well-rehearsed from playing the sixteen dates on the West Coast tour. We gambled that Mia's voice would be stronger after performing every night.

Just after leaving the studio, we got news that L7 and 7 Year Bitch had decided to play a pro-choice tour and wanted The Gits to join them on the road. Rock for Choice was an organization created by L7's bass player, Jennifer Finch, to counter the increased activities of the anti-abortion movement. It was called the Rock for Choice tour, though we thought of it as "the anti-pope tour." We would be playing the same cities where the Pope would be speaking on his American tour. All told, it would be three months of touring. We would have to quit our jobs and either sublet or give up our places. I believed that if we worked hard enough, we could build a war chest of show revenue and, at the end of tour, split up money.

When I showed up at the meeting place the morning we were to leave for the tour, Mia was already waiting. Her ratty blonde dreadlocks were gone. She had cropped her hair short and dyed it black. Red highlights glistened in the morning sun.

"Hair looks good, Mia," I said.

Mia ran her fingers through her still-wet hair. "Yeah, man. It's too hot. Had to lose the white-boy dreads. I just put my head upside down and chopped it off, then I dipped my head in a bucket filled with black hair dye. Done. No fuss, no muss."

She was a little shaky but sober, ready to begin a new life and to forge a tighter, healthier Gits. We loaded up the truck and hit the road for the first stop: Portland, Oregon.

Mia on stage, June 1993. Photo by and courtesy of Ed Goralnick.

Al's Bar, downtown Los Angeles. Photographer unknown.

LOSER BABY

28

We played on the floor—no elevated stage and face to face with the audience, just how we liked it. We played as well as ever. Mia was in top form already. I could tell she was anxious and uncomfortable. She hardly addressed the audience and simply concentrated on singing. I wished this could have been the vocal recordings in the studio a week before. Her throat was clear, and she had regained the power in her voice. At the end of the set some teenage fans lined up for autographs. It was unnerving, yet we complied without a complaint. The emcee at the show gave me a live recording of the set. Ten years later, I would discover the tape in a box while moving house in Seattle.

We left for a show in San Francisco right after we played. There, we played at a tiny spot on Valencia Steet with J Church and the Flesh Eaters. A guy named Fat Mike excitedly introduced himself to us after we played. He claimed to be starting a record label and wanted The Gits to be his premier release. His band, NOFX, was a very popular punk band that toured the U.S. and Europe frequently. We thanked him for considering The Gits to be on his label and promised we would get back to him. We never did, and his label turned out to be wildly successful.

Mia was alert and sober at the end of the night. A bartender at a hole in the wall at 16th and Albion Street invited Mia to play an after-hours show at his bar, the Albion. Mia had been privately working on her solo set, and she accepted the gig—so she could practice, she said.

After playing a sold-out show at the Covered Wagon with The Gits, Mia slipped out to sing at the other bar. We joined her an hour later, and for the first time I was able to sit in the audience and relax while Mia performed solo. Andy accompanied Mia on a clean guitar through a small amp.

There was a tiny theater at the back of the room for unplugged performances. There was seating for as few as twenty rocking theater seats. She played acoustic versions of Gits songs such as "Precious Blood," "It All Dies Anyway," "Cut My Skin," and "It Makes Me Human," to name a few. The titles of the songs indicate the introspective, shadow side of Mia's personality. Listening to her bluesy vibrato, I was reminded of why I'd dedicated my life to backing this brilliant, slightly broken woman.

It gave me goose bumps to witness Mia perform. The little theater was packed and you could have heard a feather drop when she began to sing "Precious Blood," a song she had written with Andy. "There are these things, I want the most. Usually one step from my reach, but they always stand close enough, to take me to the next drink . . . "

Jimmy, the bartender, who was also the guitarist in the band Strawman, handed Mia $150 after she had exhausted her repertoire of encores. She tried to give the money to Matt.

"That's not band money. That's your money, Mia," Matt said. She shook her head. "No fuckin' way, man. It's band money."

Matt pushed the cash into Mia's cutoff pockets and ran into the men's room.

Obviously tickled, Mia counted the money, then pushed it back into her pocket. She'd left Seattle carrying a single $20 bill, which she had borrowed from a roommate. The next morning we continued down the road to Los Angeles. We rolled into Los Angeles for the third time in twelve months in June of '93. It was blistering hot when I set eyes on the famous Capitol Records building, looking like a massive stack of 45s on white vinyl. My father had worked for Capitol Records—label home of the Beatles—in the '60s. He had stories about the label's famous artists, including Frank Sinatra, the Beach Boys, George Shearing, Julie London, and Lena Horne. But Dad didn't care for the rock music, and he lost his job as America's popular music grew hair long and got dirty.

Our tour manager, driver, and roadie Mikey Nichols fired up his Boy Scout camping stove on the side of the street to boil water for Top Ramen noodles. I noticed brown cockroaches scurrying about the gutter. Appetizing! They reminded me of that Steve McQueen movie *Papillon*, where he is banished to a prison colony in French Guiana and has to eat cockroaches in solitary confinement to survive.

“Maybe today’s a good day to fast,” I said to no one. “Mia, you wanna take a little stroll to the Capitol Records building?” It was an excuse to walk around, as the Capitol Records building was miles away. In L.A., when asking directions, any place is just a few blocks away, yet is often miles.

Mia shrugged. “Sure.” She was always up for an adventure. Mia and I had made a game of visiting Seattle’s seediest, toughest dive bars. Mia could get along with just about anybody, so she was a great partner for urban adventures.

While the others enjoyed the ramen, Mia and I took a stroll. Al’s Bar sat in the dead heart of an urban ghost town, at the edge of Los Angeles’s iconic Skid Row. Outside the bar it felt like a set for some zombie B movie. Garden hoses used as urine aqueducts snaked out of broken windows of the abandoned buildings. We made sure to walk down the center of the deserted streets, which were strewn with filth. Homeless people shuffled about the tent homes and shanties that lined the streets. Those who didn’t sleep in the makeshift shelters on the sidewalks slept alongside giant rats in the irrigation service tunnels they had breached. Everywhere we looked, we saw shopping carts full of personal belongings. It reeked of urine and burning rubber. Some cursed and sparred with invisible demons; others defecated or masturbated in plain sight. Crack was available in $5, $10, or $20 rocks. Toothless prostitutes signaled for johns who cruised by in Chevy Impalas and Lincoln Continentals, shopping for human attention in the era of AIDS.

When darkness fell, the zombies appeared, wearing overcoats and layered puffy jackets, in spite of the summer heat, better days hidden under leathery skin. They moved about erratically, spastically, searching for something to subjugate or consume, anything. Fires burned in oil barrels, giving the scene an end-of-days feel.

An emaciated woman wearing a FIFA soccer outfit of a child created her personal studio inside a portapotty. There was a dead Rottweiler next to a baby stroller filled with old computer parts. A man played an out-of-tune cello remarkably well seated on a bucket. His ragged homeless entourage shuffled in place and nodded blissfully to the music and Thorazine.

“You gotta go through hell if you wanna get to heaven,” said Mia. “Steve Miller Band, right?” I asked.

“Yeah, man.”

“Think he’s from Tacoma.”

This was a containment zone for the have-nots—and the site was shocking. The poor, mentally ill, addicted, and dismembered souls could disappear, be forgotten, and die, away from the rest of us. Across town, the deluded haves in the Hollywood Hills occupied a containment zone for the flinching Hollywood movie heirs. Would they survive even a single night on Skid Row?

Our evening stroll had become a nightmare tour of social ills. It is brutal to be up close and personal with such suffering, while the respectable and polite society simply looks away. Punk rock straddled the fence, allied firmly on the side of underdog. These were our people too.

The smell was overwhelming, and we were lost.

"Let's get the hell outta here," said Mia. "I don't hang in no dumps."

"*Vamanos,*" I said.

We wandered among the old warehouses and burning trash cans until we thought we recognized the area. San Julian and over to Fourth Street, we came to what we thought was Al's bar, but it didn't seem like the right place. A sign on the door read simply, "*Hoy, Quinceañera.*" I explained that a *quinceañera* is like a bat mitzva for Mexican girls. Mia looked confused. We heard Mexican music blasting inside: reggaeton and cumbias. We asked a homeless man in a three-piece suit for directions to Al's Bar. He told us he didn't know no Al, but we were standing in front of a bar. This must be it.

The *quinceañera* party was raging inside. Teens and drunken adults were swinging a pool cue at a Pancho Villa piñata hanging above the tiny stage. Everyone hooted and whistled as a blindfolded fifteen-year-old girl dressed to the nines whacked away at the piñata. Every time she swatted it, the cowboy-suited crowd yelled, "*¡Viva Zapata!*" Whack! "*¡Viva la revolución!*" Whack!

Eventually the *quinceañeristas* filed out of the bar and dispersed to big, beautifully detailed pickup trucks with oversized tires. Some had eight wheels in back and chrome semi-truck horns on the roof. One of these super-trucks, perhaps belonging to the birthday girl's father, played "La Cucaracha" through its horns, and the convoy roared off in the direction of Skid Row.

Somebody dropped a Patsy Cline record on the old jukebox, signaling the surrender of the bar to the outsiders. Mia and I walked in. The place was a mess. A young woman wearing a Bikini Kill T-shirt ran out from behind the bar, where she was collecting a string of brick-red raffle tickets from the barkeep. Those tickets were hard currency for thirsty bands.

Al's Bar was on the ground floor of a decrepit, low-rent apartment building. There was no marquee out front, not even a sign, just a heavy red door that led into a small, low-ceilinged barroom with twelve barstools, a single pool table, disgusting toilets, and a jukebox full of 45s. Next to the barroom was an even smaller band room with a slightly higher ceiling, but there were no tables or chairs to speak of. The room was empty except for a tiny stage, a four-inch drum riser, and an old pool table. There was space for an audience of about sixty people, which was probably for the best because the sound system was shit. There was no ventilation to speak of, and it got so hot and muggy that condensation dripped from the ceiling, giving the room the feel of a sweltering rainforest.

"Hi, I'm Toast from Paper Tulips," said the woman. "I booked you guys. Thanks for coming down from Seattle. This is so awesome! Do you want some drink tickets?" Pointing to the stage, she said, "Something died under there, so it sorta stinks, but don't sweat it. The sound guy should be here by the time the show starts. Oh, and don't talk to the bartender 'cause he hates bands. I'll get your beers for you."

I reached out a hand to shake, but she playfully brushed it aside and gave me a warm hug. "I love your music, man. You're so awesome! I also booked you a show tomorrow night in Glendale. It's really close. Only about two hours without traffic."

I wondered how long it took with traffic.

"It's a bowling alley. We convinced 'em to do a show in their karaoke bar. It's totally rad. Awesome sound! You're playing with Pop Defect, Catherine Wheel, and my band, Paper Tulips. You guys will play first of four bands. It's gonna be totally rad!"

"Awesome," I said as she handed me the drink tickets.

We had some time to kill before the show, so I put some quarters into the slot on the pool table, brushed Mexican candies off the green velvet, and racked the balls. I invited Matt to play. He nodded and lit a cigarette. I bummed one.

Crack! Matt smacked the cue ball into the triangulated mass of balls with such force that it caused the cueball to skip off the table, bounce on the floor, and roll into the jukebox. Matt surrendered the lone sticky warped cue stick to me. I scratched, then Matt took over and I didn't get the opportunity to take a second shot. Matt proceeded to sink every solid and finally the eight ball. Mia then stepped up to challenge the winner.

Andy chatted with someone at the bar while Mikey Nichols changed the strings on his guitar. We all knew that this was going to be one of those ill-attended, shitty shows that we'd grown accustomed to playing. We just had to sit and wait for people to trickle in, then play fourteen songs, then break down. We would try to sell a T-shirt or two, then collect our forty bucks, load the van, and find a place to crash.

We waited a lot while on tour. We waited in the van en route to the shows. We waited to load in our gear. We waited to soundcheck—if we even had a soundcheck. We waited to play our set. We waited for the other bands to play. We waited to get paid—if we got paid. Since time immemorial, musicians have been hurrying up to wait. It's part of the job.

The bar was almost totally empty when the opening act walked up to the stage. A lanky blond kid barely twenty-one years old carried an old acoustic guitar with a broken string. He was followed by a girlfriend, who carried an old boombox. She placed it at the foot of the stage and hit play. A drumbeat dribbled out of the tape machine. He wore a floppy leather hat, its brim low, making him look like a hippie throwback with a lost-baby face. I loved his stars-and-stripes bell-bottom pants.

While he played, Toast walked up to me and leaned into my ear, saying, "He's cool. He lives upstairs in a room . . . sorta. We let him open the shows sometimes. He cleans up and stuff." I got the impression that she was trying to say that he wasn't quite right in the head.

As he played his five-string guitar, he rarely looked up. No one watched the kid. Except Mia. She was drawn to the stage.

Waving me over, she said, "I like this guy, he's . . . cool. He's got something going on, and he's funny."

After giving him a listen, I agreed with her. There was something about him. He had the appearance and stage presence of an awkward teenager, but he was compelling.

Matt pocketed the eight ball, then asked, "Who's next?"

Over my shoulder, I noticed another band loading gear through the beat-up front doors. It wasn't uncommon for us to be on a bill with three or four other bands. A disheveled fellow in a dirty, oversized T-shirt and Coke-bottle eyeglasses slipping from his nose extended a hand. It was Bob Lee, the original Gits drummer. I hadn't seen him since Mia, Matt, and Andy had unceremoniously asked him to leave the Sniveling Little Rat-faced Gits in 1986 and asked me to join.

When they asked him to leave, I imagined him saying something like, "I'll show you!" Then he disappeared from the college thereafter, not to reappear until tonight. He *must* have borne me some ill will.

"Hey, Steve! Good to see you!" he said, his voice quivering. He was taller than I remembered. "One of my bands, the Lazy Cowgirls, is playing with you guys tonight. My other band, Clawhammer, just signed a contract with Interscope Records. Snoop Dogg is on our label."

"Damn," I said, lifting an eyebrow.

"And I'm working with Mike Watt of the Minutemen on his solo record and with Wayne Kramer of MC5 and with Toast in Paper Tulips." He said it all in one breath.

"Impressive," was all I could muster. These were all very good bands. How had he become so prolific?

Andy appeared behind Bob and tapped his shoulder. Arms outstretched with palms up and head slightly tilted, Andy offered Bob a generous embrace. Bob blushed, then welcomed Andy to his adopted hometown.

"When I left Yellow Springs in '86, I moved to L.A. and started practicing," Bob explained.

I turned around to find Mia, I saw that she was speaking with the singer we'd just seen perform; his name was Beck, and his single "Loser" was about to break. I was glad Mia wasn't drinking, but before I could say hi, Toast signaled to me to let me know that it was time for us to play. I said goodbye to Bob and hurried to set up my drums on the stage.

The sound guy got mad about something and went home, and Toast had to run sound, which was for the best. The smell on the stage was awful. I guessed that the sound guy who had fled the scene had stashed a body under the drum riser. It wasn't impossible.

Like squatters and train-hobos, band members often left little messages for other bands in odd places within clubs. On a column that stood dead center on the stage, someone had written in Sharpie, "NO JUMPING!" and "WE LOVE THE GITS, Love Stefanie." That second one put a knot in my throat. A little message from beyond.

When Mia introduced the set, she added a dedication, "This song is dedicated to our good friend Stefanie, who died just one year ago today . . . and to all those who loved her."

I struck my twenty-inch Zildjian K Heavy crash cymbal with such force that the metal cracked. The crash sent the band headlong into the intro of "Absynthe." Off to the races.

Valerie and Selene, who were in town for a press junket and for meetings with their new record company, strolled into the bar with a few friends, including their new guitarist, Rosian, and their manager, Stacy Slater. Minutemen's bassist, Mike Watt, stood with Bob Lee. They stood watching from the side of the stage, smiling up at us with something like pride, their eyes filled with tears. It was good to see familiar faces, but I also felt a pang of sadness and longing. I was still in love with Valerie.

Members of some notable bands showed up too. Jennifer Finch, bassist for L7, Bobby Schayer, who was drumming for Bad Religion, and Beck, who would be notable in six months.

We bashed out "Seaweed," "A," "Ain't Got No Right," "Precious Blood," and "Sign of the Crab," all without so much as a sip of water between songs. The heat was nearly unbearable, and the sound quality on the stage was terrible, but we could play by muscle memory at that point. We ripped through fourteen songs, back to back, closing with "Second Skin," the closest thing we had to a hit.

Mia's voice was brilliant. She was on day twelve of her sobriety, and I could see in her eye a grit born of suffering and determination. We sounded tight. The songs were mature and more complex than they seemed, but we played with unbridled energy and excitement. We had command of the dynamics and a feel for the diverse styles we wrote into the tunes. We were too good to remain ignored for long. The pace of our gigs and band commitments was intensifying. On stage, we delivered in spades. We commanded the stage and often bands that followed us would pale in comparison. We were ready to take the world by storm.

Did we stand at the edge of our dream of a sustainable music career?

As we were toweling off after the set, Selene asked if we wanted to crash on the floor of their room at the Hyatt Regency on Sunset Boulevard. Lemmy from Motörhead was staying there, after all! After a brief band meeting, we politely declined her offer.

We hung out with Jennifer Finch for while after we played, and she invited us over for a nightcap. She had air conditioning! The four of us crashed with Jennifer on her big waterbed, along with Lisa Nardoni of Black Angels Death Song and a couple of her friends. Eight people surfing the waves of the California king waterbed.

Matt asked Jennifer if she was in a band or something.

"No, I just collect L7 shit and put it all over my house because I'm a super fan," she replied.

"What?" asked Matt, oblivious. That wasn't the first time that Matt had put his foot in his mouth. He made the same honest mistake when members of Metallica came to see us at a small San Francisco club called the Bottom of the Hill. He simply didn't know anything about Metallica and certainly not what they looked like.

To her credit, Jennifer wasn't fazed. "Yeah, L7. We just got back from Brazil on a tour with a band from up in your parts. I think they're called Nirvana or something?"

"Oh yeah, we know those guys pretty good," Mia added.

Humor was at the core of just about everything we did. We all learned well how to take good-natured ribbings from one another, and no one was immune to becoming the butt of a joke. Laughing made even the most preposterously demoralizing gig tolerable. We would have been lost without the ability to mock ourselves and make fun of anything and everything.

Mia rolls a spliff in Bern, Switzerland, c. 1991. Photo by author.

MOSS BAY

29

JABBERJAW

The next of our three gigs in greater Los Angeles was at a place called Jabberjaw in the Arlington Heights neighborhood. It was a dirty, single-story stucco building typical of Southern California urban sprawl. It reminded me of a storefront church or an AA meeting space. No frills. It had a low ceiling, a six-inch riser for a stage, and no air conditioning. From the stage, if you jumped just a little bit or lifted your arms above your head, you'd hit the ceiling. And the show started at 3:00 in the afternoon. Another weird gig to add to The Gits' résumé of weird gigs.

Over the years, we had rehearsed so much and knew our songs so well that we could play a set without cues from one another. We didn't need to hear each other on stage, which came in handy when we encountered a club's crappy sound system. It wasn't fun to play that way, but we figured that when we started playing bigger clubs we would have access to much better sound systems. We were just paying our dues, but none of us paid as dearly as Mia did. The feedback that screeched through the

Andy and Mia overheated at Jabberjaw, Los Angeles, June 1993. Still image from fan-made live performance video.

stage monitors was terrible. It is a high-end squeal emitted from the stage monitors when the sound coming from the amplifiers is too hot for the speaker's ability to filter it. The feedback is so piercing that it can make ear drums spam and cause ringing, tinnitus, and pain. It can even cause permanent damage. The monitors are set up directly in front of the singer at center stage, so Mia got the worst of it.

When we were loading in, two young women were leaning against the wall by the side door. Mia was helping me with the drums, per her custom.

"Are you a riot grrrl?" one of the leaners asked Mia as we brushed by carrying my cymbals.

"What's that?" Turning to me, she said, "But I tell you one thing—I ain't no girl, that's for sure."

I shrugged. I'd heard someone mention something about this being a riot grrrl show, but I had no idea what the term meant. We were late, so we didn't bother to engage with the riot grrrl inquisitors.

A couple hundred kids were queued up around the block, waiting to get into Jabberjaw in the working-class Latino barrio. They were mostly in their teens and early twenties, and they stood out like sex workers at Disneyland. Neighborhood guys in low-riders and Chevy Broncos slowed down to gawk at the locos standing in the sun with their green hair and strange clothes. It could have been a casting call for a sequel to *Sixteen Candles*.

We were playing with a band from Olympia called Bratmobile. For me, their name evoked memories of the old family station wagon: "Come on, you little wankers. Everybody get in the Bratmobile. It's time for school!" The riot grrrl bands had very particular branding, and it wasn't hard to see a pattern: Huggy Bear, Potty Mouth, Heavens to Betsy, Bratmobile, and Bikini Kill, who were the queen bees of the scene. They were mostly nerdy, middle-class white girls and women, the daughters—and occasionally sons—of professors from Evergreen State University in Olympia. Local teens who were bored into action growing up in the quaint state capital, many had no musical training apart from listening to records and attending shows. The independent record labels K Records, Kill Rock Stars, and Chainsaw Records released 7-inch records and albums by many riot grrrl bands. The raw, garage-rock brashness of the sound echoed early English punk bands like the Slits and X-Ray Spex, and it struck a nerve with young women. The new-wave voice of feminism was spreading as the music was in demand worldwide. Bikini Kill, Bratmobile, Team Dresch, and Sleater-Kinney records could be found in stores alongside those of the "Big 5" Seattle boy bands: Soundgarden, Nirvana, Pearl Jam, Alice in Chains, and Screaming Trees.

Several of the women who performed in the bands were also prolific writers. Their song lyrics were expounded in band manifestos or in self-published zines. Articles about the riot grrrls appeared in respected radical feminist publications like *Bust*,

Bitch, and *Ms.* They challenged the sexism, homophobia, transphobia, and toxic masculinity that lurked around the edges of the punk-music scene. The lyrics were broad social indictments, or unapologetically violent words designed to provoke confrontation and direct action. Unlike their mother's brand of feminism, riot grrrl bands respected very few boundaries of convention and parodied macho hubris and toxic masculinity in rock by becoming caricatures of themselves. Instead of songs about polite empowerment, Bratmobile's songs expressed themes of same-sex fucking, bondage, dominance, and sadomasochism—perhaps inspired by X-Ray Spex's "Oh Bondage! Up Yours!" Punk rock has a way of galvanizing youth into grassroots action. The riot grrrl swell was one of the catalysts of contemporary feminist movements like Me Too. It injected accountability for poor behavior into the worldwide punk scene and opened doors for young women to play instruments and form bands. They revived the energy and feminist ire of the punk movement of the late '70s with a radical mandate: to dismantle and subvert sexism, racism, and trans- and homophobia in the written word from the stage. They held their mothers' feminism of the '70s and '80s in high regard, while exalting no one as the new generation of idols and ideologues.

The riot grrrls found a voice in the freedom of expression that punk rock afforded. They picked up instruments or found objects and bashed out songs, whether they had music training or not. The riot grrrl anti-fashion statement mixed themes of violence with cutesy imagery (think Hello Kitty with a switchblade and a hankering to cut your face). The look was thrift-store retro '50s housewife, complete with horn-rimmed glasses and Jackie O-style pillbox hats—evil Lolita meets tomboy temptress, if you will (or won't). They carried lined notebooks and children's lunchboxes with *Brady Bunch* or *Munsters* designs. The fashion was unflattering and self-deprecating yet could be portrayed as a pedophile's wet dream turned black nightmare—a booby trap, if you will.

Mia was not a riot grrl but I enjoyed seeing the next wave of punk bands embrace politics in their music. The Gits, as a band, was political by action, not by declaration. I sometimes felt that espousing a unified political stance for The Gits was warranted. But the older I got, the more I recognized nuance and hypocrisy in any political affiliation. The four of us rarely entirely agreed on a political stance. For me, playing punk rock was in and of itself a political stance. I stand by that today.

There were plenty of riot grrrls and boys in the crowd when we took the stage at Jabberjaw. We began the show by blasting out the bass and drum intro of "Absynthe." A few kids in the audience moved toward the stage and jerked their bodies to the music. Others simply sat on the edge of the stage and wrote in their notebooks or traded Garbage Pail Kids cards with other overage adolescents. Were they trying to insult us?

They were obviously confused by the three sweaty men in combat boots, cutoff T-shirts, and tattoos backing the "older woman" (all of twenty-seven) in cutoff jeans and a stained black T-shirt.

It was a tough crowd, but Mia did everything she could to engage the kids. She spat out the words while looking people straight in the eyes. Slowly but surely, the kids began shifting their weight from left to right in time with the music. Then they swung their arms. By the fourth song, Mia had them rattling their lunchboxes and dancing.

She turned to me during an instrumental section of a song, and with her left hand she made little dancing people by wiggling her fingers in the palm of her right hand. Then she made a fist and crushed it into her palm. It was her way to mime that she planned on converting the naysayers. The audience was helpless against Mia's powers of vocal persuasion and the music of the mighty Gits. When we paused for a moment so I could fix my broken bass-drum pedal, I recognized the fire-red hair of the singer of Bratmobile, Allison Wolfe, and her identical twin sister, Elizabeth. They stood stage left, rapt, watching Mia's every move. When Allison clapped, the tough crowd followed suit. With Allison's help, we soon won over another audience.

In the back of the house, I saw a tall guy with long, curly hair. He wore a black silk Armani jacket, which seemed like a form of self-torture in that unbearable heat. He made the L7 sign with his thumbs and forefingers, like an old-fashioned movie director framing a shot. He looked out of place, like somebody's dad. But then I suppose, we did too in that crowd.

When we finished playing, the reception was anything but riotous. I'd describe it as "polite." Allison stared at Mia. I don't know if she was impatient or awestruck, but when Bratmobile took the stage they were ferocious. Mia wasn't an easy act to follow—none of us were—but Bratmobile were good.

The last tour. Al's Bar, Los Angeles, summer 1993. Photographer unknown, from the author's archive.

LET'S DO LUNCH

30

The tall man with the silk Armani jacket approached us after the show. "Tim Sommer, Atlantic Records," he said. "I would like to take you all to lunch tomorrow. Are you busy at 11:25 a.m.?"

Food sounded good, so we accepted his invitation. Matt wrote down the restaurant address on Sunset Boulevard.

We sat at a table with white linens, several sets of silverware, white plates (small, medium, and large), and water and wine glasses. Our waiter's name was Étienne. We were famished, but it wasn't clear who would pick up the tab, so we all ordered the cheapest dishes on the menu. I knew Mia and Andy were flat broke, and I had exactly $26 in my pocket, but that was supposed to last us through the remainder of the tour.

Tim ordered himself an Amstel Light and began with a well-considered explanation of how Atlantic Records could help our music career. "Bands signed to Atlantic can maintain control of their music publishing and the recording process. Atlantic handles the production, manufacture, and distribution of the records, tapes, and CDs.

Steve, Mia, and Andy on stage at the Off Ramp, Seattle, c. 1992.
Photographer unknown, from author's archive.

We put the bands on salaries, and we cover your health insurance, your cash tour support, music gear, transportation, and music lessons if you want."

"That's very nice for the bands on your label. But how does that help us?" asked Matt.

"Well, we'd like—"

"May I be excused?" Mia interrupted; her hand raised.

I smiled at her elementary-school manners. "I'm fresh out of hall passes at the moment, but you may be excused." I handed her a cloth napkin, which she shoved into her bag.

Leaning into my ear, she whispered, "Can I borrow some change for a phone call?"

I handed her the loose change in my pocket, then she scurried outside.

Mia called her dad, who was living in Vancouver. A couple months after this meeting, he shared with me what they said.

"Dad, it's Mia, your daughter."

"Yes, Mia, I know you're my daughter. How are you, darling? Are you in trouble? Are you okay?" he asked.

"I'm in a pickle, Dad. This guy took us to this fancy restaurant in Hollywood for a meetin,' and I don't have any money to pay for my lunch. I can't ask the guys, and I don't want this Mr. Fancypants guy to think I'm a moocher. I think he's from a record company, and I want to be professional. It's very embarrassin.' Can you talk to the waiter and give a credit-card number or somethin'?"

"Don't worry, Mia. That's how they do things in L.A. They wine and dine bands they want to work with. The guy is planning to pay for it, honey. Order whatever you want, and don't worry about it. Just call me later and tell me how the meeting went."

Mia returned to the table looking relieved. She ordered a shrimp cocktail and some cake, and we all enjoyed the first decent meal of the tour. We agreed to stay in touch with Tim.

After that meeting, 7 Year Bitch's manager Stacy Slater referred us to a Beverly Hills lawyer named Rosemary Carroll, who was the ex-wife of the New York author, poet, and musician Jim Carroll, one of Mia's favorite artists of all time. We arranged an impromptu meeting that same day. The ball was rolling fast.

We looked like homeless ragamuffins sitting in the chairs arranged in front of Rosemary's immaculate, modern, Dutch-style hardwood desk in the center of her imposing office. Not a piece of paper cluttered her leather desktop. The place vibrated esteem and power.

Rosemary sat up straight, her hands folded on the desk. A long, respectful silence followed. The conditioned air felt beautiful, and the cucumber in the water was a splendid touch.

"May I get any of you tea, cappuccino, or Perrier?" she asked.

Rosemary's then husband, Danny Goldberg, had signed Nirvana and Hole. He had been part of Patti Smith's team since the '70s, and he had moved from New York to

L.A. to head Atlantic Records. Danny revived the career of Bonnie Raitt, another of Mia's favorite artists.

Goldberg had even worked with Led Zeppelin and Bruce Springsteen. This guy had been on the ground floor during the heyday of American punk in New York City.

But we knew none of these details at the time. We only knew that Rosemary was one of the most influential and important music attorneys in Hollywood. Everyone who knew her told us that she would ensure that we would get the best deal possible from a record company, be it an indie or a major label. We still weren't convinced that one was better than the other. Until we met Rosemary Carroll.

Her platinum-silver, waist-length hair shimmered in the light of the high windows of the office. I have never believed in auras and all that New Age woo-woo crap, but sitting there was a woman with a glimmering aura that radiated integrity, intelligence, importance, and benevolence. (I have only ever seen such an aura on one other occasion—while I was sharing a glass of champagne with Yoko Ono on New Year's Eve 2020 many years later.)

Rosemary spoke first. "Ask yourselves this: what is most important to you as a collective, as a family of four? Do you want to do this for the long term?"

She spoke for quite a while. I was awestruck by her presence, and I have forgotten much of what she said. But I remember her telling us that we should retain the rights to our songs and that we must be well-informed before making any moves.

"Knowledge is power," she told us.

We sat mesmerized before this goddess. We simply nodded and mumbled something like, "Yes, please help us with all of this." There was no discussion among us four Gits. We immediately agreed to partner with Rosemary, to make her our legal counsel.

It was years before I realized the importance of that short meeting, that brush with genius.

We were being courted by the most artist-friendly, progressive, and innovative independent record company in the country. We would have the same legal team as Nirvana, Hole, Patti Smith, Lou Reed, Jim Carroll, Television, Bonnie Raitt, Steve Earle, and Willie Nelson. My God, how did we end up there?!

What was clear to the music-industry professionals was impossible for us to understand from where we stood: The Gits had matured into an incomparably talented and original band fronted by one of the greatest rock singers in the world. Despite our suspicions and our insularity, The Gits could bridge the gap between grunge and riot grrrl. We were on the verge of commercial success at a moment when punk was attracting attention from mainstream labels.

Matt put it this way: "We were good. We just didn't know how good."

This fact wasn't lost on Sommer, Goldberg, or Carroll. They could see that The Gits were capable of writing and performing powerful and relevant music that would stand the test of time. With their assistance and guidance, we would earn creative and commercial success—which up to this point were two mutually exclusive phenomena in the music business.

We assumed our accustomed places in the old van and headed north on I-5 for a few more shows before returning to Seattle on July 4th. No one spoke for hours after our meetings with Carroll and Sommer. I tried not to dwell on the future, even if all signs indicated that unmitigated success lay that way. Just keep doing what you do, and whatever will be will be, I told myself. *Que sera sera.* I supposed the other Gits were having similar thoughts.

"The cream rises to the top—that's what Tim Sommer said at lunch," Andy stated. It had taken a while for us to rise through the muck and noise of the Seattle grunge scene, but it seemed that seven years of arduous work and so many dead-end gigs were finally paying off. Could we really make a living playing music around the world?

"You think we'll meet Patti Smith?" Mia finally asked as we rumbled down I-5. Would Mia be the next Patti Smith?—that was the real question.

As we drove through "the Grapevine," California's reeking meat basket for a fast-food nation of finks, Matt cried out, "Cowschwitz! Windows up!"

We again rolled up the windows, despite the stifling heat. We weren't in the promised land just yet.

Mia sings truth on the last tour in 1993. Photographer unknown, from author's archive.

DEAD MOON
THE GITS
STRANGE FRUIT
FRI 14 MAY
OFF RAMP

ALMOST HOME

31

We arrived in Portland with minutes to spare. We played a show with Sister Double Happiness, featuring Gary Floyd of the Dicks, and Dead Moon. We were scheduled to tour Europe with Dead Moon in just a few months. The opener was Everclear, a band that would achieve double-platinum status within weeks of this gig. After the sold-out show, the other bands showered us with praise. We returned words of praise.

The next morning, July 3rd, we set course eastward, traveling along the Columbia River Gorge to an all-ages show in the Tri-Cities in eastern Washington, the last gig of the tour. We were scheduled to play at a place called the Tri-Cities Hoedown Center. Mia didn't think that the venue hosted real hoedowns (whatever those were), but she was thrilled at the prospect of playing a square-dancing barn. It turned out that the place was a Moose Lodge. The Tri-Cities were a thirty-minute

Dead Moon and The Gits poster. Poster by Jeff Klinesmith.

drive from the Hanford Site, the worst toxic-waste Superfund site in the county at the time. The plutonium for the first atomic bomb was produced there, and nuclear isotopes were released into air and onto the rural farming community to determine the possible outcome of a Soviet bomb dropped on an unsuspecting American population. The logo of a local high school football team, the Richland Bombers, included a mushroom cloud and the symbol for plutonium on the periodic table of elements.

We rolled up to the venue. It housed a basketball court with the hoops cranked horizontally at each end. It was echoey inside, and a band called Sicko was introducing pop-punk to a couple hundred young flannel-waving, irradiated teenagers.

Small rural town shows were often fun because the kids had nothing else to do. No cable TV, no after-school programs, and certainly no Internet. When a band came to town, it was a happening, a phenomenon even, and people came from miles around to attend. It didn't matter if they had heard of a band or knew anything about the music. It was something to do.

The audience ranged in ages from eight to forty-eight. People hovered excitedly around the van as we loaded the gear into the venue. Some kids offered to help carry our gear or to fetch beer or water.

"Come back to my house and party before the show," suggested one fan. "It's only four hours up the road."

Matt politely declined the offer, saying, "Thanks, but maybe next time, dude."

John Book, possibly the only African American man in the Tri-Cities region, had organized the show. He was only nineteen years old, but he was already a prolific music critic who published his own music and arts zine. He was an excellent writer who had written a glowing review of our first album. He greeted us warmly as we loaded in our gear. He was obviously enamored with Mia, and, just as he was about to introduce himself to her, someone announced that it was time for us to take the stage.

Two or three hundred kids were drinking beer, chasing each other with sticks, and hanging from the raised basketball hoops.

"We'd better get started," I said to the other Gits.

Thanks to playing hundreds of shows over seven years, we could take the stage, set up our gear, and start playing in under ten minutes. Still buzzing from our meetings in L.A. and eager to get home to Seattle, we went to work. We decided that we'd stick with our typical fourteen-song, forty-minute set.

As I was preparing to count off the first song, Andy struggled to tune the D string on his guitar. He winced at the ugly harmonics coming from his amp, but eventually his well-used Les Paul rang true. He adjusted the tuning peg flat, sharp. Then, varoom! He strummed a sweet power chord that rattled the hoops and changed the barometric pressure in the hall. Andy adjusted his strap, shifted the weight of the Les Paul forward, and looked stage right at Matt, who nodded. Ready.

Mia turned to Andy and smiled. Then the three of them peeked over their shoulders at me. I nodded, and Mia made the squishing gesture with her hand.

"Let's crush these hicks."

I drove the ride cymbal in the up tempo swing pattern that is the intro to "Absynthe." The song demanded attention from the audience and drew them to the foot of the stage. Matt dropped his walking bass line after eight bars, and then Andy came in with a devastating E minor seventh chord before breaking into a staccato picking to accompany Mia's lyrical indictment of the lying, pretentious posers that made the music business so unpleasant.

A dozen boys in flannels and ripped jeans started a mosh pit, swinging their arms and bumping into each other—rather clumsily. This was a far cry from the hardcore matinees at CBGB, where Andy and Matt had learned to love punk rock in the '80s.

I counted off "Social Love" and played the simultaneous thirty-second note crescendo on snare and floor tom. I held fast to the drumstick in my right hand while Andy and Matt matched the buildup in perfect syncopation. Mia came in singing on cue. "I don't need your social love . . . " Mia made her point in a tight one minute and fifty-six seconds.

Next up was "Beauty of the Rose," one of our newer songs. But Mia was struggling with her mic stand, so I paused. We often played three or four songs in succession, then we took a tiny break to drink water, tune guitars, or adjust a cymbal stand before counting off the next song.

When I looked out from behind the drums, the audience was rushing out the entrance. In fact, everyone was clearing out, even the sound guy. I assumed that the police were raiding the gig. What else is there for a cop working the Tri-Cities to do?

Only John Book, the pioneering punk publisher, remained in the audience.

"What's up?" I shouted out to John where he manned the merch table for the bands. "It's the stupid fireworks show," he yelled back to me.

"But it's only July 3rd."

"I know." He sounded apologetic. "They always do it early."

On stage, we shared eye rolls and head shakes, then I counted off the next song. We played our hearts out to John Book, our benevolent host in the Tri-Cities. It wasn't the first time we'd played for a single fan.

Outside, the locals reveled in the glow of the great fireworks. Dry sage and sulfur clouds collided with the tan-colored nuclear cooling towers, then descended along the great mesa, which housed the semi-secret nuclear facility. The exploding skyrockets were our competition for the audience. Andy tuned up his guitar and signaled to me to count off the next song. "Here's to Your Fuck," "Sign of the Crab," "It All Dies Anyway," "Seaweed," "Guilt Within Your Head," and, finally, "Second Skin."

We played "A Change Is Gonna Come" as an encore to one lucky person. The moment we finished, Andy reached behind his amp and flipped the switch. He patted Matt on the back, then hugged Mia with one arm.

"Nice playing, man," Andy called back to me. "Now let's get the fuck outta here."

"Yeah, I don't hang in no dumps," said Mia.

We accepted an offer and crashed at some kid's house while his parents were away trying to fix their marriage.

We awoke at 7:00 the next morning, and we were on the road by 8:00, feeling an exhaustion born of years of constant work. While we drove home, Mia confided in me that she had always wanted to record a solo album. Well, not exactly solo. Just more acoustic and less loud than The Gits. But she was concerned about what we would think.

"Think they'll be mad?" she asked.

"I don't think so," I said. "It'll only add to what we bring to any label."

"Can you help me?" I nodded. "Hell yeah. I'll help you." She grinned. "Cool, man."

Finally, we approached the three-bedroom house that Mia was renting with Julian and Carla. She spoke again as she gathered her books and things from inside the van. "I don't feel right returnin' to Seattle. I wish we could just keep goin', just the four of us. Just keep drivin' the hell outta Seattle."

"It's only two days, and we will be gone again," I said.

She nodded. "Yeah, you're right. I can do two days. I am ready to finish singing in the studio, finish the album, and get back on the road."

"Exactly, I know," I said.

Matt pulled up in front of Mia's place, and she climbed out of the van carrying her army rucksack and a plastic grocery bag of personal items and a half a burrito from a few nights before in San Diego. Mia had been in top form during every single show. She was mature and commanding on the stage. No dilletante, Mia was a serious musician and song writer. She drew from a range of jazz, blues, and rock influences; she was inspired by Nina Simone, Billie Holiday, Iggy Pop, and Bowie. And through sheer determination she stayed sober the entire tour.

We arrived in Seattle on July 4, 1993. I didn't bother to unpack my bag from the tour because we would be leaving for New York City for the first gig of an East Coast U.S. tour.

We had just enough time for Mia to complete the vocal tracks and redo ones she was unhappy with. On July 7 th we were to fly to New York City. We would be on tour for the better part of the autumn and winter. It was the most definitive plan I had ever had for the future. I would be away from the darkness and rain.

Mia was reliable and present throughout the tour and she had proven her abilities as a performer and musician. She sang with confidence and passion as if all our lives depended on it. Mia had achieved success for all of us. She had overcome alcohol by sheer force of will, and the support of her real friends. Mia led The Gits to the open door of a most promising musical career that, if carefully managed, would maintain our collective and individual careers for a lifetime.

So, it was a success.

I kicked back in a La-Z-Boy recliner I dragged in from the street before leaving on tour and turned on the TV. David Letterman was interviewing Michael Jordan about quitting the NBA after learning his father had been murdered by a stranger at a rest stop in Florida. How horrifying, I thought. If something like that happened to my father, I would at least have my band.

I sat back in the stuffed chair and kicked out the footrest. I was twenty-seven years old, on the cusp of a major record deal and multiple tours, and I had achieved the first major goal of my life—to make a life playing music. I was on top of the world. I crashed and it was the best night of sleep I'd had for years.

WHIRLWIND
EPILOGUE

I awoke one morning after meeting Mia in a park in a dream. We sat on a park bench and chatted casually about our lives. Mia told me she was living in New York, singing jazz standards in underground blues bars and generally staying out of the public eye. I told her that I loved her and missed her, but I understood that she had a new life. We hugged, and I wished her the best, then I woke up. A peacefulness and calm came over me. I put on one of the now out of print Gits records. I turned up the volume on "Absynthe." Then I turned it up a little more, and more. An excited shudder ascended my spine. I wanted to hear it even louder. The windows shook as the chorus of the song slid into the drum solo and back to the chorus. I could barely hear the phone ringing. I reluctantly switched off the amplifier and picked up the phone.

I was sure it was the lady upstairs. I didn't know how she tolerated me, but she did, and I was grateful. I began, "I apologize, I'll turn it down. Just got carried away again . . . " I hung up without a response. By the rotation of the final cut on side one of the album, the volume had inexplicitly increased to near deafening levels once again. The phone rang like before. I shut down the stereo amp and reluctantly answered the phone again.

"Steve, Steve Moriarty?"

It was not the lady upstairs.

"Don't hang up! My name is so and so. Remember? We went to college together at Antioch. I saw your band play . . . uh, it was . . . I mean you were . . . The Gits, with Mia Zapata. I'm a writer and I live in Miami, and I work at a newspaper here, the *Miami Herald*. Well, I know this will sound strange, but I can prove it to you."

We had sat for dozens of interviews for daily papers, fanzines, college radio stations, and filmmakers. I was in graduate school; the band was over, and I was not in the mood to repeat myself. It could be yet another amateur private investigator or another psychic with news from beyond the grave. The sun was shining, and I was enjoying a breakfast of coffee and very loud music. I didn't want to stir the terrible feelings that had been the dictating voice of my life for the past ten years. "Look, um, Steve Moriarty is not here at the moment. Can I take . . . "

The voice on the line interrupted before I could hang up. "Steve, is that you? I have it on good authority that the Miami–Dade County police department have someone . . . a man in custody. A man locked up who, they think, murdered Mia Zapata."

It had been a decade of mental combat with the unknowable past. I would have to relive my dear friend's death once again. Managing the ghosts, the intrusive thoughts, and my own brute rage had been my life's work since then. A kind of compressor/limiter effect switched on in my mind. I could not tolerate the ploy of another attention-seeking sycophant calling with a new set of cockamamie theories about the murder case. I wanted to get back to my rock and roll music.

"They have him in jail. Don't believe me," she said. "I can send you proof. I will fax you a copy of the letter I got from the sheriff. It says it right there. He is being extradited to Washington from Florida. The Seattle district attorney has already been here and interrogated him. I will fax something to you shortly."

"Ok then, I will wait," I replied.

I long ago knew better than to get my hopes up. The rug could no longer be pulled from beneath my feet without due warning. It kept me from expecting a miracle and acting foolish. Mia was gone and nothing would bring her back. Composed, I picked up the phone and called my bandmates.

Before the fax arrived, the journalist's credentials and statement were confirmed by a barrage of calls from other journalists seeking "the first interview" from members of The Gits. Word had gotten out, but after the ten-year private murder investigation had not turned up a real suspect I fantasized about this day, yet I could not allow myself to believe that it had come.

When the prosecutors disembarked their plane in Miami and collected their guns, badges, and luggage from airline officials, their suitcase bore tags indicating the departure airport, Miami International Airport, and serendipitously read, "MIA."

The man was convicted of the murder and sentenced to thirty-six years. He didn't know her, and no one knows why he did it. He died in prison of Covid-19 in 2022.

The music of The Gits can be found on vinyl records and online. I encourage readers to explore the music and find inspiration and courage from Mia's words and our songs.

7/22/89

I found this page on the floor of a club called"Dreamers" in Chicago. They have any bands there so, they can take us. I saw the shitiest bands there, I imagine that's all they could get. I realize that there isn"t going to always be an addience that gives a shit. I saw that night and other nights in other places,..if they haven't heard of you. Oh well, Andy said if they can't understand or get into it we don't want'em. Good ribbens to the ones that live without, within, with harmony.
I'm mainly writting you to lead up to a letter I wrote you long ago, while in Portland. I fell across it and thought you should have it because it still applies.
I stink like a bleeding woman and an unsanitary one. I'm also alone and am carring wieght. Wieght of feeling deserted by friends I thought would always be willing and understanding. My mother told me that friends turn out to be for certain times and it's surprising which ones end up standing near you always. Well Sarah pisses me off and so does Duog. Oh so self absorbed is oh so apart, and do they see it? No. They turn to say things that hold them so "safe", though they wouldn't see it. I'm sounding a little baligerent because I am a little pissed off and put aside, but maybe it passes,...Yeah, but I feel like screaming at the earth with all this space these secret torments provide in me. I imagine the music we create will surfice it, but it kills me still. Must let go of what's close in order to know closness again. That's what I'm learning.
So my dear I think we'll be seeing you soon, huh? My birthday is Aug. 25. I'll be twenty-four. Ooops, it's time to get started. I remember as I grew up I'd hear of these musicians that would be with the "big time" and they would turn out to be like 20 or 21, well now I no I don't like the idea with th"big time and that the younger the more nieve, foolish, apart from what's really important. I feel the efforts in me are ready though. I feel what I want because I don't like anything else, basiclly. I'm a sniviling little rat faced git. Anyway, you like all this stuff, Ican tell cause you run off the track of conversations, you start talkin to just be doing it as if nothing matters. I'm glad you'll be playing drums with us to start out somewhere with us. At this time I don't care for how long, I just think that your part of what helps alot to say what we feel as a philosophy. As an impulse that has a distinction. A hard thing to come bye. Andy and I have desided to live together. I think it will work out well cause I need him as much as he needs me so the see-saw will become a latter,...I hope. He wants to help me with guitar.
Anyay, my dirty old friends are giving me all kinds of things to write about, so the songs are going to be pumpin. Yeah, and I'm down on dancing music, yeah I want to shake it loose.......... I want to get fucking loose, and I'll do it on my own huh? Yeah it proves whose going to stick up for you when they do...

goodnight my sweet,

Love Mia.

Personal letter to Steve while students at Antioch College, July 22, 1989. From the author's archive.

ACKNOWLEDGMENTS

Feral House Books, Christina Ward for her endless patience in editing, her vision and friendship. Jessica Parfrey for believing in the project and publishing the book. The story might not seem true without the contributions of the brilliant photography of: Charles Peterson, Jackie Ransier, Lucy Hanna, Lynn Peterson, Chris Sievanen, James Moriarty, and Zannah Noe for reaching out to me with the cover photograph. Independent Arts and Media, and Kickstarter Patrons of the Arts. Jeff Klinesmith, Art Chantry, Doug Prey, Andrew Kessler, Matt Dresdner, Rachel Flotard and the Zapatas. Leah Batemen for her initial project management. And, especially, Ivonne Bustamonte in Mexico, Jimmy and Sarah, C/Z Records and my family. Pat Moriarity for his artistic integrity, inspiration, and unparalleled creative hand.

Isabel Allende for her wisdom and encouragement to: Write my heart and my hand will follow. Laura Close, Jeremy Herman, Michelle Gorthy, and Gina Sanfilipo.

All the musicians with whom I have shared a stage, studio or basement floor across North America, Europe and Asia. Emily, Joan, Andy, Matt, Carla, Julian, Hoagie, Valerie, Selene, Liz, Roisin, Scotty, Bruce, Walter, Ben, Roger, Adrian, Steve and Tia, Gilbert, Gretta, Joe, John, Mikey, Jay, Tim, Toast, Gary, Scott, Roseann, Tess, Robin, Carrie, Susan, Dave, Joan, Jenny, Scheet, Ernie, Tom, Rachel, SubPop Records, Michael Millett of Broken Rekids, Revolver Records, Empty Records, U.S. and Big Flaming Ego Records.

To my friends, family, and musicians who continue to inspire: Stefanie Sargent, Kurt Cobain, Mark Lanegan, Chris Cornell, Gary Floyd, D. H. Peligro, Tom Pig Champion, Steve Hanford, Charlie Mastrapolo, Fred Cole, Andrew Loomis, Mia Katherine Zapata, and my Dad.

THANKS